# ATLANTA

PUBLISHED BY LONGSTREET PRESS, INC.
A subsidiary of Cox Newspapers,
A subsidiary of Cox Enterprises, Inc.
2140 Newmarket Parkway, Suite 118
Marietta, Georgia 30067

Printed in the United States of America

1st printing, 1996

Library of Congress No. 95-77262
ISBN: 1-56352-265-9

This book was printed by Quebecor/Kingsport,
Tennessee.

Color separation and film preparation by
Advertising Technologies, Inc., Atlanta, Georgia.

**DIRECTOR, ENTERPRISE DIVISION**
Nancy Bauer

**MANAGING EDITOR**
Erica Fox

**ART DIRECTION AND PRODUCTION**
Graham & Company Graphics, Inc.
Atlanta, Georgia

# ATLANTA

## A VISION FOR THE NEW MILLENNIUM

By **PHYLLIS S. FRALEY**

*Photography by* **RON SHERMAN**

*Enterprise Profiles by* **LESLIE BAYOR**

LONGSTREET PRESS
ATLANTA, GEORGIA

PUBLISHED IN COOPERATION WITH
THE ATLANTA ECONOMIC DEVELOPMENT CORPORATION

# CONTENTS

$A$tlanta is a city of dreamers, a place of visionaries and idealists. Our past details a distinguished record of accomplishment and, at times, storybook success. And yet our future promises even more.

Time and again, we have redefined the city we want to be. And time and again, we have enjoyed the leadership and the collective determination to become that city. We rose from the ashes of the Civil War to become the capital of the New South. We are a center for commerce, transportation, and telecommunications. We are rich in culture and art. And, as the birthplace of the civil rights movement, we have made a solemn covenant to ensure that the flame of justice, freedom, and equal opportunity burns bright in our city.

I have seen the many faces of our city, heard the varied stories of its people, and witnessed with pride the confidence of those who live, work, and invest here. As the 20th century comes to a close, there could be no better symbol than the Centennial Olympic Games to recognize the achievements of Atlanta's past and the incalculable promise of its future.

Atlanta, now firmly established as one of the world's great cities, will continue to grow and prosper into the 21st century. But we will nurture our brave and beautiful city with care so that tall, gleaming buildings, multinational corporations, and global banks will be only one part of the story. The best part will always be the people, their neighborhoods, and the sense that Atlanta is a good city, a city whose bounty and promise are open to all.

As a city of dreamers, Atlanta is continually creating its future. Come share its vision for the new millennium.

MAYOR BILL CAMPBELL

CITY OF ATLANTA

# PREFACE

*I*ronically, 10 years ago, an editor at *Atlanta* magazine asked me to write a newcomer's guide to the city. It included an article on a native's perspective that ended up rekindling this native's hometown pride. The notion of hometown pride was new to me, a corny concept, I called it, that southerners in their syrupy drawls bragged about endlessly. But in the course of interviewing many newcomers, and it seemed the city was being bombarded with transplants—as I referred to them—at the time, I began to understand what all the excitement was about.

My parents and I moved to Atlanta when I was one. In fact, we arrived on my birthday. We had come from Europe, where my parents, Holocaust survivors, had been liberated after the war. Here in Atlanta, they saw the promise of a new life in a new land where they would be free to live peacefully and prosper with their children; a blessing beyond belief. And now, all these years later, to be the author of this ambitious book that so enthusiastically celebrates our extraordinary hometown is meaningful in many ways.

Though technically I am not quite among that rare breed—native Atlantans—who have watched a small city evolve into a stunning urban American success story, it is from this perspective that I appreciate how brilliantly Atlanta has surpassed even the most optimistic expectations.

No other contemporary American city, and few in the world, has created such an inspiring case study of why the journey toward success is as valuable and, in Atlanta's case, as rewarding as reaching the goal.

Atlanta's personality is one of notorious self-promotion, boosted by lots of fanfare, yet Atlanta epitomizes southern elegance and style. Its diverse, proud people are passionately committed to prosperity. It has been this way since before the Civil War.

The moment of truth arrived when Atlanta was bestowed the ultimate honor of hosting the world for the 100th anniversary of the modern Olympic Games, and in that moment, this was suddenly a city of soul mates. When the Atlanta Braves won the 1995 World Series Championship, the spirit of this soulful city was once again recharged. Each time Atlanta appears at the top of surveys ranking the best cities in the world, the spirit is reinforced. *ATLANTA: A Vision for the New Millennium* was created to spread the word about this truly international town.

I want to thank the many publications, newspapers, organizations, business and government leaders, and the Atlanta History Center for research assistance. Among the many people, more than can be named here, who encouraged my own dream in bringing "the Atlanta book" to fruition—a labor of love filled with more than its share of challenges—I want to thank the staff of the Atlanta Economic Development Corporation, especially Margaret McClure, executive vice president, for her unwavering support; Erica Fox, my editor, for her temperament and tireless commitment; Barbara Morgan, confidant and co-conspirator for her wisdom; my friends, who heard it all; and my family, who had the good sense to make Atlanta our home.

I called hometown pride corny a decade ago. No longer. Now my hometown pride, like other Atlantans', is from the heart.

PHYLLIS S. FRALEY

AUTHOR, *ATLANTA: A VISION FOR THE NEW MILLENNIUM*

# INTRODUCTION

The moment had come for the world to find out if dreams really do come true. That was all Atlanta's bid for the 1996 Centennial Olympic Games was—a dream someone conjured up that caught on and, before anyone knew it, became bona fide reality. And with that, a southern city with a history of progressive leadership, innovative public-private partnerships, determination, and an abundance of optimism—a city that 131 years earlier had been left smoldering in the ashes of the Civil War—proved to anyone who may have doubted it that Atlanta had arrived. The economic leader of the burgeoning New South had leaped into that coveted clique of premier international cities. And in that moment of glory, as city promoters would later proclaim, Atlanta instantly became "hometown of the American dream."

Though the city's chief boosters acknowledged the significance the world's greatest sporting event would have on its host city, little did anyone realize the impact would be so immediate and so boldly catapult the transportation, communications, and financial leader of the southeastern United States into the global arena and into the next millennium.

*"It is no accident that Atlanta is so remarkably successful.... Atlantans share and nurture a single-minded commitment to progress and prosperity for all, which is seldom found elsewhere."*

BILL CAMPBELL, MAYOR OF ATLANTA

share and nurture a single-minded commitment to progress and prosperity for all, which is seldom found elsewhere." It is no secret that a special kind of creativity and cooperation have distinguished Atlanta from other leading urban centers, making it, according to the people who live and work here, the most exciting city anyone could want to call home.

Long shots—far-fetched notions like Atlanta hosting the $1.5 billion Olympic Games or the Atlanta Braves "Cinderella" baseball team coming from the bottom of the National League in 1991 to win the pennant in one of the greatest comebacks ever in sports history—are somehow nurtured here. Such successes seem to foster the belief that Atlantans can achieve the unimaginable and, some say, create a self-fulfilling prophecy.

Almost overnight, the momentum from the Olympics announcement began generating the kinds of economic development coups urban centers only dream of. A flurry of major corporate expansions and headquarter relocations produced scores of multinational business activity.

Not all cities hoisted into Olympic fanfare automatically get such economic plums. But then, according to Atlantans—notoriously big on boosterism, self-confidence, and hometown pride—Atlanta is a city like no other.

This is a city where progressive and positive attitude has become the collective mantra. For despite all the self-promotion and hype, the fact is, Atlanta delivers. Along with its prime location, temperate climate, high-quality workforce, and a cost of living equal to or lower than that of other major metropolitan areas, Atlanta has excelled in every important way a city can: unparalleled transportation, a harmonious mix of diversified cultures, high quality of life, recreation, education, business, sports, and art.

Atlanta is the fastest-growing market in the fastest-growing region of the world's largest, most diverse economy. Boasts the city's leading promoter, Atlanta mayor Bill Campbell, "It is no accident that Atlanta is so remarkably successful. In a multiracial and ethnically diverse environment, Atlantans

"The great thing about this city," says Billy Payne, president and CEO of the Atlanta Committee for the Olympic Game (ACOG), "is that people make things happen here. This is not a city that buys solutions. This is a city that gets 30 people around a table and someone says, 'Okay, we have this opportunity, or this problem; what's the next step?' Then assignments are made and they commandeer 30 more people and so on down the line until whatever it is simply gets done.

"The legacy of the Olympics," Payne adds, "will not be in the venues it constructs or even the visibility that we get. It will be just be one more entry in a long list of Atlanta successes where people working together made the difference."

A penchant for visionary leadership working closely with an active, hands-on private sector has been the foundation of the premier city of the South, where favorite son Dr. Martin Luther King, Jr., forged and forever changed the social conscience of a nation. Strong cross-racial alliances working and achieving together underscore Atlanta's successes and show other cities how diverse ethnic groups can work in sync.

Journalist Frederick Allen, former political commentator for CNN and author of *Secret Formula*, the definitive history of the Coca-Cola Company, notes, "Atlanta was invented as a convenient place to put railroads in the 19th century—the first flat place south of the Appalachians—and long runways in the 20th century." Of contemporary factors that have contributed to Atlanta's prominence: "Atlanta had a business leadership that gave ambition and paternalism a good name, and the amazing grace of race relations—people willing to do business together that, at the time, was unheard of in most other southern cities."

Distinguished in its earlier years by the astute leadership of mayors William B. Hartsfield, Ivan Allen, Jr., and

Atlanta mayor Bill Campbell (left) and ACOG president and CEO Billy Payne share a light-hearted moment during Olympics planning.

INTRODUCTION

Atlanta—A Vision for the New Millennium

Sam Massell, a strong foundation for the city had been solidly laid. Under the stewardship of Atlanta's first African-American mayor, Maynard Jackson, Atlanta entered a new era of coalescence. First elected in 1973, Jackson returned for a third term in 1990, following two terms by Andrew Young, who brought to the position the portfolio of a U.S. congressman and former ambassador to the United Nations and a unique expertise vital to Atlanta's Olympic bid success.

"Very few cities are blessed to have leaders so deeply committed and active in their local community, working with and

Home state Georgia benefits from former president Jimmy Carter's visionary initiatives.

mobilizing the public and private sectors," says Walter R. Huntley, Jr., president of the Atlanta Economic Development Corporation (AEDC), the city's public-private economic development arm. "Our leadership has been ahead of its time, proactive and strategic, and has always planned in anticipation of accommodating growth."

The Atlanta Project, launched by former president Jimmy Carter and the Carter Center in 1991, illustrates the point. An unprecedented community-based program, the Atlanta Project was created to attack social problems related to poverty plaguing U.S. cities, beginning with Atlanta. Unveiling the Atlanta Project, former president Carter noted, "Atlanta is the city on earth, certainly in this country," where such an undertaking could succeed.

The initiative exemplifies one of Atlanta's most treasured assets: an inherent, keen sense of involvement shared by a broad-based cross-section of Atlantans, particularly apparent within the city's corporate community.

Ingrid Saunders Jones, vice president of corporate external affairs for the Coca-Cola Company, headquartered in Atlanta, and a member of the 30-year-old Action Forum, a prestigious group of business executives committed to Atlanta's multicultural focus, notes that the doors to community involvement in Atlanta, whether individual or corporate, are well marked and wide open for everyone to enter. "If someone wants to make a difference, wants to get involved and give of their time and resources," she observes, "Atlanta, unquestionably, is the city that will make the most of it."

T. Marshall Hahn, Jr., honorary chairman of Atlanta-based Georgia-Pacific Corporation, the world's largest manufacturer and distributor of pulp and paper products, notes, "We didn't just move to Atlanta to do business; we came here to be part of the community. This has been the philosophy of virtually all businesses here."

Sharing a well-worn observation of the city's character, Atlanta historian and author Franklin M. Garrett says, "Atlanta has never been the typical moonlight and magnolias, slow, sleepy southern town novelists like to write about." Reflecting on Atlanta's quick recovery from the Civil War, he adds, "Atlanta has always been gung-ho for progress, strong and spirited and not to be underestimated."

From its unceremonious beginnings in 1837, when a railroad linesman, Stephen B. Long, selected a site in the wilderness as the southernmost point for two rail lines to converge, a little town called Terminus, later renamed Marthasville, was born. Several years later, it became Atlanta. It continued growing until the Civil War, when it was annihilated by General William T. Sherman. Atlantans rebuilt their city in record time, but they were careful to protect their trees and a splendid natural setting of rolling, hilly streets and leafy neighborhoods. As the city commercially flourished, so did its charm and hospitality.

Today, the same city that sentimentally ushers in each spring with a spectacular dogwood display has evolved into one of the world's leading international urban centers.

"People easily forget that this is a young city," observes Wesley E. Cantrell, president and CEO of Atlanta-based Lanier Worldwide, Inc., a $1 billion wholly owned subsidiary of the Harris Corporation. "This is a city that has survived devastating destruction, yet had the capacity to rebuild, prosper, and outgrow other major metropolitan centers."

> *"The great thing about this city is that people make things happen here. This is not a city that buys solutions."*
>
> BILLY PAYNE, PRESIDENT AND CEO, ATLANTA COMMITTEE FOR THE OLYMPIC GAMES

Atlanta is also young in another way. The median age is 30.5 years old, about two years below the national average, according to Donald Ratajczak, director of the Economic Forecasting Center at Georgia State University. "Two years may not sound like much, but it is," he says. The reason Atlanta is such a magnet? "People think there are opportunities here. Many people have benefited from being in Atlanta, and word gets out."

Though each newcomer to the city has a unique story, the similarities are undeniable. Ronni Baer and her husband, Steven Elmets, moved here from New York in 1991. "The quality of life in New York was not what we wanted," she recalls. "We didn't have space to move around in. We were both working around the clock, and with a preschool son, we couldn't take advantage of the reasons we had moved to New York in the first place."

She was working as assistant curator of drawings and prints at New York's Cooper-Hewitt Museum, while her husband, an architect, worked in a small firm. After considering several major American cities, Atlanta won out. "This will sound corny, but we are thrilled to be living here. This is a dynamic urban environment that also offers us the quality of life, a normal, stress-free environment we want for raising a family. And aside from that, this city is beautiful."

Doug MacIntyre, president and CEO of Atlanta-based Dun & Bradstreet Software, says, "Of key North American cities, Atlanta has positioned itself as a dynamic international and domestic leader. This is why talented, high-performance people make Atlanta their home: success breeds success."

Some of the most significant corporate successes that began and have blossomed in Atlanta and that still base

> *"When I came to Atlanta, I didn't know anyone, but I soon realized Atlanta is one of the few cities that you can come to as an outsider and, in a relatively short period, can become a part of the city's fabric, part of the vision, and take part in crafting that vision."*
>
> STEVEN J. LABOVITZ, CHIEF OF STAFF FOR MAYOR BILL CAMPBELL

global operations here include the Coca-Cola Company, Cable News Network and Turner Broadcasting System, Inc., and Home Depot.

Arthur Blank, president and CEO of Home Depot, the world's largest home improvement retailer and, with sales of $12.5 billion in 1994, the 10th-largest overall retailer in the U.S., notes how the home improvement giant came to be headquartered in Atlanta. He and partner Bernie Marcus were living in Los Angeles 16 years ago when they developed the full-service, warehouse-style retail concept. Earlier in Blank's career, he worked in Griffin, Georgia, and had become familiar with Atlanta as a "growing, affordable city, open and welcome to newcomers."

"There is a strong focus on home ownership in Atlanta," Blank says. "Housing is very affordable here, most homes have backyards, and incomes and demographics are broad-based.

"One of the things I like most about Atlanta," he adds, "is the opportunities it provides for people like Bernie and me to become a part of the community, put our shoulders behind the wheel, and see not just our dreams but Atlanta's dreams become reality."

Other industry giants that have contributed to the city's impressive corporate roster and job market and to the state's robust economy include Georgia-Pacific Corporation, BellSouth, Inc., and Delta Air Lines, Inc.

Pro-business in the biggest of ways, metropolitan Atlanta led the nation in 1994 by adding 97,100 net new jobs. Atlanta's job market increased by almost 12 percent from 1992 to 1994, the third-largest increase in the nation.

More Japanese investment is in the state of Georgia than in any other state except California, and 80 percent of that investment is in metropolitan Atlanta. The city's prominence in the international marketplace is supported by more than 950 international companies, including some of the largest Japanese manufacturers in the U.S.

Location, combined with cutting-edge transportation, is the driving force behind Atlanta's fast-track domestic and international commercial success. Within the city limits, Atlanta is identified from its southern tip to its northern boundaries by Southtowne, downtown, midtown, and Buckhead, each with a distinct personality, while overlapping and supporting one another.

Surrounding and complementing the city is a flourishing 20-county metropolitan region with a population of 3.4 million. With its communities of neighborhoods, educational

Under the leadership of maestro Yoel Levi, the Atlanta Symphony Orchestra has risen to world-class status.

institutions, striking office parks, and high-rise commercial development, the metropolitan area provides a well-balanced, unspoiled natural suburban environment enhancing the centerpiece city of Atlanta.

Having attended Emory University law school, Steven J. Labovitz came to Atlanta from Pittsburgh in 1972 and liked the city so much he made it his home. Today, the attorney is chief of staff for his former law partner, Mayor Bill Campbell, and praises all Atlanta offers, professionally and personally .

"Across the country, even throughout the world, people recognize Atlanta's uniqueness," he notes. "We have all the prerequisites that make a city great—wonderful climate, employment opportunities, and a business community that demonstrates a willingness to work with the governing bodies to tackle the difficult municipal issues that cities face every day.

"When I was a student here, the city was smaller, but a terrific place to be. After graduating, and looking at cities to live," Labovitz adds, "it was clear that this was where I wanted to make my home, raise a family, and enjoy the lifestyle, the beauty, the excitement and opportunities that you will find only in Atlanta. I'm not alone in this belief. All you have to do is spend some time here and before you know it, you're a believer."

As home to 36 colleges and universities providing more than 350 programs of study to more than 95,000 students, the metropolitan region contributes significantly to Atlanta's well-trained labor force.

By the end of the last decade, service jobs accounted for almost one in three jobs within the city of Atlanta. Since local industry is diverse and well balanced, Atlanta has not experienced the economic fluctuations and cycles other major cities have undergone. This helps support Atlanta's enviable unemployment rate, consistently lower than the rest of the nation.

Because of the increased worldwide emphasis on innovative technology, Atlanta has become a strong contender in the high-tech arena—so strong that the city's technical capacity to handle the Olympics was one reason Atlanta won the bid for the 1996 Centennial Games.

The Georgia Research Alliance is a unique collaboration between the state's research universities, business community, and government, creating science- and technology-driven economic development. William J. Todd, president of the alliance, says, "Atlanta and Georgia are rapidly dominating the multifaceted high-tech industry, a

phenomenon we intend to drive home by producing a high-tech Olympics. Just look at the resources we already have in place. We are more fiber-optically connected than any other city in the U.S. When the Olympics get here, we'll be able to demonstrate to the world that Atlanta is truly going to be the best place to see the future from."

Andrew Young lends his international experience to diverse hometown projects.

Hand in hand with high-tech is Atlanta's advancing position as a leading telecommunications center. Tom Johnson, president of Cable News Network (CNN), recalls, "People told Ted Turner he was crazy if he thought an international all-news network could succeed anywhere outside New York or possibly Los Angeles." But a string of successes proved critics wrong, "and it also showed just how powerful the attraction of Atlanta is."

The telecommunications frontier in Atlanta seems virtually as unlimited as the vision of CNN's originator, broadcast news mogul Ted Turner.

AT&T Atlanta Works, the largest fiber-optics and copper cable manufacturing facility in the world, also chose Atlanta as its home base. Its metro Atlanta Network Control Center is one of the company's most important facilities, managing 75 to 80 million calls each business day. The global communications and computer company has its second-largest employee population in the world in Atlanta and another 200 work locations throughout the state.

Atlanta's status as a leading high-tech and telecommunications center is the reason that in 1991 Holiday Inn Worldwide moved its global headquarters

> *"If someone wants to make a difference, wants to get involved and give of their time and resources, Atlanta, unquestionably, is the city that will make the most of it."*
>
> INGRID SAUNDERS JONES, VICE PRESIDENT, CORPORATE EXTERNAL AFFAIRS, THE COCA-COLA COMPANY

here. "To maintain our strong competitive edge," underscores Holiday Inn Worldwide chairman and CEO Bryan D. Langton, "we needed the information and communications infrastructure available in the Atlanta area."

Though already blessed with its own ample resources, Georgia's capital city gets a big boost from its partnership with the state. Addressing top national executives at the governor's mansion during an annual Red Carpet Tour—an exclusive Georgia Chamber of Commerce-sponsored economic development "look-see" through the state—Georgia governor Zell Miller sums up the state's virtues: "First in transportation; center of finance and commerce; unsurpassed technology research and telecommunications; top bond rating; pioneer in employment training; one-stop environmental permitting; low corporate, personal, motor fuel, and sales taxes with no hikes during the recession; a strong economy that has outpaced the nation."

Incentives for business include Georgia's Quick Start training program, which has contributed to the state's high productivity level—50 percent above the national average and the highest per capita output in the Southeast. Enterprise zones in Atlanta and the Atlanta Foreign Trade Zone near Hartsfield Atlanta International Airport further help attract business. Georgia's 6 percent tax rate has not changed since 1969, and the sales tax has risen by only 1 percent in more than 40 years. Further, Georgia is a right-to-work state.

Georgia has a $300 million film and television industry and is on its way to becoming the third-largest entertainment center in the U.S. And at the heart of the state's entertainment, cultural, and arts offerings, Atlanta has a stellar lineup of major recording stars taking up local residence.

> *"Atlanta's community leaders are willing to step outside the traditional parameters and define a new vision for themselves and the community. They will take chances on what is new, what is innovative, and what is daring."*
>
> SHIRLEY C. FRANKLIN, SENIOR POLICY ADVISER, ATLANTA COMMITTEE FOR THE OLYMPIC GAMES

With so many transplants moving to Atlanta, how do native Atlantans, that rare breed, feel? One such Atlantan is Herman Russell, chairman and CEO of Atlanta-based H. J. Russell & Company, the nation's fourth-largest African-American-owned business.

"I'm one of those unique Atlantans who has watched this city grow during the past 60 years," Russell says. During the

late 1950s, he left Atlanta to attend college, but returned. "I have watched the sun rise and set on Atlanta's beautiful skyline. I have watched this city create opportunities for all people, from all walks of life, and I have witnessed a tradition being created—a tradition of welcoming newcomers who can find opportunities for growth and prosperity here. There is room for everyone in Atlanta."

Shirley C. Franklin moved here in 1972. The Philadelphia native served as chief administrative officer for the City of Atlanta and is now senior policy adviser for the Atlanta Committee for the Olympic Games. "What I find unique in Atlanta is that it has always been a community that believes in itself, and believes that it can accomplish the impossible.

"Atlanta's community leaders are willing to step outside the traditional parameters and define a new vision for themselves and the community," she says. "They will take chances on what is new, what is innovative, and what is daring. When I think about when Atlanta began its bid for the Centennial Olympic Games, I think back to 1895 and the Cotton States Exposition held here—a bold assertion that Atlanta was the New South—and the vision Atlanta leaders had of a great city. Now, 100 years later," she notes, "Atlanta will host almost 200 nations for the Olympic Games and continue its character and vision for the next century."

Former Olympic athlete and Atlantan Dennis Berkholtz, who serves as local marketing consultant for the U.S. Team Handball Federation, adds, "As the Olympics come and go, Atlanta will still have a forceful sports component to its economic development push. Atlanta will offer one of the best places in the country—the world—to play competitive sports. There's no stopping Atlanta now. We are bringing home the gold."

**Right:** The gold-domed Georgia State Capitol, across the street from Atlanta City Hall, is part of Government Walk, the largest government complex south of Washington, D.C. Pages 11-12: Hosting Super Bowl XXVIII in 1994 gave the world a preview of Atlanta's ability to stage the Centennial Olympic Games.

Introduction

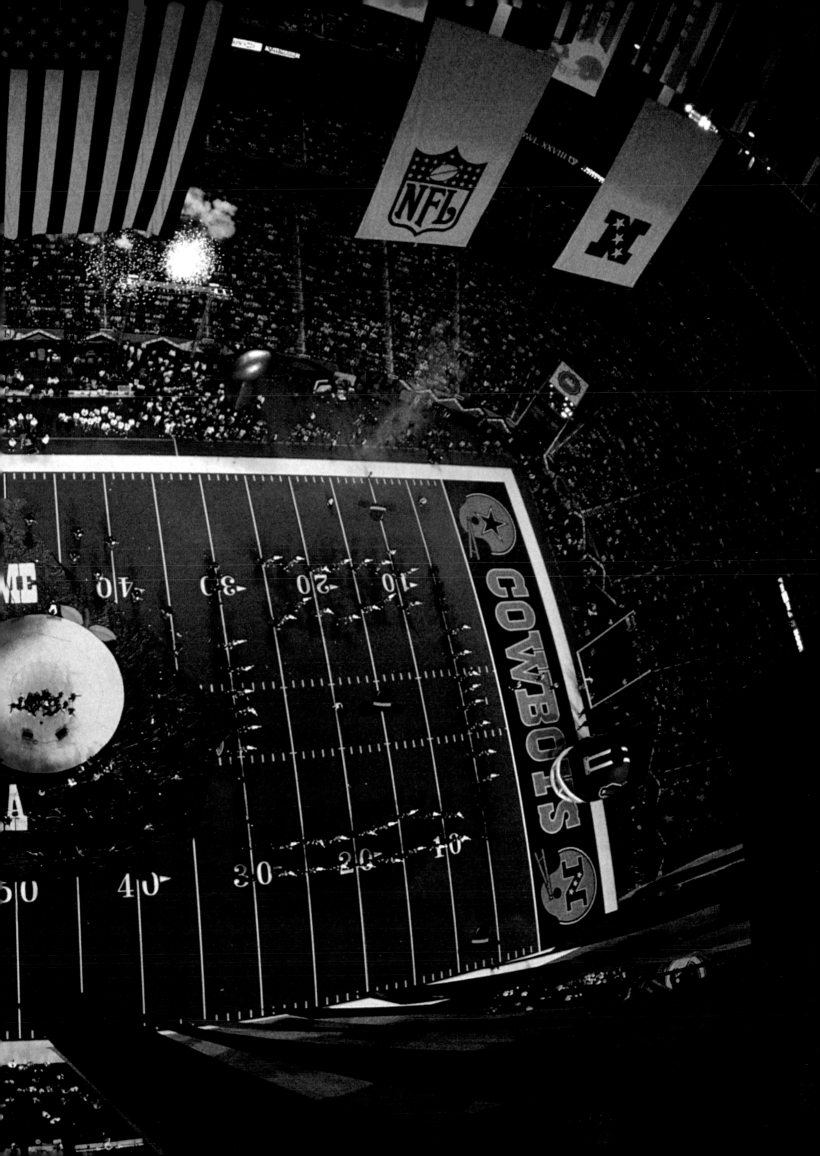

*T*he most heavily forested city in North America, Atlanta blossoms with spectacular foliage each spring.

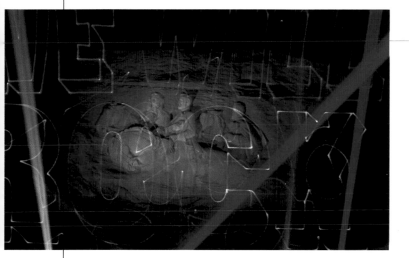

Busy Atlantans take time out to enjoy the city's informal street life entertainment, lazy afternoons on the Chattahoochee River, and Stone Mountain Park, site of the world's largest chunk of granite.

When the Atlanta Braves "finally" won the World Series in 1995, the victory was sweet indeed.

FOLLOWING PAGES: Atlantans celebrate winning the Olympic bid during a spectacular downtown parade. The festivities continue at Underground Atlanta, where street entertainment delights crowds nonstop. Downtown workers are equally delighted as children romp on the high-rise rooftop playground of the Downtown Child Development Center.

Atlanta—A Vision for the New Millennium

INTRODUCTION

*A*tlanta-based Delta Air Lines has been bringing people to the city for such major league events as Braves games and the 1988 Democratic National Convention.

From the quick pace of CNN Center in the South Central Business District (top left), to the stately ambience of the Carter Presidential Center (bottom left), to the serenity of nearby Lake Lanier (right), Atlanta's diverse attractions suit all tastes.

# CHAPTER ONE

# SUPER SPORTS CITY

*A*tlanta and world-class sports have become synonymous. In this city where sports and outdoor recreation find a near-perfect year-round climate, recent major professional sports coups and the city's ability to attract more professional teams have transformed even the most blasé Atlantans into die-hard fans.

Where else can fans find contenders like hometown hero Evander Holyfield winning back boxing's heavyweight championship, or the Atlanta Braves coming from oblivion to first place in the National League in 1991 and then, four years later, clinching the World Series championships?

But the surprising triumph Atlantans will savor forever was winning the bid to host the biggest sporting event of all time, the 1996 Centennial Olympic Games.

It was September 18, 1990, when Atlantans became the beneficiaries of this most sought-after opportunity for global attention, economic expansion, international cultural enrichment, and public-private coalescence in the world. Atlanta had been selected not only to host the world's greatest sporting event, but to do so during the 100th anniversary of the modern Olympic Games. Atlantans had brought home the gold, and with that heady distinction, the city became the focus of world-wide attention overnight.

"Although Atlanta was considered to be a long shot to host the 100th anniversary of the modern Olympic Games," notes Andrew Young, co-chair of the Atlanta Committee for the Olympic Games (ACOG), "those of us who have lived in this incredibly creative and resourceful city knew better. In fact, judging from Atlanta's history, it may well have been the challenge to prevail despite the odds that saw us to victory in winning the 1996 Olympic Games bid."

The former congressman, U.S. ambassador to the United Nations, and former mayor of Atlanta was keenly instrumental from the beginning in helping the city pursue the Olympics. "Now that we have the opportunity to showcase our city to the world," he says, characteristically confident, "Atlanta will be taking a place as a leader among international cities and international sports."

> *"Now that we have the opportunity to showcase our city to the world, Atlanta will be taking a place as a leader among international cities and international sports."*
>
> ANDREW YOUNG, CO-CHAIR, ATLANTA COMMITTEE FOR THE OLYMPIC GAMES

A projected two-thirds of the world's population will see the 16-day Olympic event on television—the largest gathering of nations and most watched event in history—from July 19 through August 4, 1996. Another two million visitors will witness it first-hand, 15,000 of whom will be members of domestic and international media.

The economic impact is equally staggering. The $1.5 billion event will have an estimated $5 billion impact on the state of Georgia, and there will be 80,000 permanent and temporary jobs created and another 40,000 enlisted volunteers.

But hosting the Olympics means more than revenue for the city. The numbers don't convey the momentum and incalculable exposure an Olympic event bestows.

As the focal point of Atlanta's Olympic development, Centennial Olympic Park will welcome visitors and locals sharing the awesome experience. The 21-acre park will be the site of ACOG's "Festival of the American South," staged during the games.

From a terrace in ACOG's high-rise headquarters overlooking construction of Centennial Olympic Park, a smooth, albeit anxious, Billy Payne, ACOG president and Centennial Olympic Park CEO, checks construction progress daily. Having pioneered and shepherded the city's Olympic bid dream, he easily transmits enthusiasm for the eternal significance the grand park will hold for generations to come. "I believe a major legacy of the 1996 Centennial Olympic Games will be our city's Centennial Olympic Park, a beautiful, permanent gathering place and showcase commemorating the spirit of the 1996 Olympic Games and the centennial celebration of all Olympic games."

### WORLD SERIES CHAMPIONS

Centennial Olympic Park will not be the first packed park in town. Though former Atlanta mayor Ivan Allen, Jr., brought the Atlanta Braves to town three decades ago, it was not until 1991 that the city's investment by fans finally paid off.

Only a year after Atlantans celebrated their Olympic bid victory, they saw almost impossible odds dramatically defied again, this time at the ballpark. The Atlanta Braves, about to become professional baseball's Cinderella team, had been ranked at the bottom of the National League. Thirteen months later, in one of the greatest comebacks in sports history, the Braves became the National League champions and were one game away from winning the World Series. A year later, the Braves were once again National League champions and clambering for another shot at a World Series title. Then, for a third consecutive

Ted Turner has been a major league force in Atlanta's emergence as a leading sports center. Turner and his wife, Jane Fonda, cheer on the winning Atlanta Braves throughout the season.

Atlanta Braves legend Hank Aaron gave the city's early baseball fans a taste of world-class sports thrills when his 715th home run shot out of the park in 1974.

year, the Braves were in another dead heat for major league baseball's top trophy. For a city that had spent years waiting for a professional sports victory, such back-to-back breathless triumphs boosted fans, business, and a tremendous sports industry almost overnight.

Acclaimed throughout the National and American leagues for their on-field performance, the Atlanta Braves have set unheard-of franchise attendance records. What's more, the Braves have become a regional team; almost half the fans at Braves games live 100 or more miles away.

Stan Kasten has watched Atlanta become a professional sports center since moving here almost two decades ago when he joined Turner Broadcasting, first as an attorney for the Atlanta Braves and Atlanta Hawks National Basketball Association team, then as assistant general manager of the Hawks, and then as general manager. Since 1986, he has been president of both clubs.

Of the Braves' phenomenal following, Kasten asserts, "The fans are there, the support is there, and they're hungry for signs of success. When the Atlanta Braves team came here in the mid-1960s, it was the only major team south of Baltimore. We were the only professional baseball team in this whole quarter of the U.S., and as those fans grew up, they became big sports fans.

"Up to three years ago, we were drawing 900,000 attendance a year. In 1993, we drew 3.9 million. No other American city," he says, "has ever been able to sell

On the heels of the Olympics, Atlantans will be hosts once again, this time to the 10th Paralympiad, the world's second-largest sporting event, at which 119 nations will be represented by 3,500 elite, world-class athletes with physical disabilities.

Jogging down Peachtree Street after a full day of meetings with delegates in Atlanta from around the world, Canadian Bob Steadman, president of the International Paralympic Committee, shares his perspective on the long-term benefits of hosting the world's greatest athletes. "When you look at hosting a major worldwide festival—the International Paralympic Games—you are building community pride, community spirit, and a lifelong legacy. Not just a legacy of venues and facilities," he says, "but a legacy of enthusiasm, pride, and particularly attitude—and that's what the spirit of the Paralympic Games are about. When you witness the performance of these extraordinary athletes, there is a tremendous exhilaration that's contagious. Once you've been there, it's with you forever."

out virtually every game for an entire season."

The Braves' stadium is being replaced by a new structure on the same site that will accommodate the grand opening and closing ceremonies of the Olympic Games. After the Olympics, the stadium will become a gift to the citizens of Atlanta and will be converted into a new stadium for the Braves. The 56-acre, $209 million facility will seat 85,000 people and when converted to a baseball stadium will seat 45,000 to 50,000.

Planned to benefit some of the city's oldest adjacent communities, the stadium will include street-level retail shops and a park at the entrance area. Its design is among the structure's hallmarks and features the dramatic downtown skyline in clear view.

According to Kasten, "The new stadium will be the finest place ever built both to play and to watch professional baseball. The new stadium will be a destination, it will be a tourist sight, and people will be coming here even on nongame days."

Much of the Braves' impact on the city's economy and the growing numbers of fans can be attributed to the team's astute general manager, John Schuerholz, who came from Kansas City to Atlanta in 1990 when the Braves had finished last three lonely years in a row. Of the team's surge in attendance, he notes, "In addition to the fact that we've drawn over 3 million fans, it's interesting that so many of our new fans are female. So many women and so many husbands have told me that their wives have become fans of the team," he says. "There's a clear-cut phenomenon going on."

### A City for Summer and Winter Sports

Local sports curiosities don't stop with baseball. Atlanta, amazingly, has the second-largest ski club in the Americas, although there are no local ski slopes close to town. The attraction to winter sports also has been boosted since the city landed the Atlanta Knights professional hockey team franchise in 1992, which in two short seasons became the 1994 Turner Cup champions.

More in keeping with the city's choice climate, Atlanta is home to the largest local tennis organization in the world, the Atlanta Lawn Tennis Association, second only to the U.S. Tennis Association. Tennis is further boosted by the recently formed Atlanta Thunder professional team and the annual spring AT&T Challenge, bringing leading men's players to Atlanta from around the world.

> "Up to three years ago, the Braves were drawing 900,000 attendance a year. In 1993, we drew 3.9 million. No other American city has ever been able to sell out virtually every baseball game for an entire season."
>
> STAN KASTEN, PRESIDENT, ATLANTA BRAVES AND ATLANTA HAWKS

Internationally ranked runners, along with local and domestic seriously driven joggers, hit Atlanta's hot pavement every summer during the world's largest 10K, the annual Fourth of July Peachtree Road Race. Drawing more than 50,000 participants, the race begins at Buckhead's Lenox Square Shopping Center, continues along and up what is not so affectionately called Heartbreak Hill, and finishes in midtown's plush Piedmont Park.

For golfers, Atlanta is the only city in the U.S. to have an event every year from each of the major golf tours. Atlanta's golfing legacy started with the biggest name in golf, Bobby Jones, who took the top prizes in 1930 with an unprecedented grand slam. Today, PGA's annual BellSouth Classic, the Atlanta stop for top international male golfers, is held at the Atlanta Country Club each May, and the annual LPGA tour comes to town for the Chick-fil-A Charity Championship, drawing professional female international golfers in April. For senior international male golf professionals, Atlanta annually hosts the Nationwide Championship at the Golf Club of Georgia.

International tennis players are no strangers to America's premier southern city, where tennis courts abound.

## A SUPER STADIUM

When 750 million fans watched Super Bowl XXVIII in 1994—the most watched American sporting event in the world—it kicked off Atlanta's passage into professional football's most heated gridiron event. Played in the then newly constructed 71,000-seat, $210 million Georgia Dome—built for the city's professional football team, the Atlanta Falcons, and the playing field for the annual Peach Bowl—the 1994 Super Bowl generated an estimated $166 million for the city. The Dome's total 1994 impact was $1.5 billion.

Leeman Bennett, who served as executive director of the Super Bowl Host Committee, was head coach of the Atlanta Falcons from 1977 to 1982 and twice named National Football Conference coach of the year. "By winning the Super Bowl bid," Bennett says, "Atlanta is perceived as one of the top sporting cities in the world, and hosting the Super Bowl certainly gives our city the impetus to host other world-class sporting events. I believe our Super Bowl coup may have influenced our winning the Olympic bid.

"The Georgia Dome gives football fans in Atlanta one of the best places in the U.S. to watch a game firsthand," the sports veteran adds. "This is not only because the Georgia Dome is a great playing facility, but because the city of Atlanta will be attracting more top athletes who want to work and live year-round in this area."

## A CITY FOR BASKETBALL LOVERS

For hoop fans, the OMNI Coliseum is home to the National Basketball Association's Atlanta Hawks. The team entered a new era under the direction of head coach Lenny Wilkens, who guided a winning streak of 14 games during his first season here in 1993. In 1995, Coach Wilkens

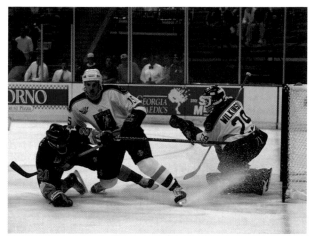

The 17,000-seat OMNI Coliseum draws fans to Hawks basketball games, Atlanta Knights hockey games, and events and concerts year-round.

became the NBA's all-time-winningest coach, and he was named head coach of the U.S. Olympic Basketball Team for the 1996 Centennial Olympic Games. He has participated in more games as a player and/or head coach than anyone in league history.

Atlantans love college basketball, too. In fact, because Atlanta is home to so many colleges and universities, an enormous fan component is built in.

In 1993, the city hosted the National Collegiate Athletics Association (NCAA) Women's Final Four Championship, and it has been tapped to host the 2002 NCAA Men's Final Four Championship. For the first time, the Southeastern Conference (SEC) Basketball Tournament was held in Atlanta in 1995, and the city has slam-dunked the SEC tournament for 1998.

## PARTNERS IN LAUNCHING THE OLYMPICS

• The city's Olympic responsibilities are spearheaded by the Corporation for Olympic Development in Atlanta (CODA). It is charged with developing the environment/public spaces surrounding Olympic facilities, Olympic transportation corridors, and parks/public gathering spaces.

• The Atlanta Committee for the Olympic Games (ACOG) serves as developer of all Olympic venues and facilities. It stages the Olympic events in cooperation with the International Olympic Committee, the United States Olympic Committee, and international federations.

Robert Dale Morgan, executive director of the Atlanta Sports Council, established by the Atlanta Chamber of Commerce, observes, "With facilities like the OMNI, the Georgia Dome, and the Georgia Tech Coliseum, Atlanta is clearly a prime choice for major college basketball tournaments and increasingly is competing and winning bids to host the sport's most prestigious tournaments."

Add to that Atlanta's winning bid in 1994 to host the Mobil Indoor Track and Field Championships for the next decade.

### SPORTS ENTHUSIASTS EXTRAORDINAIRE

Atlanta's most notable auto racing track is Atlanta Motor Speedway, the number-one sports attraction in Georgia, with an estimated annual economic impact, according to the State of Georgia, of $455 million. It draws during its two weekend events each year more than half a million spectators. Competing here is the NASCAR Winston Cup series and the NASCAR Bush Grand National. Having doubled its attendance in three years, the Atlanta Motor Speedway is becoming the showplace of American motor sports.

"As fast as we can build seats—and in the past three years we've added more than 40,000—we fill them," says a spirited Burton Smith, chairman and president of Atlanta

A near-perfect climate makes Atlanta ideal for professional and amateur golfers. Right: Football fans cheer a winning home team at Georgia Tech's midtown stadium.

Motor Speedway. "If someone wants a ticket for our annual November race," the proud promoter cautions, "we sell out in August and have a waiting list."

The city's sports momentum started with the efforts of Ted Turner, sports enthusiast extraordinaire, who has had a powerful hand in promoting the city through his television empire and ownership of local professional sports teams. Owner of the Atlanta Braves, the Atlanta Hawks, several cable television sports outlets, and the company that manages the OMNI Coliseum, Turner has been a 20/20 visionary. Turner Network Television presents NFL and NBA competition and operates SportSouth, the regional cable all-sports station. WTBS, the superstation that started the sports surge with Braves cable telecasts nationwide, brings in ongoing revenue for the team as well as tremendous exposure for the city.

Atlanta's physical environment, its public and private leadership, and the spirit Atlantans share have made sports here a full-time preoccupation and the city one of the world's hottest sports centers. Even more compelling than cutting-edge sports venues and facilities, there exists a core of leaders nurturing powerful public-private partnerships committed to making miracles happen here.

Ten years ago, while other American cities were relying on manufacturing, banking, tourism, and more traditional tried-and-true vehicles for economic development, Atlanta's business, government, and hospitality leaders recognized sports as a powerful economic and quality-of-life draw. With that, they combined resources to make Atlanta the pioneer in proactive sports marketing, and their plan has paid off.

When he's not managing the country's number-one FOX television affiliate in Atlanta, Jack Sander, chairman of the Chamber of Commerce's Sports Council, has his eye on the city's sports future. He believes, "Topping the Olympics and Paralympics cannot be easy. The Atlanta Sports Council has spent the last three years developing and implementing a long-range master plan to ensure a solid schedule of sporting events into the next century."

The Sports Council's former chairman, Ralph Jernigan, under whose tenure the city snagged the Super Bowl and the Olympic Games, concludes, "When the Sports Council was created in 1985, its goal was to make Atlanta the number-one sports city in America by the year 2000. Many believe we're already there."

*L*oyal fans of the Atlanta Braves pack the stadium in record numbers.

*A*mateur sports enthusiasts fill neighborhood parks and playgrounds throughout town.

The Atlanta Falcons touch down at the Georgia Dome, also the playing field for the annual New Year's Eve postseason college football Peach Bowl and the site of the 1994 Super Bowl.

RIGHT: With a tradition of heart-stopping comebacks, the Atlanta Braves won the 1995 World Series title for this super-sports town.

Marlene Karas, Staff Photographer, *Atlanta Journal and Constitution*

The Peachtree Road Race, the world's largest 10K, brings together 50,000 international and local runners and super athletes every July 4.

$S$eriously driven cyclists wind through city streets during annual local and international competitions.

FOLLOWING PAGES: Atlantans, young and old, go for the gold.

ATLANTA—A VISION FOR THE NEW MILLENNIUM

*A*tlanta's new Olympic natatorium at Georgia Tech creates a world-class venue for international competitive swimmers.

*D*ressed to the nines, Atlantans wine and dine at the annual gala Steeplechase.

$\mathcal{U}$nder the direction of the NBA's all-time-winningest coach, Lenny Wilkens, the Atlanta Hawks have been slam-dunking their way to victories.

RIGHT: World-class free-style wrestlers compete at the OMNI Coliseum during 1995 pre-Olympics championships.

# CHAPTER TWO

# SOUTHTOWNE

## TRANSPORTATION AND TRADITION

At first glance, from several thousand feet, Southtowne is a lavishly green, glittery surface viewed by millions of people each year hovering above the city. Here, aviation underscores Atlanta's prominence in global transportation.

Southtowne—a name given in recent years to the city's southwest quadrant by the Atlanta Economic Development Corporation—is a curious mix. From its southernmost tip at Hartsfield Atlanta International Airport to its northern edge in downtown's South Central Business District (SCBD), Southtowne contributes to making Atlanta a uniquely efficient city for business and pleasure. Meshing state-of-the-art transportation with some of the city's top tourist attractions and recreation, Southtowne is also the hub of regional government, a center for media/communications, education, and convention and sports venues, all charmingly woven into the richly textured tapestry of some of Atlanta's oldest neighborhoods and traditions.

At 23, and having been raised in Atlanta's southwest area, Alicia Stacey Hunter only fleetingly contemplated living elsewhere, even elsewhere in town, after graduating from an elite New England college in 1994. "This is the best place to be in Atlanta," she maintains. "The southside area is close to everything. It takes me 10 minutes to get to the airport, 10 minutes to get to Buckhead; I jump on the expressway and go. Atlanta is not a good city because of the Olympics," she asserts, "it's a good city because of the people; they're open enough to accept the nontraditional, new ideas, different ways of seeing and doing things. The Olympics is an expression of our city's creativity and ability, and that's why people like me want to live here."

Adds her mother, Cecelia Corbin Hunter, a management/operations consultant who has lived in Atlanta for 30 years, "Over the years, African-American leaders have been accessible to the community and have lived in the community, which is unique not only in major urban centers in the U.S. but around the world. It is a tradition in Atlanta's southside to socialize with our leaders, who are also our neighbors."

### PLANES, TRAINS, AND AUTOMOBILES

First dubbed the "Gate City" in the mid-1800s, Atlanta was selected as the end point in the wilderness that connected the new Western and Atlantic Railroad with points west. Today, the city's full combination of transportation amenities include an efficient, modern system of major highways, Interstates 75 and 85, Interstate 20, the Metropolitan Atlanta Rapid Transit Authority (MARTA) rapid rail, and the region's largest intermodal rail yards. These modes of transit define the Southtowne corridor.

At the heart of this unique, diverse community is Hartsfield Atlanta International Airport, which has put Atlanta and the entire southeastern United States on the map. The airport

> "For more than 50 years, Delta has worked with city and state officials to develop one of the finest transportation systems in the world. Through this partnership, Delta has been able to achieve consistent growth, which has meant economic development and opportunity for the city, state, and region."
>
> RON W. ALLEN, CHAIRMAN, PRESIDENT, AND CEO, DELTA AIR LINES

With more than 2,000 scheduled arrivals and departures each day, Hartsfield International Airport links people and places with ultra-efficiency.

generates about $22 million a day—$8 billion annually—making it the largest economic center in the Southeast and the largest employment center in Georgia.

Ranked consistently among the top two busiest airports in the world for aircraft operations, Hartsfield places Atlanta within only two hours of 80 percent of the U.S. population.

Aggressively preparing for the next century and Atlanta's prominence as a primary global link, the airport has recently added a $300 million international concourse, the largest in North America, through which more than 2.7 million passengers already travel annually. And construction is beginning on a fifth runway designed for commuter air traffic, which will increase airport traffic by a whopping 25 percent.

Close to a fifth of the population of the United States passes through Atlanta's airport each year. Hospitably accommodating this huge volume of passengers is the $18 million Atrium—the central meet-and-greet area—with shops, restaurants, a business center, and more.

Yet even before the first plane took off, Hartsfield Atlanta International Airport was a success. Lauded by industry experts for its "advanced technology, functionality, and intelligent, innovative design," Hartsfield is distinguished from other U.S. airports by its consumer convenience and smooth operations. "Efficiency has always been our hallmark," emphasizes Angela Gittens, general manager of Hartsfield Atlanta International Airport, "and it is at the core of our long-term strategic plan for the next century."

Delta Air Lines, the largest private employer in Georgia, with some 25,000 personnel locally, anchors the airport. Delta's Atlanta hub is the largest airline hub in the world, and Delta has more transatlantic service from Atlanta than any other airline.

Casually leaning back in a chair in his office overlooking the one-block Delta complex at Hartsfield Airport, Ron W. Allen, Delta's chairman, president, and CEO, beams, "Delta's growth over the years and its recent expansion have gone hand in hand with Atlanta's emergence as an international city. For more than 50 years, Delta has worked with city and state officials to develop one of the finest transportation systems in the world. Through this partnership," adds the Atlanta native, "Delta has been able to achieve consistent growth, which in turn has meant economic development and opportunity for the city, state, and region."

Atlanta's booming air transport industry includes a major air cargo component: more than 1.5 million square feet. The Atlanta Perishables Complex and Equine Complex have created excellent opportunities for goods to be transported. The city's Cargo Trade and Development Initiative has added further incentives for freight businesses.

To better connect Atlanta to the region, Southtowne's interstates have recently undergone $108 million in improvements.

Atlanta is also a leading U.S. freight center. CSX and Norfolk Southern railroads have the largest rail classification yards and intermodal freight yards in the Southeast. The port of Savannah, the largest freight commerce port on the South Atlantic seaboard, is just four hours away via interstate highways.

Rounding out Atlanta's superior transportation network is MARTA. The $2.3 billion public transit system is new, quick, clean, and efficient. Linking 29 stations in two counties, and augmented by a $1.6 billion network of superhighways along the metro area's perimeter, MARTA is even available in the airport terminal. Ultramodern trains carry passengers east and west as well as north, straight through downtown and midtown, then on to Atlanta's northern border, known as Buckhead, and to metro points beyond.

### HOME TO SOME OF THE CITY'S OLDEST NEIGHBORHOODS

Among Atlanta's oldest, most popular, and diverse residential communities are Southtowne's West End and Grant Park, where restored Victorian homes and new affordable housing meet the demands of an evolving community.

With its rich history and cultural and ethnic diversity, West End, Atlanta's oldest neighborhood, is a genuine Victorian village dating back to the mid-1830s. Named after the London theater district, West End was incorporated in 1868 and annexed to the City of Atlanta in 1894. Atlanta's neighborhoods south of Interstate 20 emerged from West End.

The 18-foot-tall bronze "Phoenix Rising from the Ashes" statue, symbolizing Atlanta's rebirth following the Civil War, has been renovated by the Corporation for Olympic Development in Atlanta and now stands proudly in Woodruff Park.

Festive entertainment at Underground Atlanta celebrates international customs and traditions.

The Ralph David Abernathy/Cascade corridor is enjoying a rebirth and wealth of development. Several upscale, exclusive residential subdivisions, including The Cascades and Spring Lake, are being complemented by new high-end commercial and retail business.

Supporting its resurgence, in 1992, West End received Historic District designation, making it the first neighborhood in Atlanta's southside area to receive such status. Sharing a passion for their community's treasured past and a penchant for Victorian indulgence, West End homeowners ardently boast about their neighborhood's unique urban charm.

Architect Wade Burns, former vice chairman of the Atlanta Urban Design Commission, is a West End resident and long-standing proponent of the area's commercial viability. "A successful inner-city neighborhood attracts thinkers, contributors, and risk takers," Burns says. "West End has an abundance of such people, and the successful socioeconomic mix is what we're most proud of."

Burns's preoccupation with West End began with sketches for commercial improvement in the area in 1969 while working for a local architectural firm. Within a year, he bought a 20-room Victorian home in West End, on Peeples Street.

During the next four years, Burns purchased 25 homes in the Peeples Street vicinity, later known as the West End restoration effort. Today he lives in a house built in 1856, believed to be the second-oldest house in Atlanta, which is four doors down from his first West End residence.

Burns's home was built on 200 acres before the Civil War. All of West End's earlier prominent families, such as former U.S. Secretary of State Dean Rusk and Clark Howell, founder of the *Atlanta Constitution*, built homes on sub-parcels of that original lot.

Fourth-generation Atlantan architect Bill Stanley, who is committed to West End's commercial and housing revitalization, notes, "What is so unique about this community is that it is multicultural and largely African-American." In fact, the southwest Atlanta area is the richest black community south of Washington, D.C., and east of Chicago.

Mary N. Long travels extensively as vice president of government affairs for the Atlanta-headquartered National Arthritis Foundation, but she doesn't worry about leaving her Peeples Street home alone. A former resident of nearby Grant Park, Long moved to West End a decade ago and appreciates the built-in neighborly security system in her community.

"We have a community of families, children, singles, varied races and ethnic cultures right here," she says. "We all know each other, and while some of us are relatively new to the area, some of my neighbors have been here for 30 to 40 years."

Long's home, built in 1907, is among nine houses on Peeples Street, which is listed in the National Historic Register.

The West End community also lures residents looking for new, contemporary neighborhoods, for here affordable, high-quality housing is abundant.

### ENTERTAINMENT GALORE

A community for families, the Southtowne corridor, not surprisingly, includes some of the city's most wholesome playgrounds. Here lies Grant Park, Atlanta's oldest park and home to the Cyclorama, a spectacular three-dimensional painting and diorama said to be the largest in the world. Created in the 19th century, it depicts the 1864 Civil War campaign of the Battle of Atlanta.

Zoo Atlanta, a futuristic biopark, covers 40 acres within historic Grant Park. Established as Atlanta Zoo in 1889, it became Zoo Atlanta almost a century later, spearheaded by the efforts of Atlanta City Council president Marvin Arrington, and is now an important and nationally recognized resource.

When MCA Concerts, a division of Los Angeles-based MCA, Inc., was considering sites for a new facility, it chose property in Southtowne. Today, on balmy summer nights, the $18 million Coca-Cola Lakewood Amphitheatre showcases major recording stars, entertaining crowds of up to 20,000 fans.

Drawing locals and tourists to the northern edge of Southtowne where it meets downtown is Underground Atlanta. This retail/entertainment complex—the largest attraction in Georgia—is located at the site of the Zero Mile Post, staked out in 1837 as the point where the rail line that spawned the city began. By the late 1800s, the first paved streets in Atlanta encompassed a business district in the Underground Atlanta area.

The question, about 120 years later, was what to do to give the area modern commercial appeal. City leaders decided that if the streets were elevated, traffic would increase. So a viaduct system was put in place in 1928, bringing merchants one street level higher. Old storefronts were left for storage and service, while the Georgia Railroad Freight Depot, built in 1869, remained at the original Underground location and today is the oldest building in central Atlanta.

The five-block Underground area became a historic site in 1968, and a year later Underground Atlanta opened as an entertainment attraction. For a decade, it thrived as the city's most festive place. But over time, Underground Atlanta lost its allure. Again, city leaders joined forces, looking for a solution, and in 1989, with the expertise of urban/environment-attraction specialist the Rouse Company, scores of new exciting shops, restaurants, entertainment, and activity made Underground Atlanta an urban success once again. Today, Underground Atlanta generates $65 million in sales annually and draws 10.5 million visitors a year.

It is fitting that the history of Atlanta's most celebrated commercial product is housed right next door. Each year, nearly 1 million people come to the World of Coca-Cola to experience the chronicled century-old history of the world's most popular soft drink. And next to the World of Coca-Cola, across from Underground Atlanta, is the site where the Atlanta Economic Development Corporation and Zoo Atlanta plan to build a world-class aquarium.

The 45,000-square-foot, $15 million World of Coca-Cola attraction was built in 1990 and features international product tasting, a soda fountain of the future, a replica of a 1930s–40s soda fountain, museum-quality artifacts, and state-of-the-art technology, including a high-definition video projection movie theater. Touch-screen TVs are housed in

Transporting Atlantans throughout the city, MARTA trains are safe, quick, and convenient.

# THE COCA-COLA LEGEND

The brew that today is called Coca-Cola was created in Atlanta in 1886. Legend has it that the Coca-Cola empire began with John Styth Pemberton, a local pharmacist who created a syrup in a brass pot in his backyard, then carried it down the street to Jacob's Pharmacy, at the corner of Peachtree and Marietta Streets, where it sold for five cents a glass as a soda fountain treat. At some point, carbonated water was combined with the syrup, creating a "delicious and refreshing" drink. Pemberton's partner and bookkeeper, Frank M. Robertson, is credited with creating the famous trademark name "Coca-Cola."

In its first year, "sales averaged a modest nine drinks a day," the company says, noting that Pemberton had little clue of the marketing magnitude of his concoction. Gradually, he sold portions of his business, and eventually Asa G. Candler, an Atlanta businessman, took over the company's control.

Today, Coca-Cola is the number-one soft drink company in the world. It has a 45 percent share of worldwide carbonated soft drink sales, represented by 685 million products served every day in more than 195 countries. More than 4 trillion Coca-Cola products have sold since the company was founded.

eight-foot-high Coca-Cola cans that allow participants to learn about a five-year segment of history while also learning about the evolution of Coca-Cola.

An estimated 94 percent of the world's population recognizes the Coca-Cola symbol displayed outside the World of Coca-Cola in a 12.5-ton revolving neon sign. Yet there is another "product" that even more literally links Atlanta with the farthest reaches of the world.

### COMMUNICATIONS CENTRAL

CNN Center, headquarters for Cable News Network, brings Atlanta into homes worldwide via the global communications empire created by Georgia's favorite son and media maverick Ted Turner. CNN brings the news and home base Atlanta into about 64 million American homes—24 hours a day—and 146 million homes in more than 210 countries and territories.

Telecommunications and the high-tech industry are big business in Atlanta, underscored by CNN's global prominence. An enormous news organization in itself, CNN is only part of a larger company, Turner Broadcasting System, Inc., a multifaceted news, entertainment, and sports empire created two decades ago and headed by Ted Turner. As of this writing, there are plans to make Turner Broadcasting System part of Time Warner, creating the largest media company in the world.

Ed Turner, no relationship to Ted, is CNN's executive vice president and has lived in Atlanta since 1979, when he moved from CBS in New York to the capital city of the South. Turner says, "Our job in organizing, putting together, and launching CNN would have been infinitely more difficult in the traditional media centers in the Northeast. There, you have a thousand naysayers for every person who says we can do it. Here, the attitude is 'why not?' There's a positive, 'can-do, tackle-anything' approach here that you just don't find in other parts of the U.S."

Only slightly distracted by the eight television monitors running simultaneously, nonstop, in his office, CNN's executive vice president/senior executive producer Bob Furnad adds, "With satellite technology, CNN could be anywhere in the world, but it's essential that a worldwide operation like CNN be located near a large international airport. Obviously, Hartsfield fills the bill."

The news veteran emphasizes that "when people come here or are recruited here to work, and sometimes reluctantly at first, they fall in love with the beauty and quality of life. The fact that the cost of living in Atlanta is lower than in so many other major cities often clinches the deal."

A few blocks away from CNN Center are the newsrooms of Atlanta's daily newspapers, the *Atlanta Constitution*, founded in 1868, and the *Atlanta Journal,* which in 1883 began to "Cover Dixie Like the Dew." On Marietta Street, near the newspaper building, is a statue that pays tribute to Henry Woodfin Grady, the *Constitution's* visionary editor and civic crusader, who campaigned, most notably in a speech made in New York in 1886, for an industrialized "New South."

The newspapers are owned by Atlanta-headquartered Cox Enterprises. The 14th-largest media company in the U.S. in revenues, Cox has subsidiaries and investments in related businesses and new media technology.

### CONVENTION AND SPORTS CENTER

Joining Southtowne and the southern tip of downtown, the South Central Business District takes over where the Southtowne corridor leaves off, but not before a grand exit along Interstate 75-85, leading into Olympic Stadium, built for the 1996 Centennial Olympic Games and the new playing field for the Atlanta Braves.

When Atlanta hosted the 1994 Super Bowl, all eyes were on the Georgia Dome, the second-largest domed stadium in the world, home of the Atlanta Falcons National Football League team and major entertainment events. Next to the Dome is the OMNI Coliseum, home to Hawks basketball and Atlanta Knights hockey games, along with events and concerts year-round.

The Georgia World Congress Center (GWCC) is the heart of Atlanta's thriving convention industry. It consistently makes Atlanta one of the nation's leading convention and trade show centers, attracting 17 million visitors annually. At 2.5 million square feet, the GWCC is the nation's second-largest convention complex. Coupled with the adjacent Georgia Dome, the two make up one of the world's largest convention/sports/entertainment complexes.

### THE REGION'S GOVERNMENT CENTER

Within the SCBD lies the regional center of federal, state, city, and county offices and employees.

Totaling about 40 square blocks is Government Walk, the largest concentration of government offices south of Washington, D.C. This includes the Sixth District Federal Reserve Bank, Atlanta City Hall and annex, the Georgia State Capitol complex, the U.S. district court house, the Fulton County government complex and courthouses, the Richard B. Russell Federal Building, and the newest addition, Atlanta Federal Center.

At the site of the former landmark Rich's downtown department store, a local institution whose forerunner, M. Rich and Co., opened in 1867, Atlanta Federal Center will become the largest, fully occupied office building in metro Atlanta. Consolidating some 8,000 federal employees, the $260.5 million federal office complex is being developed by a joint-venture partnership of the Atlanta Economic Development Corporation and Prentiss Properties and is financed by the Atlanta Downtown Development Authority for the U.S. General Services Administration. When completed, the 1.3 million-square-foot facility will anchor federal, state, and city government campuses, creating an enormous opportunity for robust revitalization within the SCBD.

### A PLACE TO BE EDUCATED

Campuses of another type—those of Georgia State University (GSU), in the South Central Business District, and the

Atlanta University (AU) Center of Higher Education, within the Southtowne corridor—bring additional energy and personality to the city's southern quadrant.

The world's largest consortium of African-American private higher education institutions, Atlanta University was founded in 1865 and boasts such distinguished alumni as Dr. Martin Luther King, Jr.

AU's six campuses include Spelman College, Morehouse College, the Morehouse School of Medicine, Clark Atlanta University, Morris Brown College, and the Interdenominational Theological Center.

Spelman College, the oldest historically African-American college for women in the nation, has the largest enrollment, currently at 2,000, of any women's college in the state. It has garnered prestigious national recognition, including a 1993 ranking of number one on *U.S. News & World Report*'s

*"Spelman is a very special place. Here we educate African-American women to be leaders in science and mathematics; for careers in law, business, and medicine; to become teachers and astronauts and poets. Perhaps most important of all, our students also learn that it is their responsibility to help others know the success that is theirs."*

JOHNNETTA B. COLE, PRESIDENT, SPELMAN COLLEGE

SOUTHTOWNE: TRANSPORTATION AND TRADITION

"America's best colleges" list of regional liberal arts colleges of the South. In 1995, Spelman was recognized as eighth-best "college value" in *Money* magazine's survey of 100 colleges.

Entertainer Bill Cosby and his wife, Camille Cosby, donated $20 million to Spelman in 1987. The college received another gift of $37 million from the DeWitt Wallace/Reader's Digest Foundation in 1992; it represented the largest financial donation ever made to a historically African-American institution of higher learning.

Founded in 1881 to educate freed women slaves, Spelman is headed today by nationally recognized educator Johnnetta B. Cole. "Spelman is a very special place," Cole explains. "Here we educate African-American women to be leaders in science and mathematics; for careers in law, business, and medicine; to become teachers and astronauts and poets. Perhaps most important of all," she adds, "at Spelman, our students also learn that it is their responsibility to help others know the success that is theirs."

Another AU Center school is also gaining acclaim, having been ranked in 1993 by *U.S. News and World Report* among the best regional liberal arts colleges in the South. Steeped in almost 130 years of tradition, Morehouse is the only all-male, four-year liberal arts African-American college in America. Current enrollment is just under 3,000, creating a close-knit community of students from around the country perpetuating what is known as the "Morehouse mystique."

The Morehouse School of Medicine has the distinction of being the first predominantly African-American medical school established in this century in America.

Clark Atlanta University's forerunner, Clark College, moved to the AU Center in 1941 from its original site in South Atlanta, where the school was established in 1869. It flourished on a 450-acre campus until consolidating with AU and becoming Clark Atlanta University in 1988. Today it boasts a co-ed enrollment of more than 5,000 students.

The Southtowne corridor also is home to Atlanta Metropolitan College, a two-year unit of the University System of Georgia, and the Atlanta Area Technical School.

Georgia State University, founded in 1913, is the second-largest institution of higher education in the state's university system. Bringing aspiring professionals to where many will make their mark, the 21-acre GSU campus, adjacent to Government Walk, attracts more than

> "All you have to do is walk out the door at GSU and you feel the energy of a great city at work. It makes you want to get out there and be part of it."
>
> CONNIE RUBIN, LAW STUDENT, GEORGIA STATE UNIVERSITY

24,000 students, creating a 24-hour-a-day inner-city population that fortifies the area's residential, educational, and professional amenities.

"In my classes there are pilots, retired military officers, software and computer professionals, social workers, psychologists, real estate executives, corporate ladder climbers, even an archaeologist," says 48-year-old Connie Rubin, an "almost empty-nester," whose GSU College of Law classmates range in age from 23 to 50.

Rubin attended Cornell University, then moved with her physician husband from New York to Atlanta in 1977. A part-time law student, she drives from her northern suburban home in Sandy Springs to school and is parked in only 20 minutes. "There are people in class," she says, "driving from as far as Athens and Rome."

Jubilantly, Rubin explains, "I'm in the heart of the city, the fast pace, where there is diversity, stimulation. All you have to do is walk out the door and you feel the energy of a great city at work. It makes you want to get out there and be part of it."

GSU received a surprise boost in 1992 when NationsBank donated a landmark 14-story, 91-year-old Beaux Arts building at Five Points to GSU's business school, creating a west campus.

GSU's School of Music is also in the midst of positive transition; it is moving to an abandoned, once-popular movie theater being renovated in downtown's historic Fairlie-Poplar area. The Atlanta Economic Development Corporation acquired the property for the School of Music with funds from the Woodruff Foundation.

Making GSU the ultimate urban model for higher education is the clear goal of its energetic president, Carl V. Patton. "Our movement into Five Points and the Fairlie-Poplar area will provide much-needed academic space for our high-quality programs and bring life and vitality to the streets," he says. "Our goal is to help this area become a wonderful place to live, work, study, and play."

Signs of revitalization are abundant throughout the SCBD. Small mom-and-pop shops, restaurants, art galleries, and converted loft housing inject energy into this diverse community. For many, the SCBD's main attraction is a unique backyard view—an unexpected treat, for in the SCBD, you can see and feel Atlanta's downtown heartbeat.

**Right: Within the Atlanta University Center complex, Morehouse College is distinguished by its 128 years of tradition.**

51

$C$NN brings Atlanta to the world by broadcasting news to homes 24 hours a day.

RIGHT: The 45,000-square-foot World of Coca-Cola dazzles 1 million visitors each year with the Spectacular Fountain, artifacts, and more.

SOUTHTOWNE: TRANSPORTATION AND TRADITION

Two of Atlanta's most popular attractions are South Central Business District's Underground Atlanta (left)—drawing 10 million visitors each year—and Southtowne's Coca-Cola Lakewood Amphitheatre—bringing top-notch entertainers to town.

$\mathcal{S}$outhtowne is home to some of Atlanta's most upscale, contemporary subdivisions, such as The Cascades, as well as to the city's oldest neighborhood, West End, where the charming Victorian homes on Peeples Street, listed in the National Historic Register, date back to the mid-19th century.

SOUTHTOWNE: TRANSPORTATION AND TRADITION

*T*he Atlanta University Center of Higher Education offers students a variety of academic and social experiences on its Southtowne campus.

Clark Atlanta University is one of the six AU institutions of higher education. The others are Spelman College, Morehouse College, Morehouse School of Medicine, Morris Brown College, and the Interdenominational Theological Center.

Southtowne is a curious mix. World-class corporate facilities, such as the Hartsfield Centre office and luxury hotel development, dramatically overlook the airport's north runway. Natural environments, like Grant Park, house Alan the orangutan, who luxuriates in his palatial Zoo Atlanta home.

# CHAPTER THREE

# DOWNTOWN

## HOSPITALITY AND HISTORY

*A*tlanta's downtown skyline is more than high-rise powerhouses expressing the aesthetic signature of one of America's great international cities. More accurately, it reflects the passion of a dynamic urban business environment where world-renowned architects have masterfully captured the synergy of high-stakes global commerce and a thriving world-class hospitality industry.

Yet, juxtaposed with this striking scene, at its eastern border, downtown shifts to a more sobering pace. For here lies the historic community of Sweet Auburn. The center of local African-American tradition, Sweet Auburn is actively revitalizing its place in Atlanta, echoing the profound legacy of Dr. Martin Luther King, Jr., who changed the social conscience of a nation and whose birthplace, King Center, and supporting facilities attract millions of visitors each year.

Conventioneers from around the world make Atlanta one of the top-ranked meeting sites each year.

If strong ties to the past and an appetite for the future are any measure, downtown Atlanta is loaded with the additives and adjectives of a city for the world. "Great international cities don't just happen," says Atlanta mayor Bill Campbell. "It takes commitment and partnership, an understanding and appreciation for change and diversity, history and potential. Fortunately, but not by accident, Atlanta is a city that has always attracted the best and the brightest, and anyone who has ever walked through the streets of downtown Atlanta sees and feels exactly how such talent and promise are manifested."

As in other 19th-century American cities, in its early years downtown Atlanta served a dense population that later expanded into other areas as the city's size and citizenry grew. Coaxed during the 1870s by the introduction of mule-drawn trolley lines, the city's four most prominent streets became downtown's Peachtree, Marietta, Whitehall, and Decatur. Peachtree Street distinguished itself as Atlanta's most prestigious residential address and matured into the city's center of commercial development: Atlanta's Central Business District.

### Downtown Starts with Peachtree

Legendary Peachtree Street, Atlanta's most important, famous, and traveled thoroughfare, is said to have derived its name from a number of disputed sources. According to historian Franklin M. Garrett, in *Atlanta and Environs*, it was named after an Indian village, "Standing Peachtree," on the frontier between the Creek and Cherokee nations, where Peachtree Creek flowed into the Chattahoochee River. Whether the name Peachtree came from what the Indians called "pitch tree," later "corrupted" into "peach tree," will never be known. And since peach trees are not indigenous to the locale and pine trees are, the ambiguity remains.

Even so, today Atlanta is filled with beautiful, blossoming peach trees, and dozens of Atlanta streets carry the prestigious Peachtree name. Peachtree Street itself runs north and south straight through town, beginning at downtown's southern tip at Five Points, where Peachtree and Marietta Street—the widest street in downtown—intersect, all the way through the city's northern boundary in Buckhead and beyond.

Atlanta's history can be traced through Peachtree. By 1890, Atlanta's population was at 65,000. Atlanta had successfully staged the International Cotton Exposition of 1881, marking an era of prosperity for the "New South" and enticing many people to move here. In the heart of downtown, within the bustling Central Business District, landmark business buildings were constructed in the last quarter of the 19th century and early 20th century along Peachtree and its surrounding downtown arteries.

"Business buildings grew taller, intruding upon the steepled skyline," writes Elizabeth A. Lyon in *Atlanta Architecture—The Victorian Heritage: 1837–1918,* published by the Atlanta History Center. "Railroad tracks, in an ever widening band, continued to dominate the center of the bustling city. Large business blocks took over former central city residential space, but the Downtown functioned still as a mixed-use district where many shopkeepers and workers lived above and behind new buildings. . . . Picturesque-eclectic High Victorian styles prevailed for all building types and were an appropriate expression for a young city working to establish itself as a regional center."

Renovated lavish Victorian landmarks still dot the downtown skyline; they create a bold contrast to today's stunning contemporary high-rise wonders.

The Candler Building, "a 20th-century business palace" built in 1906, is still one of downtown's most important addresses, along with the Healey Building, built in 1913 at Forsyth Street. The 10-story Empire Building, built in 1901, considered at the time "the epitome of a great banking hall," became the landmark Citizens and Southern National Bank, later NationsBank, which donated it to nearby Georgia State University. The Flatiron Building, built in 1897, at 74 Peachtree, was Atlanta's first tall office building and "predates New York's more famous Flatiron Building by five years."

Contemporary downtown began taking shape during the 1960s. Once again, talented architects redefined the design and direction of what was destined to become one of the world's leading business centers. A dramatic building boom later, new high-rise office buildings made their imprint. None were more revolutionary than the first three Peachtree Center buildings, created by world-renowned architect, developer, and favorite son John Portman.

Today, the Peachtree Center area—the highest elevation point on Peachtree Street—thrives with pedestrian, street-level activity. Where Peachtree Center borders Peachtree Center Avenue are Portman's Marquis Towers One and Two office buildings and the Marriott Marquis Hotel.

Portman's newest endeavor, One Peachtree Center, soars 60 stories, while a magnificent 32-foot-high bronze sculpture, "Ballet Olympia," delights pedestrians at street level. Down the street, along the Peachtree Center ridge, are the classic 50-story One Ninety One Peachtree Tower, designed by John Burgee in association with Philip Johnson, and the neighboring pink-marbled and tiered 52-story headquarters of Georgia-Pacific, designed by Skidmore, Owings and Merrill.

Portman's blueprint for downtown's future prevails as the foundation for its business, convention/tourism, and merchandising focus.

Portman reflects, "Atlanta is a city of aspiration. The one thing about this city and state that is different is that we think big. This is a city of people who make a difference and make this a city that works. Delegations come to Atlanta every week from all over the world, and I can tell you," he pauses, "Atlanta is perceived as the city of the future."

Portman's hand in creating that future is undeniable and revolves around the Peachtree Center complex. It has been expanded to now include multiple wholesale specialized trade centers—the Atlanta Merchandise Mart, the Apparel Mart, the high-tech showroom INFORUM, and the Atlanta Gift Mart, the largest gift center in the world.

Portman's influence has been profound on hotels as well. His original lobby atrium concept, now commonplace around the world, is carried out in three Portman-designed downtown hotels, including the world's tallest—the Westin Peachtree Plaza, with its modified atrium. His first full-blown lobby atrium was inaugurated with downtown's Hyatt Regency Atlanta Hotel. At 22 stories with bubble elevators, the Hyatt launched Portman's atrium concept in 1967, revolutionizing hotel and high-rise office design worldwide.

## HOSPITALITY, ATLANTA-STYLE

Fueled by more than 20 million visitors a year, the hospitality industry in metropolitan Atlanta is huge. Its economic impact is $6.7 billion annually, and its workforce totals more than 250,000 people, says Robert King, president and CEO of the Georgia Hospitality and Travel Association.

> *"Atlanta is a city that has always attracted the best and the brightest, and anyone who has ever walked through the streets of downtown Atlanta sees and feels exactly how such talent and promise are manifested."*
>
> BILL CAMPBELL,
> MAYOR OF ATLANTA

Concentrated in the downtown area alone are 10,467 hotel rooms, for the most part in such high-quality facilities as the Westin Peachtree Plaza, Marriott Marquis, Hyatt-Regency Atlanta, Omni Hotel at CNN Center, Radisson Hotel, Atlanta Hilton, and Ritz-Carlton Atlanta, whose parent company is based here.

Strategically surrounding downtown's hotel hub are ample white-linen tablecloth and candlelit restaurants, along with such famous hot spots as the Hard Rock Cafe and Planet Hollywood. Within walking distance are first-rate attractions, including Underground Atlanta, the World of Coca-Cola, CNN Center, the Martin Luther King, Jr., historic site and Sweet Auburn district, the main branch of the Atlanta Public Library at Margaret Mitchell Square, and the High Museum satellite facility at Georgia-Pacific headquarters.

"We're sittin' on a ham sandwich scarfin' it up," says Spurgeon Richardson, president of the Atlanta Convention and Visitors Bureau (ACVB). With typical humor and the kind of cocky candor that comes with having a colossal success on one's hands, ACVB's spirited leader notes that Atlanta is always among the top-ranked convention capitals in the United States, adding, "During the past few years, we have attracted some of the world's most prestigious events, and we know Atlanta's success is a direct result of its first-rate accommodations, facilities, restaurants, and attractions.

"In attracting meetings and conventions," he underscores, "I believe we have the best package you can find anywhere in the world for citywide meetings and conventions. We have more than 55,000 hotel rooms in metro Atlanta, and we have any kind of facility you could want to meet in. That's one of the reasons we have become one of the top convention cities in the U.S."

## A PARTNERSHIP BETWEEN BUSINESS AND GOVERNMENT

Committed partnerships forged decades ago between business and government leadership are credited with creating the foundation for downtown Atlanta's vibrancy. With some 110,000 daily workers and from 12,000 to as many as 100,000 convention visitors and tourists on a given day, downtown is supported by an enviable team of organizations working toward ambitious long-range goals.

None is more impressive in membership and achievement than Central Atlanta Progress (CAP). Formed more than half a century ago as the Central Atlanta Improvement Association, then merging in 1967 with the Uptown

Association, CAP has a blue-chip board and a nuts-and-bolts approach that have led to a national reputation.

At the helm of CAP is Sam Williams, former president of the Atlanta Market Center and executive vice president of the Portman Companies for 21 years. CAP plans to conduct a campaign to create a security service district in downtown, to be paid for by property owners and managed by the private sector, to augment regular police services.

CAP's number-two project is to create more downtown housing for students and downtown workers. This entails renovation of loft housing and the creation of new apartments and dormitories in Fairlie-Poplar and then the housing district that surrounds downtown on the railroad tracks. "There's probably a market for 4,000 to 8,000 units of housing downtown," based on CAP surveys, Williams says.

Williams and his group envision a development plan around Centennial Olympic Park, to include housing, entertainment facilities, retail, and restaurants. Approximately 40 acres of land surround the park and will represent the largest piece of real estate development in downtown since the Civil War.

Instead of operating through standing committees, CAP disbands project-specific task forces once programs are under way and long-range implementation support is secured. The Downtown Child Development Center

Street merchants enliven Sweet Auburn, Atlanta's revitalized center of local African-American tradition.

> *"People love seeing children from the Downtown Child Development Center coming into buildings, getting on elevators. It makes people smile and it says, 'This is downtown Atlanta, a place that is safe for children and a place that is fun.'"*
>
> CHERYL GIBSON SMITH, DIRECTOR, DOWNTOWN CHILD DEVELOPMENT CENTER

(DCDC) is a stellar example of CAP know-how.

DCDC's director, Cheryl Gibson Smith, recalls, "Business leaders in downtown were concerned about attracting workers to the area, and one of the most important amenities identified was available, affordable child care for the workplace." With that directive, in 1985, DCDC became the first such facility in the U.S. sponsored by major downtown businesses.

Here's how: CAP brought a consortium of businesses to the table. In 1992, the federal government joined the consortium, which relocated DCDC from its Rich's facility to a new home in the Healey Building in the Fairlie-Poplar district, with the help of financing provided by the Atlanta Economic Development Corporation.

With 120 children enrolled and a waiting list, DCDC offers much-needed care for children of downtown workers, while at the same time bringing a contrasting, refreshing ambience to downtown.

"People love it," says Smith. "They love seeing children coming into buildings, getting on elevators. It makes people smile and it says, 'This is downtown Atlanta, a place that is safe for children and a place that is fun.' We get calls from businesspeople all the time telling us that when they look out of their high-rise office windows and see the children on the rooftop terrace playground, it's a real unexpected treat."

Devotion to enhancing the character of downtown Atlanta takes many forms, like the hands-on daily beautification and physical environment improvements organized by the Atlanta Downtown Partnership (ADP), an offshoot of a CAP task force nurtured into autonomy in 1992. Remarkably, ADP is an all-volunteer organization with about 300 corporate members and 2,000 volunteers.

"Each spring we conduct a downtown cleanup," explains Ronni French, ADP's executive director. "Last year it included about 1,200 people who helped paint buildings, pick up trash, landscape, even wash windows. We have a very committed group," she smiles, "that wants to see downtown sparkle and shine."

ADP's offices are in the beautifully renovated Hurt Building, across from the 21-block historic Fairlie-Poplar district. The focus of revitalization efforts include expanding Georgia State University facilities here.

Most of Fairlie-Poplar's 68 buildings were constructed between 1890 and 1930 and reflect the distinctive architectural charm of the times. The area's cobblestone streets have been walked by many members of the L. W. "Chip" Robert family, whose architectural firm, Robert & Company, has occupied and owned area buildings since the 1930s.

When he was growing up in the 1940s, Robert remembers, Fairlie-Poplar was the center of town. "We used to come downtown on the trolley, go to the movies, and eat at the Frances Virginia Tea Room, back then in a building across the street from where the Ritz-Carlton Hotel is now. There is tradition here," he maintains, "and with the recent expansion of Georgia State University, we are seeing Fairlie-Poplar enter a new era."

## SWEET AUBURN

Change is constant is Atlanta, the legacy of a city always aspiring to reach the destiny its ambitious for-bearers envisioned.

Among the legacies Atlantans are most proud of is that of 1964 Nobel Peace Prize winner Dr. Martin Luther King, Jr., whose soul-stirring spirit and commit-ment are constant reminders of what people can do in partnership.

Of America's most visited national historic sites, the King Center comes in third, after the Statue of Liberty and the Liberty Bell. The National Park Service, which oversees the King birth home and restoration of the site, is completing a new visitors center across the street from the King Center, part of an $11 million program to restore the neighborhood.

Each year more than 3.1 million people visit Dr. King's resting place and supporting King Center facilities, which serve as the centerpiece of the Sweet Auburn district. The King Historic Site features the Martin Luther King, Jr., Center for Non-Violent Social Change, which includes exhibits, photos, and artifacts and the *Legacy of a Dream* film.

Martin Luther King, Jr.'s birth home is at 501 Auburn Avenue, a two-story, nine-room Queen Anne-styled residence built in 1895 and meticulously restored to its 1929–41 condition. The modest Ebenezer Baptist Church at 407 Auburn Avenue is a 750-seat Gothic Revival red-brick structure where Dr. King and his father, Daddy King, addressed their congregations.

Nestled within downtown's treasured Sweet Auburn community is the city's first planned residential suburb, Inman Park. Established in 1889 by Joel Hurt—developer of Atlanta's first skyscraper, the Equitable Building, in 1892—Inman Park is loaded with Victorian homes, including centerpiece "Callan Castle," built in 1902–3 as the residence of Coca-Cola founder Asa Candler.

As part of Atlanta's Olympics preparation, the Cor-poration for Olympic Development in Atlanta (CODA)

Valerie Ferguson, general manager of downtown's Ritz-Carlton Atlanta, not only works in downtown but for many years as the general manager of the nearby Hyatt Regency Hotel made that hotel her permanent address. One of only several African-American female hotel general managers in the U.S. and having managed hotels in Chicago and New Orleans, Ferguson is quick to compare Atlanta's downtown with down-towns in other major cities.

"Downtowns in other cities are often brick and mortar, institutional," she says. "But in downtown Atlanta there is always something going on. I have beautiful Woodruff Park right here with street vendors selling all kinds of merchandise, and in the summers, at Peachtree Center, there are live concerts. It's safe and the weather is wonderful, so I can take walks through Auburn Avenue, with its historic sites around the corner. Underground Atlanta is just down the street. If you like the pace, the diversity of living in the heart of one of the world's great cities, this is where you want to be."

has put in place an $8 million revitalization effort in Sweet Auburn, supported and developed by the city and its business community.

Clara Axam, CODA president and CEO, describes the initiative as a comprehensive streetscape in the Auburn Avenue corridor that includes widening sidewalks, planting trees, and placing a historical script in granite in the sidewalk from Woodruff Park to the King Center, telling the story of Sweet Auburn.

CODA's pick-and-shovel work also includes creating Dobbs Plaza, a landscaped community gathering place to be developed in conjunction with an Auburn Avenue crafts market.

The name "Sweet Auburn," former Atlanta mayor Maynard Jackson notes, was coined by his grandfather, John Wesley Dobbs, a distinguished humanitarian whose legendary achievements included receiving the Thurgood Marshall Award in 1965. Locations throughout Sweet Auburn bear his name.

In downtown's Sweet Auburn district are the newspaper offices of the *Atlanta Daily World,* along with the original building for the Atlanta Life Insurance Company, founded in 1905, and the Sweet Auburn Curb Market.

Perhaps the Butler Street YMCA, which celebrated its 100th anniversary in 1994, best attests to Sweet Auburn's tradition. Currently, the 50,000-square-foot facility is expanding to include a 14,000-square-foot, $1.5 million structure across the street. Director DeWitt Martin shares a perspective on another kind of expansion it fostered: "The Butler Street Y was always on the cutting edge of social, economic, and political agendas for both black and white populations in Atlanta. This was the first place that blacks and whites in Atlanta could come together and meet."

Since 1947, the Butler Street Y has hosted the Hungry Club Forum, a weekly Wednesday luncheon meeting where Atlantans have gathered to hear speakers from governors to presidents. "It was during those meetings that some of the progressive agendas of the City of Atlanta dealing with human and civil rights were formulated and discussed," Martin notes.

Around the corner, at Edgewood Avenue and Butler Street, is the Sweet Auburn Curb Market, a municipal market dating back to 1923. Occupying 50,000 square feet under one roof on 2.5 acres, the market takes a visitor on a trip back in time, evoking the all-senses-on-alert atmosphere of a southern state fair.

> *"The Butler Street Y was always on the cutting edge of social, economic, and political agendas for both black and white populations in Atlanta. This was the first place that blacks and whites in Atlanta could come together and meet."*
>
> DeWitt Martin, director, Butler Street YMCA

Market manager Karl Gustafson explains that the land the market sits on was cleared in the Great Fire of 1917, thought to have been started in the Grady Hospital mattress warehouse. It is said to have burned more of Atlanta than Sherman burned during the Civil War. The fire allowed for new construction in the area, and soon after, two men—then known as pinhookers (middlemen)—began selling produce from the back of their trucks on the corner of Edgewood and Butler.

"The two men became popular, and more pinhookers joined in," Gustafson says. "Soon they put up a tent over the site. Then, in 1923, the city, with the Atlanta Woman's Club, decided to build a permanent facility on the site and established the Municipal Market.

"The market has historical significance as well as a practical purpose for the neighborhood," Gustafson explains, "Daddy King and Dr. King shopped here, and we are bringing it back. Atlanta has an abundance of state-of-the-art food markets, but this uniquely is a public neighborhood market with a long tradition, made of multiple tenants in the inner city."

Architect A. Ten Eyck Brown designed the original market. By 1939, it was the largest retail food center in the Southeast. With a recent $7 million federally funded revitalization effort, the market has been completely renovated, recharging the community for the future.

George Howell, an attorney and president of the Municipal Market Company, operator of the market, has offices in downtown's beautifully preserved Candler Building on Peachtree Street, just blocks from the 105-year-old Victorian home, about half a mile from the market, he and his wife have renovated in Sweet Auburn.

Howell says, "The Sweet Auburn area represented a segment of the community during a difficult time, a time when it was oppressed. It is a history we are proud of. We want to restore the economically mixed, viable neighborhood that once existed here. We want to restore the market as a public market serving downtown and the surrounding community, where residents and people who work in the city can have fresh produce and ethnic food and enjoy a gathering place—a place for all kinds of people in the community.

"It will be unique," he assures, "and it will add tremendously to the character and strength of downtown as we move into the next century."

ATLANTA — A VISION FOR THE NEW MILLENNIUM

*T*he signature of architect/developer John Portman is evident through-out 13 blocks of downtown Atlanta. One Peachtree Center (left), his most recent project, furthers Portman's original scheme for the Peachtree Center cluster of high-rise office towers (above).

FOLLOWING PAGES: The Hurt Building is among many beautifully renovated structures in the South Central Business District.

The legacy of 1964 Nobel Peace Prize winner Dr. Martin Luther King, Jr., prevails throughout the Sweet Auburn district. The King Center, which includes his birth home, tomb, and supporting facilities, is the third-most-visited national historic site in America.

owntown Atlanta is increasingly attracting artists and professionals to converted loft housing, convenient to the recently renovated Sweet Auburn Curb Market and around the corner from the 100-year-old Butler Street YMCA.

$C$rowds converge on downtown, whether filling streets during the annual July 4 parade or packing Peachtree Center's MARTA station.

*T*he Downtown Child Development Center beckons children of downtown workers to its rooftop playground, while Planet Hollywood and, across the street, the Hard Rock Cafe are playgrounds for the young at heart.

DOWNTOWN: HOSPITALITY AND HISTORY

ATLANTA—A VISION FOR THE NEW MILLENNIUM

The Atlanta Marriott Marquis Hotel (above), with its 515-foot atrium—John Portman's trademark—connects to the architect's Peachtree Center Marquis Towers One and Two office buildings.

# CHAPTER FOUR

# MIDTOWN

## CULTURE AND COMMERCE

Mild-mannered by day, with its buttoned-up commercial edge and cozily clustered neighborhoods, midtown lets its hair down as the sun sets over Atlanta's eclectic center for the arts and culture. A cosmopolitan haven for the avant-garde, midtown has managed to remain quaint over the years, despite the glamour and extravagance, grand entrances and encores that have graced this in-town community.

With a backdrop of lushly shaded winding streets rolling through centerpieces Piedmont Park and the Woodruff Arts Center, midtown is where Atlanta's arts and leisure communities have always shared center stage. During the 1930s and 1940s, Margaret Mitchell wrote her epic novel *Gone with the Wind* in a modest apartment in midtown, on Peachtree Street. Just down the road, Clark Gable and Vivien Leigh, cheered by thousands of fans, celebrated the film's world première at the downtown Loew's Grand Theatre.

The film's superstars stayed at the luxurious, Parisian-styled Georgian Terrace Hotel, as it was then called, built in 1911 and recently converted to upscale residences. Across the street, the Fox Theatre, a 1929 grand Moorish movie palace, hosted virtuosos such as Enrico Caruso and Arturo Toscanini during their annual performances with the visiting New York Metropolitan Opera. Today, this landmark corner of Ponce de Leon Avenue and Peachtree Street is a national historic district. The Fox and the Georgian Terrace are among midtown's structures that have been beautifully renovated, redeveloped, or preserved; they reflect how midtown has come full circle.

Harold Hansen, chairman of the board of First Union Bank and chairman of the Midtown Alliance, a business and community organization diligently safeguarding the future of the area, observes, "Midtown is a model for urban revitalization. It is a 'work in progress.' Our shared vision is of a vibrant, balanced urban center, second to none, where the quality of life allows our commercial, residential, and cultural components to flourish."

Susan Mendheim, president and CEO of the Midtown Alliance, adds another perspective: "A combination of Southtowne, downtown, and Buckhead, midtown gives Atlanta its personality."

Such pride befits its popularity. Though midtown is only a 5.8-square-mile area, it is Atlanta's most densely populated area and loaded with high- and low-end everything. Its many extremes, and not all deliberate, have created a community with enormous lifestyle appeal.

Midtown's early growth is credited to Richard Peters, who, with George Adair, chartered the Atlanta Street Railway Company, the city's first trolley car line. It ran through the substantial midtown property Peters owned and developed. Many of his mansions still stand today.

By the turn of the century, with trolley cars creating easier access, midtown began tapping into downtown's market and gradually expanded as a trade area during the 1930s.

Following the fate of similar American neighborhoods in the 1940s and 1950s, midtown had its share of urban ups and downs as middle-class Atlantans fled to the suburbs and shopping malls flourished.

By the late 1960s, the hippie movement was in full swing. Making its mark in Atlanta most notably at the corner of Peachtree and 10th Streets—the hub of the Strip, as it was known—the transient, bell-bottomed, halter-topped counterculture created quite a local curiosity. By the time the movement had run its course, midtown was ready for its own re-creation.

### A BOOMING AREA FOR BUSINESS

During the 1970s, midtown residents and business leaders organized to give their community some structure. The Peachtree Walk Project, an ambitious urban revitalization effort, was undertaken. Today, its successor, the Midtown Alliance, reflects broad-based goals.

The group's agenda has steadily expanded, keeping pace with the dynamic growth that took off in the mid-1980s. It began with ambitious commercial real estate developments, including the Colony Square high-rise office building and upscale condominiums, the city's first multi-use complex, at the corner of Peachtree and 14th Streets, and the nearby AT&T Long Lines Building.

Recognizing midtown as a legitimate submarket, developers turned their attention to making it a prime site for a cluster of three signature buildings: the stunning Philip Johnson-designed One Atlantic Center, known as the IBM tower, on 14th Street; the Campanile office tower, up the street and across from Colony Square; and the First Union Tower, several blocks south.

Two key factors spawned the surge in commercial development: the consolidation of downtown and suburban offices for professional law and accounting firms and the expansion of communications technology firms, including BellSouth, AT&T, and IBM.

Midtown's main events combine food, fun, art, and culture.

With three MARTA rail stations and easy interstate access and proximity to downtown and adjacent neighborhoods, today's midtown is a major office market. During the mid-1980s, the area had about 2 million square feet of class A office space. That number has soared to approximately 9 million in almost a dozen major high-rise buildings and will soar again when midtown becomes the site of the Sixth District Federal Reserve Bank. "From a construction and absorption standpoint, it's been phenomenal," says John Decker, vice chairman of the Midtown Alliance and partner in charge of office and industrial development for Childress Klein Properties.

The hotel market has flourished, too, with the palatial Occidental Grand Hotel, the Wyndham, the Colony Square Sheraton, and Marriott Suites, all in the Peachtree and 14th Street area.

© J.D. Scott

The Atlanta Symphony Orchestra shares center stage with the Alliance Theater Company at the midtown-based Woodruff Arts Center.

## WORLD-CLASS THEATER, MUSIC, AND ART

About a block away is the Robert W. Woodruff Arts Center, named for its chief benefactor, Coca-Cola magnate and leading local philanthropist, whose empire's global operations are also midtown-based. The Woodruff Arts Center, composed of two structures, is America's only major arts complex that combines visual and performing arts.

In one of the Woodruff Arts Center structures is the Atlanta College of Art, a leading independent regional school that attracts students nationwide for its four-year program in fine art and design.

The facility also houses the Alliance Theater Company, where more than a dozen productions are staged annually. Its artistic director, Kenny Leon, is a law school graduate whose passion for theater led to a stage-directing fellowship with the National Endowment for the Arts and, in 1990, the Alliance's leading creative role. Through his artistic touch, Atlantans have been presented with theater that raises issues and is often challenging. "We have been creating a new audience," Leon explains, "more diverse, younger, and at the same time we are gaining more national support through major foundation gifts."

Leon is looking to make the Alliance the theatrical voice for the region rather than a "booking house" for work created elsewhere. "I want it to be created here and have it go everywhere."

The Alliance is housed with the Atlanta Symphony Orchestra (ASO), which performs to cheering audiences in Atlanta and worldwide under the masterful direction of Yoel Levi, the third musical director in its history.

Celebrating its 50th anniversary in 1995, the ASO was originally a regional part-time band under the custodianship of conductor Henry Sopkin. By 1967, musical director emeritus and conductor laureate Robert Shaw transformed the ensemble into a full-time orchestra and created the Grammy Award-winning Atlanta Symphony Chorus, considered among the best in the world. Shaw passed the baton in 1988 to maestro Yoel Levi, whose first ASO performance was as a last-minute substitute and conducted without a score.

Having studied in London and Rome before joining the Cleveland Orchestra, where he conducted for six years, Levi came to Atlanta with a commitment to make the ASO one of the best symphony orchestras in the world and has remarkably hoisted it from what began as "respectable to spectacular."

> *"A combination of Southtowne, downtown, and Buckhead, midtown gives Atlanta its personality."*
>
> SUSAN MENDHEIM, PRESIDENT AND CEO, MIDTOWN ALLIANCE

When pressed, the soft-spoken 44-year-old Israeli concurs with critics' reviews. The ASO is at world-class level and "can compete with any orchestra in the world." As for Atlanta's devotees, "Atlanta audiences are very sophisticated. Our audiences are critical, and if they do not like a piece or a performance, they will be very reserved. But if they 'are taken' by a performance, they definitely will show their enthusiasm. There is something very positive about the southern hospitality here."

Symphony Hall is next door to the High Museum of Art, housed within an award-winning gleaming white, glass, signature structure designed by Richard Meier a decade ago. With one of the finest collections of American decorative arts in the country, the High has operated since 1991 under the direction of Ned Rifkin, former chief curator at the Hirshhorn Museum and Sculpture Garden of the Smithsonian Museum of Modern and Contemporary Art in Washington, D.C.

Atlanta—A Vision for the New Millennium

"I believe the High Museum of Art can become a leader not by imitating an old model but by generating a new one," Rifkin says. "While the collections of American and European historic art are useful references for anyone interested in those fields, the areas of contemporary international art, photography, folk art, and African art are where we will focus our attention and resources in the future." His overall strategy is to develop innovative community outreach and educational programs that use the museum as a resource, making it more accessible to a broader range of visitors and Atlantans.

### NEIGHBORHOODS WITH CHARACTER AND HISTORY

Of his move to Atlanta, Rifkin says, "I felt this was an opportunity to lead a major arts institution into a new century." And sweetening the deal was the city's superb lifestyle. Rifkin and his family live across the street from the Woodruff Arts Center, in Ansley Park, one of Atlanta's loveliest and oldest intown neighborhoods.

In this city where quality of life reigns supreme, enchanting, long-standing neighborhoods that wind through peaceful, shaded streets are the norm. Among them are midtown's Sherwood Forest, Bedford Pines, Home Park, McGill Place, Virginia-Highland, and Morningside/Lenox Park.

Through the years, the Virginia-Highland neighborhood has evolved into a cosmopolitan, cultural attraction. The historic community, with its shaded, hilly streets and homes built between 1895 and 1930, now bustles with street-level shops, restaurants, galleries, boutiques, and cafes.

Margie Eden grew up in another quaint intown neighborhood, the Morningside community, built in 1923 as a subdivision and later annexed by the city. A communications consultant, Eden was chairperson of the Midtown Alliance's inaugural First Event, a family-styled New Year's street celebration, and coordinated the first Walk for the Park fund-raiser for nearby Piedmont Park Conservancy.

"Over the years, I've seen our neighborhood go through phases," Eden reflects, "old and new, and back again, and I've been impressed with how—even though Atlanta has gone through such dynamic growth and change—my old Morningside neighborhood has kept the charm, character, and warmth I felt when I was growing up."

Natives are not alone in nurturing midtown and singing its praises. Rabbi Mark Kunis of Morningside's Congregation Shearith Israel is president of the Atlanta

**Left: Piedmont Park lures thousands of Atlantans to seasonal festivals, like the annual National Black Arts Festival, and year-round to the Atlanta Botanical Gardens (page 86).**

Rabbinic Association and nationally prominent as chairman of the Rabbinic Fellowship of the Union of Traditional Judaism. The energetic New Yorker came to Atlanta with his family six years ago to lead worshippers at one of the city's oldest synagogues, nestled tranquilly amid midtown's plush neighborhoods.

Ironically, Shearith Israel, formed in 1905, first occupied a building erected by the Ku Klux Klan. Today, that structure houses the synagogue's educational center. With its mission to help perfect the world and make it a little brighter for others, Shearith Israel was the first synagogue in the United States to create a homeless shelter for women, still in operation.

"What's interesting about Morningside, Lenox Park, and Virginia-Highland," he says, "is that these are real neighborhoods; you have people walking in the streets, stopping to say hello, going to neighborhood shops, unlike some look-alike communities that will spring up in suburbs."

Over to the east, midtown's Little Five Points area is affectionately considered the city's bohemian center. With its homemade ambience, this community has no desire for gentrification; its highly honed niche in Atlanta is unrivaled as an oasis for the offbeat and artsy. Showcasing local talent are the 7 Stages Theatre and the Horizon Theatre, with its off-Broadway atmosphere.

One of the benefits of midtown living is the close proximity of Piedmont Park, the oldest in Atlanta. With the greatest year-round attendance of any recreational site in town, Piedmont Park and Botanical Gardens is a focal point of Atlanta. In fact, the city grew up around the 185-acre playground, dating back more than a hundred years.

Atlanta's population was not yet at 40,000 in 1881 when the city hosted the first of three international cotton expositions—the equivalent of today's world fairs—at what later became Piedmont Park. Designed to drum up attention for the city as a leading distribution center and as much a dress rehearsal in unbridled self-promotion, Atlanta's expositions were a smashing success. General William T. Sherman, who had burned down the town less than two decades earlier, not only showed up but was a speaker at the 1881 event.

The third and most spectacular exhibition was the $3 million Cotton States and International Exposition of 1895, for which a lake, a midway, and grand exhibition buildings were created that are still in place today. About 400,000 people attended, including Buffalo Bill and his Wild West Show, President Grover Cleveland, John Philip Sousa, who performed, and Booker T. Washington, who delivered his famous "Atlanta Compromise" speech.

Still luring Atlantans to major recreational and entertainment events, Piedmont Park is home to the Atlanta Symphony in the Park, the Atlanta Jazz Festival, the ary Mac's Tea Room, on Ponce de Leon Avenue in midtown, first opened more than half a century ago. It had been given different names by three different owners before Margaret Lupo took over the business in 1962. Now the retired owner of this local landmark, Lupo kept the restaurant name she inherited because "it would have cost a thousand dollars to change the sign."

"There were about 12 'tea rooms' in Atlanta back then," Lupo says. "Most were owned by women, who used the term tea room because it was very genteel sounding, and this is the South." Her lunch and dinner patrons were the people who lived in the neighborhood and business professionals from downtown, spoiled on an assortment of delicious fresh vegetables, fried chicken, and baked and roasted specialties, southern-style.

"The neighborhood had lots of artists, musicians, fine people who owned the homes from Ponce de Leon on back down Myrtle Street and Penn Avenue. The front of the neighborhood on Ponce was commercial, with a laundry across the street and Central Electric Appliances next door. Down a ways was the Blue Dot Tavern, and a fresh poultry business with chickens you could buy and have cleaned right there."

While raising a family and working 12- to 14-hour days operating Mary Mac's with her husband, Lupo also paved the way for other women in Atlanta's business community. She was the first woman to become a board member of Central Atlanta Progress, the Atlanta Convention and Visitors Bureau, the Atlanta Chamber of Commerce, and the Downtown Lions Club.

Montreux International Music Festival, the National Black Arts Festival, the Dogwood Festival, hot-air balloon racing, and the blessed finish line for the annual July 4th 10K Peachtree Road Race.

Piedmont Park's main event is the annual Atlanta Arts Festival each September, among the largest and most prestigious multidisciplinary arts festivals in North America. Commanding most of the park with curated visual arts exhibits, an artists market, and performances, the event draws visual and performing artists from around the world. Since its debut in 1953, when it was held in a backyard in Buckhead, the nine-day happening has blossomed, attracting more than 2 million visitors over the past decade.

Showcased in Piedmont Park is the Atlanta Botanical Gardens, sprawling majestically amid 30 acres of landscaped gardens, the Storza Woods, and the Dorothy Chapman Fuqua Conservatory, all supported by more than a thousand members and hundreds of hands-on volunteers.

Year long, families from all parts of the metropolitan

region enjoy midtown's entertainment attractions, which run the gamut from the Center for Puppetry Arts to SciTrek, the Science and Technology Museum of Atlanta. With an impressive learning-by-experience-and-experiment program, SciTrek is one of the top science centers in America, drawing more than 1.2 million visitors since it opened in 1988. With about 100 interactive exhibits, SciTrek was the first museum in the U.S. with an on-site research lab devoted to electric vehicle technology.

### HOME TO WORLD-FAMOUS INSTITUTIONS

Technology is part of the turf in midtown. The renowned Georgia Institute of Technology (Georgia Tech), founded in 1885, is ranked third by the National Science Foundation among all U.S. colleges and universities for engineering research and development expenditures.

Graduating more African-American engineers than any other American university, Georgia Tech enrolls 13,000 students from the U.S. and 80 countries. Since 1991, the average Scholastic Aptitude Test scores of the school's incoming freshmen have been the highest among public universities in the country.

The Advanced Technology Development Center (ATDC) at Georgia Tech, a technology incubator for start-up companies, has operated since 1981.

Mary Mac's Margaret Lupo (left) and crew serve up home cooking, southern-style.

The ATDC provides businesses with assistance in new product development and marketing, along with business and technical support. Companies formed with ATDC assistance generated $214 million in revenues during 1994.

ATDC director Wayne Hodges explains, "Many of these companies are offshoots of technology developed at Georgia Tech and other research universities in the state, and of entrepreneurs who have technology ideas they want to develop. Georgia Tech's resources are being recognized internationally."

Tech's 350-acre midtown campus is off North Avenue, where the Varsity, reputedly the world's largest drive-in eatery, is a landmark and a familiar quick stop for anyone craving onion rings, chili dogs, and fries.

Georgia Tech, the Varsity, and the entire metro skyline are the view down the street from the Coca-Cola Company's worldwide headquarters on North Avenue, where 4,000 people work for the world's largest soft drink company, whose products are sold in more than 195 countries.

Another prestigious facility with a midtown address is the Carter Presidential Center, to the east off North Avenue. The complex draws international attention to the many projects supported by the 39th president of the United States and Georgia's favorite son.

Within the center is the Jimmy Carter Library and Museum, one of nine such presidential facilities. The nonprofit center highlights key 20th-century issues, bringing people and resources together to advance peace and human rights worldwide.

The center is only blocks away from flamboyant Little Five Points, where peanuts, many produced in President Carter's native Plains, Georgia, are the main ingredient in midtown-based Sophie Mae Candies, the world's largest manufacturer of peanut brittle. Spanning a street block on North Avenue for the past half-century, the candy company has produced sweet treats for 110 years.

During Thanksgiving and Christmas holidays alone, Sophie Mae produces about 3 million pounds of the delectable confection. According to plant manager Alan Garrett, Sophie Mae's packaging facility seems to be the cause of traffic congestion year-round. "Travelers like to look inside, straining to watch us package about 6,000 boxes per hour; that's 25,000 pounds during an eight-hour shift."

Aside from the taste, such treats keep captive locals and visitors rediscovering the surprises of midtown, where an enchanting blend of contradictions is the formula for success.

> "What's interesting about Morningside, Lenox Park, and Virginia-Highland is that these are real neighborhoods; you have people walking in the streets, stopping to say hello, going to neighborhood shops, unlike some look-alike communities that will spring up in suburbs."
>
> MARK KUNIS, RABBI, CONGREGATION SHEARITH ISRAEL, AND PRESIDENT, ATLANTA RABBINIC ASSOCIATION

Atlanta—A Vision for the New Millennium

idtown's Georgia Institute of Technology (left) is among the top-ranked engineering institutions in the U.S. Another renowned institution, the Carter Presidential Center (above) brings further recognition to midtown domestically and internationally.

Atlanta—A Vision for the New Millennium

*L*earning is fun at the Center for Puppetry Arts (left); SciTrek, the Science and Technology Museum of Atlanta (right); the High Museum of Art (center, top); and the Inman Middle School (center, bottom).

FOLLOWING PAGES: The High Museum of Art.

97

*L*ocals celebrate the arts at a Virginia-Highland gallery (top), a seniors workshop at the Horizon Theatre (bottom right), and with a street performer in Piedmont Park.

*O*utdoor gatherings are a natural any time in Little Five Points (top left) and at annual events like the Dogwood Festival in Piedmont Park.

*N*eighborhoods in midtown
are known for their character,
charm, and quaint tree-lined streets.

*A*tlantans take good food seriously. Fast-food eateries, like the Varsity, serve up chili dogs and fries (top left), outdoor cafes feature music under the stars, and ethnic restaurants add spice to the exotic and unique.

FOLLOWING PAGES: The "fabulous Fox" theater has showcased the best entertainers from around the world since 1929. The magnificent Moorish structure has been meticulously renovated in recent years.

# CHAPTER FIVE

# BUCKHEAD

## GLAMOUR AND GRACE

*T*hough the name Buckhead is misleading, it contributes to its mystique. Conjuring up images of a less than elite and well-heeled setting, Buckhead is Atlanta's Beverly Hills, Palm Beach, Georgetown—the backdrop for an urban fantasy city planners dream of and city dwellers come to dream in.

Those who work and live within the affluent 28-square-mile northern tip of the City of Atlanta say Buckhead is a state of mind. This is where grand mansions and middle-class cottages coexist in a traditionally blue-blood setting; where world-class shopping, restaurants, and entertainment annually generate $1.25 billion in retailing; and where Atlanta's most prestigious residences are only blocks away from some of the region's most impressive corporate addresses.

Boosters believe that Buckhead, with its magnitude and mix, may be the largest, most diverse suburban-commercial center in America. Other parts of the country may claim a comparable commercial environment, but few, if any, have Buckhead's balanced residential component. Its varied and abundant residences range from moderately priced apartments to mansions, from middle-income subdivisions to high-rises.

Buckhead is clearly the acknowledged target of urban envy. It comes with the territory when the very best in trendy night life, cuisine, entertainment, shopping, and hotels create a constant, incredible metropolitan and regionwide draw. Rich with such manmade resources, Buckhead also is steeped in tradition, a place where the history of Atlanta's refined past and its zeal for the future enchantingly combine.

The Buckhead mystique, it is told, dates back to 1838, when Henry Irby, a former South Carolinian and local resident, shot a deer at a nearby stream and hung the buck's head on a post outside his tavern. Land Lot 99, the 202 1/2-acre tract of wilderness Irby purchased for $650, was occupied by only his tavern and combination grocery and general store. Before long, the tiny community's gathering place became a landmark; "Meet me at the buck's head," locals would say.

That area, soon called Irbyville, today is the heart of Buckhead, around the bustling intersection of Peachtree, Roswell, and West Paces Ferry Roads.

The small community was steadily growing when the Civil War erupted, leaving its mark in Buckhead with the first of four major battles fought at Peachtree Creek. At the end of the war, resilient residents repaired, rebuilt, and replenished. Today, historic landmarks throughout Buckhead's upscale Peachtree Battle neighborhood tell the story of the conflict and bloodshed that took place there.

With the turn of the century and progress—paved streets, automobiles, public utilities—Buckhead showed a knack for commerce coupled with a fortuitous location. Real estate became valuable as city dwellers, only several miles away, sought out the country crossroads. As land values climbed, business and commerce of all types followed.

"There was still a lot of farmland in Buckhead back then," recalls 74-year-old Tom Murray. His Buckhead Hardware Company, started by his father 74 years ago in the original Irby Tavern, in what is now the Buckhead triangle area, is the oldest business still operating in Buckhead. "Buckhead was a jumping-off place in the late 1920s," he says, "and one of the most prestigious places anyone could live."

He recalls the trend among wealthier Atlantans with businesses downtown and homes just north in what is now midtown to build country summer homes in Buckhead.

During the 1920s, Buckhead claimed seven brick buildings and not more than 30 stores—all in the Buckhead triangle area. In the late 1920s, business migrated about a block south onto nearby Pharr Road. During the

Seventy-five-year-old Roy Milling, a long-time retailer, remembers Buckhead in earlier times: "Little two-tent, three-night circuses were held in Irby's Alley, now called Irby Avenue, and originally 'round about the site of Irby's Tavern. The name was changed from alley to avenue," he smiles, "when somebody thought we should sound uptown."

Milling's 42-year-old business, Northside Tool Rental, is among the half-dozen stores along Irby Avenue now. All the storefront buildings on Irby Avenue where Northside Tool stands are original Buckhead structures. The Five Paces Inn—so named because it was five paces down Paces Ferry Road from Peachtree—kept the name when it relocated to Irby Avenue. From time to time, rumors fly that the block will be sold for several million dollars.

quarter century from about 1910 to 1934, Buckhead began blossoming from a country crossroads into a commercial mecca.

As more stores were built in the early 1930s between Pharr Road and Peachtree Avenue, apartment buildings sprang up and public transportation became more accessible. By the early 1950s, in the aftermath of World War II, businesses had spread a few hundred feet to East and West Paces Ferry Roads.

It was not until 1952 that the Buckhead district officially joined the City of Atlanta. By the end of the decade, the region's first retail mall opened there, turning shoppers on to a new preoccupation. Meanwhile, the U.S. Congress created the interstate transportation system. Buckhead was on its way.

With Buckhead's huge popularity as a retail center, keeping traffic flowing became a planning priority. In place today are three MARTA stations in Buckhead—at Lenox Road, Lindbergh Drive, and Peachtree at Georgia 400—as well as immediate access to a network of interstate superhighways.

Motorists can also take the new six-lane Georgia 400 extension into Buckhead. Connecting the southern point of Dahlonega to Interstate 285 in Fulton County, the 50-mile road connects to the interstate system at Interstate 85 on the edge of Buckhead.

### A SHOPPER'S PARADISE

Despite the massive numbers of people and vehicles converging in Buckhead's compact space and its contrasting cultivated high-brow appeal, this thriving round-the-clock commercial center has remained remarkably hometown.

An abundance of small shops and mom-and-pop storefronts add to the ambience. Many merchants have set up shops in converted houses along side streets and main roads. These smaller businesses coexist with skyscrapers and regional malls only blocks away.

The community's retail reputation is so enticing that "about two dozen businesses not located in Buckhead use it in their names in the phone book," notes Sam Massell, mayor of Atlanta from 1970 to 1974 and president of the exclusive Buckhead Coalition, the high-powered, proactive business group steering the community's growth.

Claiming a Buckhead address is nothing new. In its early days, people said they lived in Buckhead although they were nowhere near the Buckhead triangle intersection. "Matt Perkins, owner of the area's one-time weekly newspaper, put up signs, 'Welcome to Buckhead,'" Massell recalls, pointing to old landmarks on Peachtree and at the old Buckhead Elks Club.

> *"Buckhead was a jumping-off place in the late 1920s, and one of the most prestigious places anyone could live."*
>
> TOM MURRAY, RETIRED OWNER, BUCKHEAD HARDWARE COMPANY

Only five miles from central downtown, Buckhead is a stunning example of a bedroom community that has been transformed into a successful "suburban downtown" and touted as an edge city of the future. People can live in luxuriously quiet, forestlike seclusion on cul-de-sacs only a couple of miles from the center of Buckhead's retail bonanza. Though Buckhead's population is 61,662, its daytime population is 135,000 and its annual employment growth rate is about 1,200.

The majority of offices, retail outlets, and hotels in Buckhead are strategically located within only two square miles of Lenox Square shopping mall and near Peachtree and Piedmont Roads, Buckhead's busiest intersection.

Buckhead is well known for its abundance of great restaurants, from casual outdoor hamburger joints to fine dining rooms with white linen tablecloths.

Lenox Square, one of the first regional malls in the U.S., brought Atlantans the retail mall concept when it opened in Buckhead in 1959. Only a mile or so north of the Buckhead triangle, Lenox Square is the core of Buckhead's billion-dollar retail market, attracting more than 14 million shoppers annually. The largest shopping center in the Southeast, with 250 stores covering 1.5 million square feet, it has just completed a $60 million renovation. Phipps Plaza, across the street, offers more upscale shopping in a renovated and expanded, brilliantly polished $140 million, 822,000-square-foot facility, considered one of the country's most beautifully designed retail shopping environments.

Among Buckhead's retailers are some of the world's most exclusive boutiques and specialty and department stores, from Tiffany's to Neiman-Marcus, Saks Fifth

Avenue, and Cartier. An estimated 40 percent of expenditures in Buckhead are made by visitors from 100 or more miles away.

## CROSSROADS FOR FOOD AND FUN

Once visitors and locals come to Buckhead, there's no lack of things to do. Charity events, festivals, and professional and amateur cycling races keep Buckhead hopping, as do the annual Decorator's Show House; the St. Patrick's Day Parade; the Veterans Day Parade; the July 4th Peachtree 10K Race, which begins in Buckhead and attracts 150,000 spectators; and the July 4th Star Spangled Night fireworks show at Lenox Square, dazzling 100,000 people.

A magnet for stylish crowds after the sun goes down, Buckhead has more than 200 dining and entertainment establishments. Sidewalks fill with fun seekers strolling the Buckhead triangle and nearby Buckhead Village area, which has created a merchants association of its own.

Covering 12 blocks in the Peachtree and Paces Ferry Road area, Buckhead Village includes an amazing 120 restaurants and nightspots. These run the gamut from jazz bars to trendy good-time haunts. Buckhead Village also boasts fine art galleries, antique shops, and classic, campy, and high-couture clothing stores.

Before opening a fine art gallery in Buckhead in 1980, Fay Gold taught painting in her backyard. She combined the school with a gallery in Buckhead's Irby Avenue area until the gallery was so successful that she became an art dealer full time. Today, the Fay Gold Gallery is the largest in town.

As the pioneer of contemporary art in Atlanta, Gold observes that her gallery is "close to many of my clients; I feel safe here, there's great traffic flow, it's centrally located, and there are always people on the street." As for the increase in galleries opening in Buckhead, she says, "That strengthens us all. We are very diversified, and Buckhead has become a central location for fine art."

Accommodation is part of Buckhead's claim to fame.

> "We've produced a blueprint of what Buckhead should be like in the next 20 years, and from the looks of the research, it's very exciting. Instead of the lifestyle deteriorating, we have a great opportunity to enhance it for our children and grandchildren."
>
> CHARLIE LOUDERMILK,
> FORMER CHAIRMAN, BUCKHEAD COALITION,
> AND CHAIRMAN AND PRESIDENT, AARON RENTS

Fifteen hotels, including the luxury Hotel Nikko, Swissôtel, Ritz-Carlton Buckhead, and J. W. Marriott, offer about 4,000 rooms. Buckhead also has three of Atlanta's four four-star hotels and one of the two five-diamond hotels in Georgia.

From the Dining Room at the Ritz, to curbside shiny trailer diners, from ethnic to gourmet, to veggie burgers and fries, food is one of Buckhead's biggest attractions. And the list of the best keeps getting longer.

The Buckhead Life Group, which opened its first restaurant in 1979, sets the standard, not only in Atlanta but around the country. Its first restaurant, Pano's and Paul's, gave locals and visitors a taste of awesome edibles served in opulence. Today, the company has nine restaurants. The eight in Buckhead are distinctly different and all within a five-mile stretch of West and East Paces Ferry Roads.

Among the finest restaurateurs in America, the Buckhead Life Group consistently garners the industry's top national awards. Co-owner Pano Karatassos, whose restaurants serve some 5,000 lunches and dinners on typical Fridays, says Buckhead was the only place he and partner Paul Albrecht even considered. Now that their reputation has spread coast to coast, Karatassos routinely gets calls from people in other cities asking him to open up restaurants in their towns. "I always say," he quips, "I'd be delighted to, but do you have a street there called West Paces Ferry Road?" The entrepreneur/restaurateur explains, "There's no reason to go anywhere else. Besides, we have the name Buckhead, and no other city does."

## BULLISH ON BUCKHEAD

If Karatassos sounds a bit bullish, he is, and, in fact, he was a recipient of the "Bullish on Buckhead" award. Such recognition is annually bestowed by the Buckhead Business Association (BBA), among Atlanta's oldest broad-based forums. The longest-standing guardian of Buckhead, the BBA was established in 1951. Reflecting uncommon unity, it is as concerned with picking up litter and buying sidewalk street lamps as it is with updating retail studies and neighborhood planning. Remarkably, in the more than four decades since the group's founding, a minimum of 100 BBA members have met at 9:00 every Thursday morning for breakfast and camaraderie and to hear influential speakers.

As the BBA deals with day-to-day issues, the Buckhead Coalition concerns itself with strategic direction and long-range planning. Founded in 1988, the coalition has 75 members and a waiting list; the credential to be admitted is no less than to be CEO of a major firm. Together, members undertake comprehensive planning responsibility for Buckhead and serve as financial backers for civic programs.

"Buckhead has a unique niche in the U.S.," says founding member and former chairman of the coalition Charlie Loudermilk, a Buckhead native whose 40-year-old business,

Aaron Rents, is based in Buckhead. To keep the community from "disappearing and being swallowed up into greater Atlanta," several years ago he assembled a group of friends with real estate, business, and neighborhood interests and formed the Buckhead Coalition. "We've produced a blueprint of what Buckhead should be like, in all aspects, in the next 20 years," he explains, "and from the looks of the research, it's very exciting. Instead of the lifestyle deteriorating, we have a great opportunity to enhance it for our children and grandchildren."

The coalition's impressive roster includes developers who have contributed to Buckhead's 11 million square feet of office space—40 percent built within the last five years.

### HIGH-RISE 9 TO 5

It was during the mid-1970s that the office space explosion ignited in Buckhead. Pioneer developers were Claude Petty, who built Piedmont Center, and Charles Ackerman, whose Tower Place—a 29-story, glass-encased high-rise—has recently been spiffed up with dazzling green neon lights outlining its silhouette.

With one of the lowest vacancy rates and highest rental rates in metropolitan Atlanta, Buckhead is projected to triple its office space in 13 years. Buckhead's biggest office development is the 13-building Piedmont Center office park, developed by PC Associates and located on 45 acres on Piedmont Road between Roswell and Peachtree Roads. Recently, the 1.6 million-square-foot development grew to 1.9 million with the addition of a high-rise. Second in size is the sprawling 1 million-square-foot Atlanta Financial Center, an enormous high-rise on Peachtree Road south of Lenox Square that boosted the 1980s building boom in Buckhead with its three glass-covered connecting 12- and 19-story towers, the latest completed in 1989.

Several older areas within Buckhead have flourished into significant business centers, too. Off Piedmont Road is Miami Circle, a top home furnishings and decorator center that complements the nearby Atlanta Decorative Arts Center, the region's premier furnishings facility, open to decorators only.

Bennett Street, several blocks from the Peachtree Battle area, was a dirt road with clapboard houses at the turn of the century. Today, Bennett Street is a rustic retail area with antiques, art, fine crafts, furniture, and accessories.

On the other extreme, just blocks away, in the Peachtree Battle area, is a 60,000-square-foot decorative arts center, built in 1986. With 26 shops, the complex has an 18th-century French architectural theme that is far from the cookie cutter mold.

Sixty-seven-year-old Jane J. Marsden, developer of the center, has lived in Buckhead for 45 years and now lives in a penthouse above her store there. Buckhead is "probably the biggest market for antiques in the U.S. outside New York,"

Within a five-mile stretch of posh East and West Paces Ferry Roads, the Buckhead Life Group's restaurants, including the Buckhead Diner, have turned Atlantans on to awesome edibles.

she says, based on the quantity of containers and shipments coming to Atlanta.

### HEAVENLY HOMES

From cottage quaint to grandiose, neighborhoods in Buckhead have a flair few communities can rival. Standard sightseeing tours of Buckhead's renowned residential real estate always include Tuxedo Park, about two miles from Lenox Square/Phipps Plaza, in the West Paces Ferry Road area, where the gardens are manicured and the estates palatial. The governor's mansion is found here and, about a block away, another estate converted into the Southern Center for International Studies.

"The best of Atlanta begins with Buckhead," says Jenny Pruitt, whose seven-year-old residential real estate firm sold the Tuxedo Road home of Coca-Cola icon Robert Woodruff for $6.5 million in 1990. "Buckhead is considered by many to be the epitome of a luxurious lifestyle and the best the South has to offer," she says. "It reminds me of Worth Avenue in Palm Beach and Rodeo Drive in Beverly Hills."

Known for an aggressive marketing spirit, the Buckhead native is one of three women directors of the Buckhead

Coalition and eagerly touts Buckhead's credentials, like the fact that more CEOs live in Buckhead than in any other part of Atlanta.

"When we get a million-dollar customer," she says, "they'll seldom get to the closing table without looking at Buckhead. Nothing will match Buckhead's grace and style."

Along the fine line where Buckhead and midtown merge on Peachtree at the Amtrak station are some of Atlanta's oldest neighborhoods, such as enchanting Brookwood Hills, off Peachtree Street. Its rolling hills filled with dense foliage are across the street from Piedmont Hospital and the Shepherd Center—the nation's largest hospital devoted exclusively to the rehabilitation of patients with spinal disorders.

Collier Hills is close by, while moving northward are Buckhead's Peachtree Hills, Peachtree Heights, Garden Hills, Peachtree Park, and Pine Hills communities. Just blocks away from the old-line Peachtree Battle neighborhood at Peachtree is newly constructed, exclusive Park Place, the largest, single-purpose residential condominium building in America. One of its most famous residents is Elton John.

Buckhead's northern residential area is highlighted by

> *"The best of Atlanta begins with Buckhead. Buckhead is considered by many to be the epitome of a luxurious lifestyle and the best the South has to offer."*
>
> JENNY PRUITT, REALTOR

the green, sprawling community of Chastain Park, off Roswell Road. The only park in Atlanta that still boards horses, Chastain is also the site of the Atlanta Symphony Orchestra's annual summer concert series.

Curiously, along with its growing population of urban professionals, young families, and upwardly mobile types, Buckhead has more than a dozen residential high-rises for the elderly, the greatest concentration of such housing in the region. And off Piedmont Road in Buckhead is the highest concentration of international residents, primarily Hispanic and Asian, found anywhere in Atlanta.

The diversity in Buckhead today, combined with a glorious, upper-crust past, have created a fairy-tale community for the next century. Yet, despite the high-polish, high-brow setting, Buckhead residents have a wholesome side. This is the home of the country's largest Presbyterian church, the largest Episcopal congregation, two of the largest Southern Baptist churches, and the third-largest conservative synagogue in America.

"The spiritual health of the Buckhead community is alive and well," smiles the Reverend Joanna Adams, senior pastor of Trinity Presbyterian Church. Located at the corner of Moores Mill and Howell Mill Roads, it is the largest Presbyterian church in the U.S. with a woman senior pastor. "To me, the test of spiritual health is how we live in the world with our neighbors outside the sanctuary," Adams says, "and I have found that the people here have a great reservoir of goodwill."

It seems appropriate that the Atlanta History Center, operated by the Atlanta Historical Society, founded in 1926, is located in the heart of Buckhead. Chronicling Buckhead's prestige, its blue blood, and its bloodshed during the Civil War, this historical society has the only history museum and gardens and two different museum houses of different periods in the U.S. Along with 32 acres of gardens and trails are exhibits, a library and archives, and a new $11 million, 83,000-square-foot museum, the largest such structure in the state devoted to the history of Atlanta and among the largest in the nation devoted to urban and suburban history.

The museum's Swan House Mansion, a meticulously preserved 1920s Italian-style villa, and its 22 acres of gardens illustrate the extraordinary architecture and grand living of Buckhead long ago. Its Tullie Smith Farm House and outbuildings speak of the wild frontier and farming community of the 1840s—an era reflecting the days when Irby's Tavern, just around the corner, was distinguished by a buck's head.

Buckhead's estates are legendary. Some of the city's most magnificent, such as the governor's mansion (right), lie in the heart of Buckhead within Tuxedo Park.

BUCKHEAD: GLAMOUR AND GRACE

Atlanta—A Vision for the New Millennium

July 4 is no longer a day of leisure for many Atlantans. At last count, 50,000 runners hit the hot pavement at the Lenox Square starting line for the world's largest 10K.

LEFT: Buckhead is renowned for its real estate. Its palatial estates are a must-see on any tour of the town.

A mid Atlanta's bustling urban environment, neighborhood parks offer a peaceful retreat.

*D*espite its elegance, casual socializing is very much a part of the Buckhead lifestyle.

The Civil War left its mark in Buckhead and is chronicled at the Atlanta History Center, where the 1840s-era Tullie Smith Farm House and grounds (top right) and an 83,000-square-foot museum are major attractions for locals and visitors.

*B*uckhead is the place to be, with unsurpassed shopping, parades and festivals, and loads of neighborhood parks and pools.

The beautifully restored 1920s Swan House mansion, located at the Atlanta History Center in Buckhead, is open for tours year-round.

RIGHT: The Atlanta Symphony Orchestra performs at the Cathedral of St. Phillip in Buckhead.

BUCKHEAD: GLAMOUR AND GRACE

# CHAPTER SIX

# METROPOLITAN ATLANTA

## SHARING THE SPIRIT

*W*ide-open spaces, old-fashioned main streets and county fairs, commercial, high-tech, industrial, and corporate enclaves, and the city dweller's retreat to untampered nature all come together in the metropolitan Atlanta area. At its heart are the glory and goals of the dynamic, progressive city of Atlanta.

"The relationships that have been built between the city of Atlanta and our surrounding counties set Atlanta apart from other cities in America," says Walter R. Huntley, Jr., president of the Atlanta Economic Development Corporation. "When you look at quality of life, natural resources and amenities, and the commercial drive the metro area injects, it is not surprising that Atlanta is the performance capital of the Southeast."

Counties within the metropolitan Atlanta area flow into one another, with no distinct visual boundaries or terrain to delineate where one county ends and another begins. The broad 18-county metropolitan Atlanta area encompasses 5,147 square miles with a population of 3 million, making it the ninth-largest metro region in the U.S. As one of the country's premier employment centers, metropolitan Atlanta has among the fastest-growing job markets in the nation; more than 500,000 new jobs were created during the 1980s.

Jerry Bartels, president of the Atlanta Chamber of Commerce, observes, "As the heart of the most populous region in the United States, Atlanta commands an inherent leadership role within the dynamic surrounding metropolitan area. With approximately 20 percent of the U.S. buying power and a combined GNP bigger than all but the largest countries, the southeastern U.S. is one of the largest markets in the world, with Atlanta at its core."

Adds Bart Lewis, chief of the Socio-Economic Analysis Division of the Atlanta Regional Commission (ARC), a comprehensive regional planning organization and development center coordinating activities among 10 counties and more than 60 cities in the region, "The metropolitan region's employment base will more than

> *"When you look at quality of life, natural resources and amenities, and the commercial drive the metro area injects, it is not surprising that Atlanta is the performance capital of the Southeast."*
>
> WALTER R. HUNTLEY, JR.,
> PRESIDENT, ATLANTA ECONOMIC
> DEVELOPMENT CORPORATION

double from 901,157 in 1980 to 2.17 million in 2010, four times the growth rate of the nation."

Following the national trend, the service industry in the region will not only remain its largest sector but will increase its share of the regional economy. According to ARC, for the 10-county Atlanta region, the service industry will account for more than one in every four new jobs created between 1980 and 2010, increasing 240 percent.

Service employment currently represents 27 percent of Atlanta's total employment. Retail trade, the second-largest sector, accounts for 18 percent, with government at 15 percent and manufacturing and wholesale trade at 10 percent each. Transportation, communications, and public utilities combined represent 9 percent of Atlanta's employment, with finance, insurance, and real estate at 8 percent and construction at 4 percent.

In terms of population and economic development activity, the hierarchy of counties in the metro area has Fulton at the top, followed by DeKalb, Cobb, and Gwinnett.

"What I think is so remarkable," says ARC's Lewis, "is that this region has had a high rate of growth in population and employment for more than 30 years now. Not many regions are able to add two-thirds of a million people a decade over a protracted time period, yet the metro Atlanta region's population is projected by ARC to soar to 3.6 million by 2010—an increase of nearly two million people—continuing the remarkable historical rate of growth."

Add to that the fact that its economy is expanding faster than its resident population and it becomes clear that new residents will continue to move to metro Atlanta for job opportunities. With its high migration rate, the metropolitan region will continue to have a relatively younger population than the rest of the nation, and by 2010, the median age here will be 35.4 years compared with the nation's 38.4.

## FULTON COUNTY

Ninety percent of the City of Atlanta is within Fulton County's boundaries, which starts at its southernmost tip at Southtowne's Hartsfield Atlanta International Airport. Downtown Atlanta, much of midtown, and all of Buckhead are within Fulton County, whose residential and business directories are a virtual who's who of the Southeast. Top-notch institutions of higher learning are also concentrated in Fulton County, including Georgia Institute of Technology, Georgia State University, the Atlanta University Center, and Atlanta Area Tech.

While significant development activity has been historically concentrated in Fulton County, in recent years, greater attention has been placed on North Fulton and, more recently, South Fulton.

With a population of 710,000 within its 529 square miles, Fulton is the most populous and developed county in the metropolitan area. "We view Fulton County as 'Atlanta Plus,' " says Nancy Leathers, director of the Fulton County Department of Planning and Economic Development.

In the past several years, new high-quality, upscale residential development has begun in South Fulton County. Within it, the Fulton Industrial Area is the largest aggregate industrial area east of the Mississippi. With approximately 80 percent still undeveloped, South Fulton is a bed of opportunity, with a modern infrastructure, highways, and rapid rail surrounded by rich green natural terrain.

South Fulton is home to the AEDC's Hartsfield Centre, an $80 million business park at Hartsfield Atlanta International Airport. AEDC's Southside Industrial Park (SIP), also in South Fulton, was established in 1986 and has a total of 4 million square feet of potential build-out space. With its aggressive enterprise zone designation and freeport tax-exemption status, the SIP has attracted Fortune 500 and local companies. Its sister development, the AEDC's Atlanta Industrial Park, provides 3 million square feet of industrial space and has created more than 2,000 jobs.

North Fulton County, with more class A office space than downtown Atlanta, begins with Sandy Springs, one of the fastest-growing communities in the country. With the new Georgia 400 toll loop highway to downtown, North Fulton is expected to experience even more growth. One of the first developments was the 1.3 million-square-foot North Point Mall in the City of Alpharetta, which also is headquarters for Harry's Farmers Market, Inc., a 100,000-square-foot facility opened in 1988 and the first of four such mega stores now in surrounding metro counties.

President, CEO, and chairman Harry Blazer, whose publicly traded business had revenues of $140 million in 1994, employs 1,600 people in the metro region. Regarded as one of the country's leading retailers of fresh foods, Blazer says, "There is no question that the best fresh food offerings are available to Atlantans more so than in any other city in the U.S. Atlantans have come to expect that. The people here have high incomes, they are highly educated, families, homeowners with sophisticated tastes. There was a need," he says, "and we filled it."

### DeKalb County

Covering 270 square miles with a population of 577,000, DeKalb is Atlanta's most culturally diverse county, claiming the greatest concentrations of African-American, Hispanic, and Asian populations. As Atlanta's most urban county, DeKalb is solidly service-based; it is the

second-largest county in the state in population, business, jobs, and payroll.

Liane Levetan, chief operating officer of DeKalb County, holds the second-highest elected position in Georgia headed by a woman. "This is a county with a strong infrastructure, good transportation, excellent residential areas, multifamily housing, office, industrial, and commercial development, and," she emphasizes, "the lowest water and sewer rates in the metropolitan Atlanta area."

DeKalb also has the largest available in-use space in the 20-county region for industrial, distribution, and service industries.

Biomedical and biotechnical industries are highlighted in DeKalb. Clustered along its Clifton corridor are such leading institutions as the U.S. Centers for Disease Control and Prevention (CDC), with 4,800 employees housed in its

*"With approximately 20 percent of the U.S. buying power and a combined GNP bigger than all but the largest countries, the southeastern U.S. is one of the largest markets in the world, with Atlanta at its core."*

JERRY BARTELS, PRESIDENT,
ATLANTA CHAMBER OF COMMERCE

"The American Cancer Society moved to Atlanta because we found that it was the only place we could go to, other than New York City, where we had been located, that could provide the outstanding transportation access to our constituencies nationally and internationally," says John Seffrin, national executive vice president and chief of staff officer for the American Cancer Society.

"The reasonable cost of doing business here and the potential to work closely with institutions of the prestige of the CDC and Emory University's schools of medicine and public health were tremendously important in the decision to relocate here," he adds. "To be in a place that is attractive to our field staff who may aspire to national-level positions as they progress in their careers is very important. We have more people than ever before who started their employment in our field operation now working in our national home office staff in Atlanta."

A stone's throw from the American Cancer Society's offices is the plush, leafy northeast Atlanta campus of Emory University, ranked among the top 25 universities in the nation. With an annual enrollment of more than 10,000 students, it is noted nationally for its school of law and internationally for its medical research. Emory provides nearly one-third of all medical care to residents of metropolitan Atlanta through its Emory University System of Health Care and affiliated hospital programs.

Atlanta headquarters. Established by the U.S. government in 1942, the CDC is federally funded under the auspices of the Department of Health and Human Services and has an annual budget of $2.2 billion. As the 911 of public health services, the CDC provides a broad range of medical, laboratory, and health study services throughout the U.S. and plays a vital role in controlling and monitoring diseases internationally.

The Clifton corridor also includes the Woodruff Medical Center complex of Emory University, the Yerkes Primate Research Center, Wesley Woods Geriatric Hospital, the Henrietta Egleston Children's Hospital, and the national headquarters of the American Cancer Society.

As home to Emory University, Mercer University-Atlanta, DeKalb College, Columbia Theological Seminary, Oglethorpe University, and Agnes Scott College for women—ranked nationally by the Carnegie Foundation—DeKalb is a center of education.

Another DeKalb institution that is both educational and recreational is the Fernbank Science Center. As part of the county's public school system, Fernbank includes an impressive museum of natural history, the largest such facility south of the Smithsonian.

Callanwolde Fine Arts Center, the 1920s Gothic/Tudor-style mansion of Coca-Cola heir Charles Howard Candler, is a centerpiece in the county's Druid Hills residential community and offers outstanding programs in the visual, literary, and performing arts.

DeKalb's crowning jewel is Stone Mountain Park, a 3,200-acre landmark built around the world's largest chunk of granite. During summers, laser shows illuminate the mountain's face, while year-round, Atlantans and tourists enjoy scenic trails, a championship golf course, a ski lift, a water slide park, a 363-acre lake with beaches and boating, an antebellum plantation, a riverboat, and more.

### COBB COUNTY

Also vying for the metropolitan region's recreational/entertainment dollars is Cobb County, home to three of the Southeast's largest theme parks: Six Flags Over Georgia;

The U.S. Centers for Disease Control and Prevention is recognized internationally for its medical and scientific research.

White Water, with the largest children's water playground in the U.S., and the adjacent American Adventures children's amusement park; and "the beach within reach," Sun Valley, the largest swimming pool in the Southeast. Such attractions contribute significantly to the $800 million generated annually by visitors to Cobb County.

Cobb's natural resources also attract visitors, including Kennesaw Mountain, Lake Allatoona, and the winding Chattahoochee River. For history buffs, there are historical landmarks and museums featuring Civil War memorabilia.

Yet, of the county's many attractions, Cobb may be best known for the "Big Chicken," a gigantic four-story rooster built three decades ago to promote a local fried chicken establishment. Over the years, it has become not only a local landmark on Highway 41 off Interstate 75 but a legitimate navigational aid for pilots.

Tad Leithead, a member of the Cobb County Chamber of Commerce Executive Committee and a partner with Childress Klein Properties, is more familiar with other Cobb landmarks, such as its high-rise centerpiece, the Atlanta Galleria. Contributing to the county's almost 15 million square feet of class A office space, known as the Platinum Triangle, the Galleria was built in the 1980s as the first high-rise, mixed-use office complex in suburban Atlanta and the first taller than six stories. It is still the area's standard in mixed-use commercial development and remains the centerpiece of office and retail development in northwest Atlanta.

According to Leithead, "Once the Interstate 285 and 75 intersection was created, it became the corner of what we considered Main Street in suburban Atlanta, with the Galleria literally at the intersection." Composed of four office buildings, the 1.6 million-square-foot complex, where about 7,500 people work, includes a four-star Waverly Hotel, a specialty mall, and an attached convention center.

Cobb's population broke the half-million mark in 1995. The median household effective buying income of these residents is among the metropolitan area's highest.

The largest private employer in Cobb County is Lockheed Aeronautical Systems Co. With almost 12,000 workers, it is also Georgia's second-largest manufacturing employer.

Increasingly, international firms are finding Cobb attractive. Some 250 do business in Cobb, and one-third of these base their U.S. operations here.

State Route 41, known as Cobb Parkway, is Cobb's main strip and gives the county its edge. Running north to the Canadian border and south to the tip of Florida, with 25 miles in Cobb County, this is where all substantial retail, office, and general commercial activity in Cobb lies. By 1999, construction will be complete on Cobb's $75 million Kennedy Interchange.

## BRINGING HOME THE GOLD

Atlanta and its surrounding metropolitan counties consistently garner top rankings nationally and internationally as the best place for business:

- #1 (tie) among "Top U.S. Cities for Foreign Investment" by the Association of Foreign Investors, 1994

- #1 on American Demographics magazine's "Healthiest Cities Survey," 1994

- #1 among World Trade magazine's "Top 10 U.S. Cities for Global Companies," 1994

- #1 on Entrepreneur magazine's "Best Cities to Own a Business," 1994

- #1 on Business Traveler International magazine's "Best Airport in North America," 1989-94

- #1 on Retail magazine's National Investor Survey for CB Commercial Real Estate Top Markets for Investment, 1994

- #2 on Fortune magazine's "Best U.S. Cities for Business," 1995

- #2 on Office magazine's National Investor Survey for CB Commercial Real Estate Top Markets for Investment, 1994

- #2 on Emerging Trends in Real Estate list of "Hottest U.S. Markets," 1994

- #4 on Fortune magazine's "World's Best Cities for Business," 1994

### GWINNETT COUNTY

Drivers enter Gwinnett County via what is affectionately called "spaghetti junction," a massive network of intertwining superhighways, where I-85 is Main Street. Covering 437 square miles and beginning 30 miles northeast of downtown Atlanta, Gwinnett County ranked as America's fastest-growing county with populations of more than 100,000 from 1984 to 1988. From 1980 to 1990, its population grew 111.57 percent, making it metro Atlanta's fastest-growing county. This was due in part to Gwinnett's tremendous transportation access to all parts of the metro area, the state, and the nation.

The metro Atlanta area offers leisure-lovers the best in outdoor recreation. Right: Landmark Stone Mountain is the backdrop for exciting summertime laser shows. Scenic trails, a water slide park, golf courses, beaches, and boating provide year-round recreation.

"The icing on the cake was that we were in an excellent market in the metro area, and land for development at the time was extremely reasonably priced," explains Glenn White, a board member of Gwinnett's Chamber of Commerce and president of the Bank of Gwinnett. "Today, we're attracting a lot of younger people, married couples who will keep our county energetic. Our housing values," he adds, "are clearly one reason we attract this important age group."

Gwinnett has a population of 436,900 and an employment base of more than 239,257. The greatest concentration of residents are between the ages of 20 and 34.

A unique aspect of Gwinnett County is its lifestyle appeal. Berkeley Lake, for example, looks like a storybook community with upscale residences, cottages, winding streets, and, of course, its lake. In striking contrast, there is Norcross. The heart of the high-tech industry in metropolitan Atlanta, Norcross is a highly commercial city with a completely renovated downtown. The city's industrial component contributes tremendously to the 26 percent of Atlanta's industrial space located in Gwinnett County.

International firms operating in Gwinnett County include some 85 from Japan alone. There is even a school for children of Japanese executives, which benefits not only the county but the entire metro area.

Adding to the area's recreational amenities are Road Atlanta, a 2.5-mile course that attracts international racing stars; the Atlanta Falcons Football Team Training Center in Suwanee; the Yellow River Wildlife Game Ranch, a 24-acre "see-and-touch" wildlife preserve with more than 600 animals; and the 90-acre Vines Botanical Gardens.

Carole Kendall, president of Gwinnett Utilities, Inc., a 20-year-old piping sales business she and her husband started, moved to Gwinnett in 1970 from DeKalb County, where the couple worked. "We wanted more home for the value," she recalls, "and Gwinnett's convenient proximity to DeKalb was important." Within five to six years, "Gwinnett was starting to grow, and since we were living in what was becoming the fastest-growing county in the nation, we decided to start our own business here.

"Gwinnett offered a great quality of life. There were opportunities to become a part of a maturing county," she says. A point of concern was its fledgling arts community, in which Kendall soon became active, ultimately serving as fund-raising chair and then president of the Gwinnett Council for the Arts, which today is housed in a $1.3 million fine arts center.

"Gwinnett, like other metro counties surrounding Atlanta, gets to benefit and participate in Atlanta's dynamic growth," Kendall observes. "But, at the same time, we're able to enjoy the amenities that you will only find in a more suburban, pastoral setting. I feel very fortunate," she says, "I have the best of both worlds."

$\mathcal{M}$etro Atlanta has an array of community festivals, like the Decatur Arts Festival (left), and theatrical extravaganzas, such as the annual Renaissance Festival in South Atlanta (top right) and the Shakespeare Festival at Oglethorpe University (bottom right) in North Atlanta.

$\mathcal{L}$ocated on a magnificent estate, Callanwolde Fine Arts Center in the Druid Hills residential community offers a variety of classes in the arts.

$C$hateau Elan, the most com-plete winery resort area in the world, is among the metro area's leading attractions.

Water, water, everywhere—
though Atlanta is far from
the coast—refreshes hot Atlantans
on the Chattahoochee River (top
left), on Lake Lanier (bottom left),
and at White Water.

𝒯he Atlanta spirit means striving for the best, whether competing, learning, or producing.

$\mathcal{W}$ithin minutes, Atlantans can enjoy thrills and chills at Six Flags Over Georgia (top left), strolls at sunset along the winding Chattahoochee River (bottom left), or meandering the town square in Marietta.

FOLLOWING PAGES: A bona fide navigational tool (page 136), the "Big Chicken" is a local Atlanta landmark. Veterans of the Vietnam War are remembered at the memorial in Roswell (page 137).

Atlanta—A Vision for the New Millennium

METROPOLITAN ATLANTA: SHARING THE SPIRIT

For golf devotees, Peachtree City has about 60 miles of golf cart paths and the greatest number of golf carts per capita of any city in the U.S.

RIGHT: Education is a major component of life throughout the metropolitan area. Leading schools, such as Emory University, attract students from around the world.

FOLLOWING PAGES: "Spaghetti junction" links Atlanta to all parts of the metro area and beyond.

METROPOLITAN ATLANTA: SHARING THE SPIRIT

# PROFILES IN EXCELLENCE

A LOOK AT THE CORPORATIONS, BUSINESSES, PROFESSIONAL GROUPS, AND COMMUNITY SERVICE ORGANIZATIONS THAT MAKE ATLANTA THE #1 CITY IN AMERICA IN WHICH TO DO BUSINESS

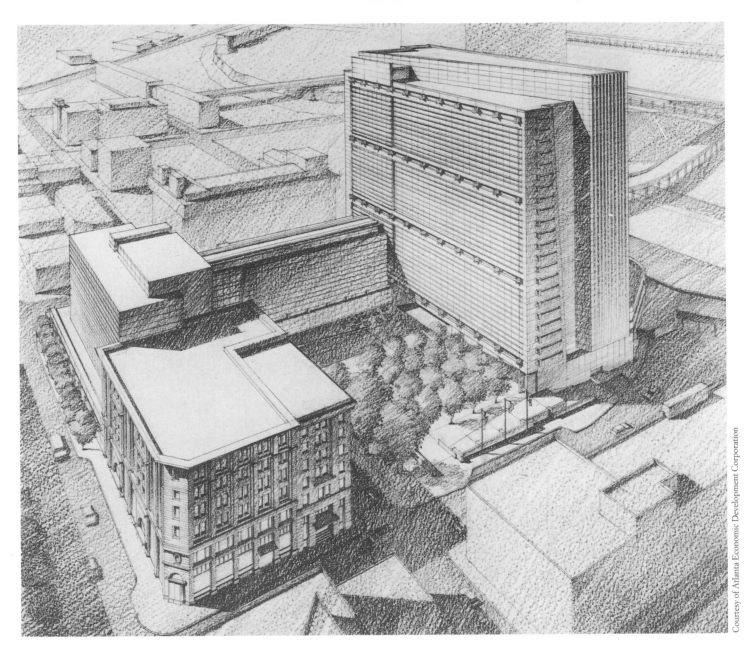

*Courtesy of Atlanta Economic Development Corporation*

Business owners no longer need to dream of having an influential relative or to rely on luck to obtain low-cost loans and cut through red tape, thanks to the Atlanta Economic Development Corporation (AEDC). AEDC provides financial and consulting assistance to entrepreneurs in opening or locating a business in Atlanta, in addition to acting as a catalyst and "deal maker" for neighborhood commercial revitalization and the development of industrial

parks. AEDC also implements innovative multimillion-dollar developments in cooperation with international investors.

Founded in 1976, AEDC was created to promote economic development in Atlanta. Its mission is to bring jobs and investment into the city, and its motto is "Building Partnerships for Progress." Since its inception, AEDC has grown to become a full-service operation.

Structured as a public-private partnership between the City of Atlanta

*Rendering of the Atlanta Federal Center*

and private enterprise, AEDC is a chartered nonprofit corporation. The mayor of Atlanta serves as chairman of AEDC's 15-member board of directors, which represents business and community leaders, including members of the Atlanta City Council Finance and Community Development committees. AEDC also has an ongoing working alliance with such key organiza-

Courtesy of Terry Manufacturing Co.

*A factory worker makes battle dress uniform coats at the Terry Manufacturing Co.*

tions as Central Atlanta Progress, which in conjunction with the city helped create AEDC, and with the Atlanta Chamber of Commerce, the Atlanta Convention and Visitors Bureau, and the Georgia Department of Industry, Trade and Tourism, as well as the region's banking/finance community.

Some of AEDC's services include development, loan packaging, asset management, value-added consulting, and the implementation of real estate projects designed to shape critical areas of Atlanta.

The agency also works with the Downtown Development Authority, which provides tax-exempt and taxable bond financing for eligible projects. Low-interest financing enables existing businesses to expand, while also keeping them healthy and within city limits.

According to Mayor Bill Campbell, "The city of Atlanta today is the national model for a number of important economic development initiatives as a result of AEDC's activities to strengthen and balance the economic viability of our city."

In the majority of its activities, AEDC functions in three primary roles: as developer/redeveloper for commercial and industrial projects, as lender and facilitator for small and minority businesses, and as catalyst and implementor for current and long-range development.

As part of AEDC's development mission, it has developed two industrial parks—the Atlanta Industrial Park, a 300-acre enterprise zone, and Southside Industrial Park, which generates more than $150 million in private investment in Atlanta, as well as jobs.

AEDC's involvement in mixed-use/commercial development is evident at Hartsfield Centre, a 31-acre, $160 million complex that includes 150,000 square feet of Class A office space and a 400-room luxury hotel at Hartsfield Airport's old terminal site.

In addition, AEDC has played an important role in revitalizing depressed neighborhoods such as the Little Five Points area and the South Central Business District, home of the Atlanta Federal Center—a $260.5 million, 1.6 million-square-foot federal office complex developed by the joint venture partnership of AEDC and Prentiss Properties and financed by the Atlanta Downtown Development Authority for the U.S. General Services Administration.

Keith Melton, AEDC's vice president of development, notes, "By identifying opportunities for development projects and bringing the needed resources together, we are able to generate jobs and amenities that further promote targeted sectors of the city, while increasing Atlanta's tax base and enhancing the quality of life."

AEDC's goal is to "Build a Better Atlanta," and since its founding, the agency has been involved in a host of complicated projects, funding and financial

*Hartsfield Centre*

Courtesy of Atlanta Economic Development Corporation

*AEDC executive staff: (left to right) Keith Melton, Vice President of Development; Margaret McClure, Executive Vice President; Walter R. Huntley, Jr., President; Lonnie Saboor, Vice President of Loan Programs*

arranged leasing of property for parking, and assisted management with construction contracts.

"We fill the gap and leverage AEDC's financial resources, making it possible for small, minority, and female entrepreneurs who otherwise may not have been able to find assistance to go into business," explains Lonnie Saboor, vice president of loan programs. Since 1981, AEDC has arranged financing of more than $41 million through its city-sponsored Business Improvement Loan Fund Program, which provides financial assistance through low-interest direct loans for the acquisition of commercial property, renovation, fixed equipment, inventory, and office equipment.

AEDC's role as a catalyst and implementor has resulted in a number of successful programs. Among the most successful are the Atlanta Neighborhood Development Partnership, the Minority Enterprise Small Business Investment Corporation, and the Venture Capital Network. According to Margaret McClure, AEDC's executive vice president, "AEDC must be comprehensive in its approach to economic development. While we constantly seek opportunities through public-private partnerships, we also provide the nuts-and-bolts, behind-the-scenes foundation for strategic, planned progress."

AEDC's president, Walter R. Huntley, Jr., believes that "Atlanta's ability to effectively manage growth, balanced with a high quality of life, has been one of the city's greatest assets and will distinguish Atlanta among international cities in the future. At AEDC, we are interested in working with businesses that want to be a part of this community and participate in shaping one of America's great international cities."

He adds, "Atlanta's emergence as one of America's great international cities has prompted unprecedented global attention and international investment. As we approach the next century and our city's next phase of economic growth, AEDC's scope and services will continue to focus on our most basic commitment and founding mission—strengthening the quality of life for all Atlantans and future generations."

strategies, incentive packages involving features such as enterprise zones, and tenant recruitment and development plans.

AEDC has been involved in projects valued at more than half a billion dollars and that have brought between 6,000 and 8,000 jobs to the city. AEDC is currently involved in several major downtown Atlanta projects valued at more than $300 million.

The agency is especially proud of its work with small businesses. AEDC is one of the only sources for start-up loans. It has provided more than 400 loans to new and existing small businesses that could not have arranged for all or some of their financing through traditional sources. As lender/facilitator for viable small and minority businesses, AEDC serves as "process broker" and intermediary, skillfully putting loans and financial packages together. For example, during the $7 million renovation of downtown's Sweet Auburn Curb Market, AEDC arranged the renovation financing, reorganized the market's board and management,

*Southside Industrial Park*

*Atlanta Industrial Park*

While most people are familiar with Atlanta, host city to the 1996 Summer Olympic Games, they are not as knowledgeable about Fulton County, whose motto is "We're Atlanta, Plus!"

Georgia's largest and most populous county, Fulton County is made up of 600 square miles in north-central Georgia at the center of the 20-county Atlanta-Metropolitan Statistical Area. The City of Atlanta, along with other smaller cities, is located in Fulton County. Because of such factors as its competitive business investment costs and excellent quality of life, Fulton County is a prime business recruiting market, attracting not only small business operations but Fortune 500 firms and over 350 international businesses.

To keep business costs competitive, the County offers development and business incentives for qualified commercial, industrial, and residential projects. In addition, property tax rates are

*North Point Mall in North Fulton County*

comparable to those of other major urban centers nationwide.

The Development Authority of Fulton County was established in 1973 to encourage high-quality development activity while stimulating and diversifying economic development. To accomplish this goal, the authority serves as an issuer of revenue bonds to help businesses finance relocations and expansions.

The County's Development Services Department (DSD) works with the Department of Planning and Economic Development to ease red tape. The one-stop department handles all permit activity, as well as zoning and variance requests for developers and companies.

Fulton County also offers high-quality education and training, excelling especially in technological education. The County's 55 public elementary, middle, and high schools are augmented by 51 private schools, many with national reputations for excellence. Georgia Tech,

*Cascade Road subdivision in Southwest Fulton County*

the Atlanta University Center, and Georgia State University are all located in Fulton County.

The County's quality of life is often envied. It is one of the most livable communities, offering moderate weather; attractive and affordable housing; efficient transportation, including Hartsfield Atlanta International Airport and rapid rail and bus service; shopping, recreation, and such entertainment opportunities as Underground Atlanta, the High Museum of Art, the SciTrek Museum, the Fox Theatre, the Atlanta Civic Center, the Atlanta-Fulton County Stadium/Olympic Stadium, the OMNI, the Georgia Dome, the World of Coca-Cola, Atlanta International Speedway, Road Atlanta, the Hard Rock Cafe, and Planet Hollywood.

World-class transportation plays an important role in attracting new residences and businesses to the County. In addition to Hartsfield Atlanta International Airport, other transportation facilities include Fulton County Airport-Brown Field, piggyback facilities for CSX and Norfolk Southern railroads, Amtrak, and MARTA rail and bus service. Fulton County is also one of the leading interstate highway centers in the nation; converging here are three major interstates—I-20, I-85, and I-75. I-285, which rings the City of Atlanta, passes through the County as well.

The County's great transportation access has attracted nearly 900 manufacturing and distribution firms, employing about 30,000 people and occupying more than 50 million square feet of space in the Fulton Industrial District in Southwest Fulton County. This is the largest contiguous industrial center east of the Mississippi.

Southwest Fulton offers excellent opportunities for development, including a positive track record of significant growth in new residential construction as well as high-quality investment by major companies.

South Fulton County offers beautiful and affordable land with superior accessibility to road, rail, and air transportation. South Fulton is home to Hartsfield Atlanta International Airport, one of the world's busiest airport terminals.

North Fulton County features a range of middle-to-upper-income single and multifamily residences, as well as all the benefits of suburban living, in addition to upscale office and commercial development space.

Sandy Springs has the benefit of a suburban lifestyle combined with high economic growth and significant office development.

Regardless of which part of the County one chooses, metro Atlanta cannot be beat for its quality of life, business incentives, world-class transportation, and affordable and upscale housing. This explains why such companies as Delta Air Lines, Coca-Cola, Chick-fil-A, United Parcel Service, Ford Motor Company, G.E. Capital, BellSouth Corporation, AT&T, and Georgia-Pacific Corporation have been attracted to the County.

*Concourse in Sandy Springs*

*Chick-fil-A headquarters in South Fulton County*

The City of East Point offers a friendly atmosphere and sense of community for both residents and businesses, as well as the conveniences of suburban living close to the fast-paced City of Atlanta.

East Point is accessible to metro Atlanta through its MARTA rail station (located in the Central Business District), to the state via every major interstate highway, and to the nation through its location in South Fulton County just seven minutes from Hartsfield International Airport.

With low property taxes and outstanding city amenities, such as 24-hour fire and police protection and electrical, water, sewer, recreation, library, community development, and sanitation services, it is not surprising that East Point has grown to become the third-largest city in Fulton County. East Point covers 18 square miles and has a population in excess of 34,364. The city has a $7 million Law Enforcement Center, which houses the police and fire departments, the municipal court, and the communications department.

East Point's daytime population expands to over 44,441, most of whom are in service and medical-oriented employment. Some of the major companies located in East Point include Pittsburgh Paint & Glass, Inc.; Owens-Brockway Glass Company; Bama F.I.S.H. (the major seafood supplier for all

*Dick Lane Velodrome, constructed in 1977, is one of only two bicycling tracks in Georgia. Cyclists from across the Southeast come to East Point's Velodrome to train.*

metro Atlanta Kroger Stores); and Mid-South Ice, which makes East Point the "ice capital of the southeastern United States." An array of chemical and R&D facilities, five air freight distributors, the only Federal Archives facility in the southeastern United States, major bank branch offices, and one of BellSouth's largest switching stations are also within its corporate limits.

East Point is home to the only full-service medical facility in South Fulton County, South Fulton Medical Center. The medical center has 400 beds, over 700 employees, and a medical building adjacent to the hospital that houses the offices of over 112 physicians.

The city's transportation system includes Norfolk Southern and CSX railways. The largest rail storage yard within Fulton County outside the corporate limits of Atlanta is also located here.

East Point was established in 1887 and has a council-manager form of government. It operates an independent water system, which has the capacity to generate up to 20 million gallons per day. It supplies water to the City of College Park and to Fort McPherson.

Educational facilities are an important part of East Point. Forty acres are home to Atlanta Christian College, a private

*South Fulton Medical Center's system of providing care has positioned SFMC at the forefront of the country's health-care providers. In 1994, SFMC was recognized as one of the top 100 hospitals in the country by the HCIA/Mercer Benchmarks for Success Survey, which also gave the facility honorable mention in 1995 for continued excellence. In addition, the SFMC was named to the official Hospital Support Network for the 1996 Olympics.*

religious college. East Point is also home to four private grammar schools, four public elementary schools, two public middle schools, and the only magnet high school with a concentration in sports medicine and the performing arts in the tri-cities area. The Fulton County Board of Education's administrative and training/technical facilities and a portion of Woodward Academy are also located within East Point's corporate limits.

To encourage new industry and business development throughout the city, the East Point Business and Industrial Development Authority and Fulton County have legislated a 100 percent property tax exemption on all three classes of manufacturer's inventory belonging to companies located within the city. This establishment as a "freeport" reflects East Point's progressive climate.

Camp Creek Parkway, the new major entrance into Hartsfield International Airport for eastbound traffic from I-285 and suburban counties west of Fulton County, is East Point's western boundary. Two nationally acclaimed developments are located on the parkway: Camp Creek Centre, developed by Laing Properties, and Southmeadows, developed by John McDonald & Associates.

East Point's careful historic restoration of two turn-of-the-century factories, the old Buggyworks and White Wagon Works, has created premier office space in a prime location adjacent to the MARTA rail station and four minutes from Hartsfield International Airport. Listed on the National Register for Historic Places, both complexes feature exposed beams and beautiful exposed interior brick walls, along with skylights and 10-foot arched warehouse windows.

The new theme for East Point, "East Point USA, International City: Community of the Future," is well suited, since East Point has a broad industrial and commercial base, as well as a significant residential population in single-family and multifamily housing. All of the city's attributes contribute to East Point's diversification and help make it a great place to live and work.

*Southmeadows, owned by McDonald Development Corporation, is home to World Span, AT&T, and Amana.*

*Camp Creek Centre, owned by Laing Properties, is home to the United States Army Reserve Command.*

PROFILES IN EXCELLENCE

# LANIER WORLDWIDE, INC.

In 1934, the Lanier brothers—Hicks, Sartain, and Tommy—opened a small Nashville-based distributorship for the Ediphone Company, the manufacturing arm for Thomas A. Edison's dictating machines. Their first business offices were the trunks and rear seats of their automobiles.

Through hard work and dogged tenacity, the venture grew. Later, they moved to Atlanta, where, in 1955, Lanier Business Products started distributing 3M duplicating, microfilm, and visual products across Florida, Georgia, and Louisiana. From those humble origins emerged one of the world's office equipment giants.

A broadened distribution pact between 3M and Lanier in 1982 moved Lanier's distribution rights out of its southern base and triggered tremendous growth. It was, however, a 1983 merger with Harris Corporation that launched the company down a road toward even more dramatic expansion. Next came a joint venture between Harris and 3M in 1986, which created a new national distributor for copiers, facsimile, and other products under the Harris/3M brand name. In 1989, Harris purchased 3M's share of the joint venture company and set Lanier Worldwide on a path toward leadership in the global office products and business communications markets. Today, Lanier Worldwide enjoys revenues of more than $1 billion and employs nearly 7,000 men and women in over 80 countries around the globe.

Lanier markets, sells, and services a broad product line. Through a network of direct and dealer offices, Lanier offers copying systems, facsimile equipment, information management systems, digital dictation and voice logging systems, PC-based health-care systems, and supplies. Lanier's goal? Total customer satisfaction. This is the route Lanier has chosen to earn recognition as the world's preferred provider of office solutions.

Lanier is led today by Wesley E. Cantrell. On impulse one spring day, Cantrell walked across an Atlanta street into the Lanier headquarters. He already had a job lined up for that summer with IBM's service organization, but he walked out a Lanier service technician.

As CEO, he has captained innovative programs like "Tell It to Wes," "Customer Vision®," "The Lanier Performance Promise," and the "Lanier Team Management Process." His Lanier management team seized on the Customer Vision theme, making it the controlling culture of the company.

Customer Vision means seeing the business through customers' eyes and responding, as a team, to their needs, meeting or exceeding their expectations.

Customer satisfaction has always been a hallmark of Lanier. This Customer Vision creed now drives decisions throughout the far-flung reaches of the company's operations. "We're betting on customers trading in and/or upgrading an average of every three years,"

*Wesley E. Cantrell, president and CEO of Lanier Worldwide, Inc., began with the firm in 1955 as a service technician.*

Cantrell notes. "If they're happy with our products, our service, and our people, a customer's next purchase will be a Lanier product. Our business will grow exponentially."

This approach has produced a unique and successful company, with growth far exceeding the market. As part of its Customer Vision goal, Lanier offers reasonable prices and expert service.

One aspect of Customer Vision is the Lanier Performance Promise. Lanier

*Lanier markets, sells, and services an award-winning array of office solutions around the world.*

guarantees 98 percent uptime or assigns a money refund for the time the equipment is down. Additionally, if a copier, facsimile system, dictation machine, or continuous recorder is out of service for more than eight hours, the customer gets a free loaner.

Lanier also operates a 24-hour, toll-free help line to assist customers with emergencies after hours. Plus, Lanier guarantees 100 percent uptime on all digital dictation systems and several PC-based health-care solutions covered by the "Intensive Care Commitment."

The Tell It to Wes program is a telephone hot line used by employees to voice ideas and concerns, in confidence, directly to Cantrell. Also, the Lanier Team Management Process (LTMP), Lanier's quality program, empowers employees to succeed and grow professionally to better serve both customers and other employees. Based on a solid foundation of business ethics, LTMP emphasizes seven additional areas in its "window of opportunity": Customer Vision, Employee Vision, Field Operations, Growth Strategy (focused on products, systems, and services), Process Management, Information Systems Strategy, and Technical Excellence.

These efforts do not go unnoticed. Tom Peters remarked about Lanier in *In Search of Excellence*: "Lanier lives, sleeps, eats, and breathes customers." That is why Lanier has earned quality awards from customers like DuPont, Pacific Bell, Comerica, and the Christian Purchasing Network and from analysts like Datapro and Dataquest. Lanier has

*Lanier's world headquarters at 2300 Parklake Drive in Atlanta*

also captured the coveted "Most Outstanding Copier Line of the Year" award from Buyers Laboratory, Inc., for two consecutive years.

Lanier had an exceptional 1995. The company boosted the number of "100 percent sold" customers and continued steady growth in revenue and profit; plus, it improved its customer satisfaction index, outpacing the industry.

The company's ongoing investment in research and development, with leadership in key areas such as digital technology, keeps Lanier a step ahead of the competition.

Lanier is a worldwide company proud to call Atlanta home.

# ATLANTA CASUALTY COMPANY

The year 1996 marks the 24th anniversary of the Atlanta Casualty Company, a subsidiary of American Financial Group, Inc. Throughout its successful history, the firm, which specializes in high-risk automobile insurance, has grown geographically as well as financially. Today, Atlanta Casualty writes more than $575 million in private passenger automobile insurance through more than 9,000 independent agents in 35 states, employs over 1,000 people, and is licensed in 41 states.

The company was established in 1972 as a subsidiary of the Alabama-based Stonewall Insurance Group to write high-risk automobile insurance in Georgia. In 1977, Atlanta Casualty Company was acquired by the Great American Insurance Company, a subsidiary of the American Financial Corporation, located in Cincinnati, Ohio.

It was at this time that the firm moved into its current headquarters in the Atlanta suburb of Norcross. The company's ultimate parent is the American Financial Group, Inc. (AFG), whose subsidiary companies are engaged primarily in specialty property and casualty, multiline property, and casualty insurance and the sale of tax-deferred annuities. AFG stock is publicly traded on the New York Stock Exchange.

Atlanta Casualty's success and growth are very impressive. The firm's expansion began in the mid-1980s when it entered other states. At that time, a corporate decision was made to expand the company's territory rather than expand the type of insurance it sells.

An example of the company's explosive growth can be seen in its financial statement. In 1982, the firm wrote $20 million in business, compared with

$575 million in 1994. Over the past five years, it averaged a healthy 34 percent growth rate each year and a remarkable 95.8 percent combined loss and expense ratio. Georgia remains the company's largest volume state with $110 million in premiums written. According to the A. M. Best Company, independent analysts of the insurance industry, Atlanta Casualty has a rating of A+ (superior).

The company is led by President and CEO Robert L. Lowe, a veteran of the insurance industry. Lowe believes that Atlanta Casualty's success is due to several factors. He explains, "We offer unparalleled stability in financial resources and rate levels. Our service to agents, insureds, and claimants is widely known to be outstanding. We maintain competitive rates due to the efficiency of our operation."

Lowe, who has been with the firm since 1979, adds, "We offer a superior level of automation for processing and are highly centralized, with most of our 1,000 employees located here in our home office.

Our efficiency is enhanced by servicing our business out of the Atlanta office through telecommunications rather than through a branch office system. This gives us a competitive advantage."

Customer satisfaction is Atlanta Casualty's strategic marketing goal for the future. Some of the services offered are full-spectrum underwriting, affordable payment plans, a direct billing system, a comprehensive discount program, state-of-the-art rating software, a continuous renewal system, an easy-to-use rating manual, and 24-hour claims service.

"Our success is dependent on the service that we render to our policyholders and agents," says Lowe, who adds, "We've established this 'mission statement' to meet our present and future challenge:

*OUR ONLY PRODUCT IS SERVICE*
*Our product's acceptance depends upon the quality each employee invests in it."*

This mission statement is a reflection of the contribution of dedicated employees and a true team effort. Competitive pricing and customer satisfaction remain key ingredients for the company's future success.

In order to offer a lower rate to high-risk clientele who improve their driving record, American Premier Insurance Company was formed in 1990 as a wholly owned subsidiary of the Atlanta Casualty Company. In 1994, Atlanta Specialty Insurance Company was added to the Atlanta Casualty's growing group.

Commenting on Atlanta as a corporate headquarters, Lowe remarks, "Atlanta has been a very pleasant work environment for a small company to grow. There is a good pool of employees, and the greater Atlanta area provides a very positive business climate. As to the future goals of the company, we would like to continue our expansion from being a regional carrier and to firmly establish Atlanta Casualty as a national company servicing insurance needs of consumers countrywide."

© Jana Lowe

© Jana Lowe

# LAING PROPERTIES, INC.

Laing Properties, Inc., is a full-service real estate development management and investment company. Founded in England in 1848, Laing established its U.S. operations in 1976 with headquarters in Atlanta, Georgia.

Laing enjoys full or partial ownership of commercial and residential real estate exceeding 3.4 million square feet and valued at more than $220 million. Its portfolio includes office buildings; business and industrial parks; high-rise apartment developments; and senior adult communities. In addition to its Atlanta office, the company has focused its business activities in Washington, D.C.; Charlotte, North Carolina; Nashville, Tennessee; and St. Petersburg, Florida.

Above all, Laing Properties is quality-driven. The firm is committed to the physical and aesthetic quality of all its projects as well as to providing the highest level of management and marketing services developed for them. Laing also offers its property management, leasing, construction, and financial services to third-party interests representing ownership of an additional 1 million square feet.

In 1990, Laing was acquired by a joint venture between two United Kingdom public companies. The Peninsular and Oriental Steam Navigation Company (P&O) and Chelsfield, PLC. P&O, the venture's managing partner, is a global organization with interests in travel, transportation, shipping, construction, development, and investment property. With assets near $10 billion, P&O employs more than 60,000 people worldwide and produced revenues near $10 billion in 1994.

Laing provides comprehensive real estate services for company-owned properties and third-party clients. The firm's expertise, refined through years of experience, includes asset management and leasing and marketing services, as well as the management of commercial, residential, and senior adult properties. Laing's goal is to provide working and living environments that are stimulating, comfortable, and efficiently operated— efforts that not only produce the highest long-term valuation of assets but that maintain the highest levels of tenant/resident satisfaction and retention.

This commitment is not only to the buildings that Laing manages but to their settings as well. For more than a decade, Laing Landscape has enhanced properties with beautifully designed and meticulously groomed surroundings. The division provides initial installations, maintenance, seasonal color, irrigation, and interior landscape programs.

The company's management philosophy is expressed in "The Laing Standard"—a commitment to the creation of premium-quality, people-oriented environments supported with the highest level of service. The Laing Standard requires its employees to pay meticulous attention to every detail and to demonstrate a concerned, responsive, innovative, and professional attitude in their interactions with tenants, brokers, and the properties. This commitment to excellence enables the firm to maintain high occupancy rates, while its management expertise helps control operating costs and justify steadily increasing rental rates.

The company upholds The Laing Standard by maintaining a qualified and responsive staff. Employees are carefully

© Chris Hamilton Photography

*Palisades office complex, located in the north-central submarket of Atlanta*

selected, extensively trained, and routinely evaluated. In addition to clearly defined business policies and procedures, Laing encourages direct and open communication between senior management and on-site personnel to ensure a quick and effective response to market dynamics.

The development phase of every Laing project draws on professionals throughout the company—marketing representatives, leasing agents, property managers, and corporate executives—who determine everything needed for an asset to succeed in the marketplace. Their combined efforts result in a project development plan that meets the following criteria: it provides a rate of return commensurate with corporate guidelines; incorporates proven design and construction standards; combines aesthetic appeal and user-friendly features at or above the market standard; and competes favorably with products in the surrounding market area.

The Construction Management Division provides quality service and professional expertise in all areas of real estate design and construction. The division's commitment to excellence ensures unwavering attention to detail throughout the entire process.

The process begins with a thorough understanding of the user's needs, which evolve into the new asset's form and function criteria. Design consultants experienced with the product type are selected and closely monitored throughout the design process. Once construction documents are completed, prequalified contractors compete through the bidding process and/or negotiations for the construction contract. Laing personnel meticulously monitor the quality of work, the construction schedule, and all project costs throughout the construction phase. The firm's ultimate goal—user satisfaction—is achieved through continuous attention throughout the design, construction, and occupancy stages.

*Photograph by Gabriel Benzur*

*The Mayfair, located in midtown Atlanta*

*Photograph by Gabriel Benzur*

*1979 Lakeside Centre, located in the Northlake submarket of Atlanta*

Much of Atlanta's breathtaking skyline can be attributed to the work of Cousins Properties Incorporated and its founder and chairman, Atlanta native Thomas G. Cousins. From metro Atlanta's northern suburbs to downtown Atlanta's Central Business District, Cousins has had an enormous impact on the Southeast's largest city.

Cousins Properties, a diversified real estate development and investment company, was founded by Mr. Cousins and his father, I. W. Cousins, in 1958. It became a public company in 1962 and has built a solid reputation for innovative development and leadership. The firm started in the residential area and grew to become the largest home builder in Atlanta by the time Mr. Cousins was 33 years old. This success enabled the company to expand into the retail industry with regional malls and community shopping centers, as well as other sectors such as office buildings, office parks, and downtown mixed-use developments.

Some of the firm's major accomplishments include rejuvenating the Ansley Park in-town community in the 1960s, investing in the Omni International complex, and playing a key role in the development of the World Congress Center. Among the projects in which the company shares ownership are NationsBank Plaza, 191 Peachtree Tower, Ten Peachtree Place, Wildwood Office Park, and North Point. In November 1992, Cousins acquired New Market Development Company to form Cousins MarketCenters, Inc. As one of the country's leading developers of large non-enclosed retail centers, this division is responsible for 25 centers around the country, totaling approximately 8.5 million square feet. Recent developments include North Point MarketCenter, Lawrenceville MarketCenter, Perimeter Expo, Presidential MarketCenter, and Merchant's Walk, all in metropolitan Atlanta. The company has received awards in national design competitions for its emphasis on tasteful architecture and landscaping design.

The key to Cousins Properties' success is that it develops properties that are substantially precommitted to quality tenants, maintains high levels of occupancy within owned properties, selectively sells assets and acquires quality income-producing properties at attractive prices, and is opportunistic and takes advantage of normal real estate business cycles.

Another element of Cousins' success is its corporate philosophy, which emphasizes service, pride, integrity, and quality; respect for the land; and attention to detail.

# PRYOR, McCLENDON, COUNTS & CO., INC.

The Atlanta office of Pryor, McClendon, Counts & Co., Inc. (PMC), the largest minority-owned and controlled investment banking firm in the United States, has become the company's cornerstone. PMC was established in January 1990 through the merger of Pryor, Govan, Counts & Co., Inc., and the Atlanta-based McClendon Capital Corporation, which opened in 1987.

While Chairman Malcolmn Pryor is based in Philadelphia and President Allen Counts is based in New York, Vice Chairman and Chief Operating Officer Raymond McClendon performs his corporate-wide responsibilities out of the Atlanta office.

McClendon has a long history of experience in finance in both federal and Atlanta government. A graduate of Morehouse College, he holds an M.B.A. from Georgia State University and formerly was the City of Atlanta's chief investment officer and vice president of multifamily activities for Fannie Mae.

In addition to his impressive credentials, McClendon has been active in professional and community organizations. A partial list of his leadership roles include chairman and national treasurer of the National Association of Securities Professionals, president-elect of 100 Black Men of Atlanta, Inc., and chair-elect of the Atlanta Business League.

The firm is a member of the National Association of Securities Dealers, the Securities Investor Protection Corporation, and the Public Securities Association.

PMC provides a full range of financial services, including municipal, corporate, structured, and international finance, fixed-income and equity sales and trading, financial advising, and, through an affiliate, asset management. Since the 1990 merger, the staff has almost doubled to include 50 employees with nine offices in major cities.

Pryor, McClendon, Counts & Co., Inc., is ranked first among minority- and women-owned investment banking firms. Since 1991, the company traded several billion dollars in government securities, and it is ranked among the top 20 firms in municipal finance. PMC is also the first minority-owned firm to lead manage a publicly offered taxable transaction for the federal government.

The firm's success is attributed to its technical ability and its focus on client service. The combination of experience, technical expertise, resources, and standard of excellence has been the key to PMC's growing reputation as a leader in investment banking.

© Bud Smith Photo

*PMC's Vice Chair and COO Raymond McClendon*

NationsBank, the third-largest banking company in the U.S., has played a major role in the changing banking industry since its inception in December 1991. The banking institution is headquartered in Charlotte, North Carolina, and has over 1,875 banking centers operating in nine states and the District of Columbia. As of June 30, 1995, NationsBank had $184 billion in assets.

NationsBank is also the largest bank in Georgia, and NationsBank of Georgia has assets in excess of $16 billion. There are 172 banking centers in the state and in cities as far reaching as Albany, Valdosta, Carrollton. and Athens.

The company credits its success in Georgia and across the country to its associates. NationsBank has responded with a commitment to its associates. The bank's associate benefits program has been nationally recognized and helps associates create an important balance between their responsibilities to their families and to the workplace. For example, liberal maternity and paternity leave policies allow new parents to take six months without pay, and the firm encourages school volunteering by allowing two hours of paid time per week.

President and Chief Executive Officer Hugh L. McColl, Jr., takes pride in NationsBank and sees it as a tight-knit group of people working toward a common goal—and helping each other along the way.

"I want the company culture to be very supportive. If someone has a personal problem, we offer our support; if it is a business problem, we solve the problem. To me, that's what it's all about." McColl adds, "I don't know a company that is more willing to let you go home and look after your children—that actually understands that you want to see your son play basketball or your daughter dance in a school play."

McColl believes that because of Nations-Bank's size, it can be more effective in the marketplace and in the community, "Large can be better if it is managed well. We will set the standard of service in every community where we are present," notes McColl.

NationsBank has set the standard in a number of different areas, including community lending. In 1992, the company unveiled a $10 billion, 10-year commitment to community lending. The program was designed to attract minority and lower-income customers who have been historically underserved by banks. In 1995, only three short years since the launch of the program, NationsBank is close to meeting its goal.

The bank is furthering its commitment to Atlanta communities through the work of its subsidiary, NationsBank Community Development Corporation (CDC). The CDC is currently in a working partnership with the Historic District Development Corporation to renovate and develop housing in the Martin Luther King, Jr., Historic District of Atlanta. The district will be a tourist attraction for the many visitors to and residents of the Atlanta area.

As a corporate sponsor of the 1996 Centennial Olympic Games, NationsBank has been a major part of Atlanta's preparations. The bank extended a $300 million line of credit to the Atlanta Committee for the Olympic Games. NationsBank is also the official banking institution for the Olympic Games and will operate temporary banking centers in the Olympic Village and other Olympic venues.

Some other examples of NationsBank's many charitable contributions include donating funds to the Atlanta Ballet for a new production of "The Nutcracker," funding an endowment for business school scholarships for the colleges of the Atlanta University system, and helping the Woodruff Arts Center with funds for needed construction.

NationsBank plans to continue its traditions of community involvement and economic growth in Atlanta—and all the cities it serves—well into the future.

PROFILES IN EXCELLENCE

Montag & Caldwell was established in 1945 by Louis A. Montag as the city's first independent investment counseling firm. As Montag & Caldwell celebrates its 50th anniversary, the firm still has the same dedication to pursuing its clients' objectives and, as a result, ranks among the country's top financial advisers. Louis Montag always believed that "you have to take the clients' concerns very seriously because the money nerve runs straight to the heart." That philosophy has helped the firm succeed throughout its history.

In 1994, the company became a member of the Alleghany Corporation family of companies. Listed on the New York Stock Exchange, Alleghany is a diversified company that owns Chicago Title and Trust Company, the world's largest insurer, and several other independently managed companies. Montag & Caldwell, in combining with Alleghany, has been able to maintain its autonomy, investment style, and collegial environment while benefiting from the capability to manage two new mutual funds and having additional financial resources available.

The firm's assets under management have grown steadily through the years. It now manages nearly $5 billion for individuals, trusts, corporations, employee benefit plans, foundations, and educational institutions. The reasons for the company's success include its emphasis on professionalism and service, the depth of its experienced staff, and its logical, consistent, and risk-averse investment approach. The firm possesses complete capability in equity and balanced portfolios, including fixed-income management. A further advantage is its focus; investment management is Montag & Caldwell's only business.

The company's successful investment philosophy is based on selection, diversification, timing, and balance. All portfolio decisions are guided by the client's objectives and tolerance for risk. With an emphasis on fundamental investment research, Montag & Caldwell also has superior record keeping and reporting systems, which are handled in-house, using state-of-the-art software.

In the area of equity selection, the decision process is a low-risk, growth stock approach. Valuation is the key selection criterion. Growth characteristics are also emphasized, since the firm seeks not only companies whose shares are attractively priced but those that should experience strong earnings growth relative to other companies.

Montag & Caldwell has served some individual families for over 40 years and a number of institutions for more than 20. Its size is ideal: with a staff of 38, it is small enough to provide individual service and to be responsive to clients' needs, yet large enough to manage portfolios exceeding many millions of dollars.

A proud moment in Montag & Caldwell's history was its establishment of the first mutual fund in the state of Georgia in 1967. This common stock fund, originally

© Ed C. Thompson

*Back row: President Ronald E. Canakaris and Executive Vice President David F. Seng. Front row: Chairman Solon P. Patterson*

named the Alpha Fund Inc., was renamed the Enterprise Growth Fund in 1987. The firm recently added two new no-load mutual funds—the M&C Balanced Fund, which seeks long-term total return through investment mainly in a combination of equity, fixed-income, and short-term securities; and the M&C Growth Fund, which seeks long-term capital appreciation consistent with investments primarily in equity securities.

While teamwork is one of the firm's main assets, successful leadership is also important. Montag & Caldwell is headed by Chairman and Chief Executive Officer Solon P. Patterson and Ronald E. Canakaris, president and chief investment officer. Patterson, who is an Atlanta native and Emory University graduate, joined the firm in 1962 and was named president and CEO in 1973. He was elected chairman of the board in 1977.

Ronald Canakaris joined the firm in 1972 and became director of research in 1973. He has held his current position since 1984.

Founder Louis Montag was an early board member of the Investment Counsel Association of America, which is dedicated to upholding the highest ethical standards, and the firm continues to be a member of the association. The company is also registered with the Securities and Exchange Commission, and all investment counselors are members of the Association of Investment Management and Research.

*Montag & Caldwell officers: (back row, left to right) Janet B. Bunch; Homer W. Whitman, Jr. ; Elizabeth C. Chester; Richard W. Haining; William A. Vogel; Carolyn Tyson (retired); Brion D. Friedman; James L. Deming; David F. Seng; Grover C. Maxwell III; Jane R. Davenport; (front row, left to right) Ronald E. Canakaris, Solon P. Patterson; Charlotte F. Fox. Officers not shown: Debra Bunde Comsudes; C. Jefferson Hagood; Becky Keister; Brian Stahl; Scott Thompson; John S. Whitney III*

PROFILES IN EXCELLENCE

# JOHNSON & HIGGINS

In 1845, two young insurance clerks, Henry W. Johnson and A. Foster Higgins, opened a firm on New York City's Wall Street that specialized in marine insurance coverage. The Golden Age of American merchant trade—with its tall master clipper ships and transatlantic steamers—was well under way at the time and the business expanded quickly.

From its modest beginning, Johnson & Higgins has grown over the past 150 years to become the world's largest privately held insurance broker, with more than 8,400 employees in over 260 offices worldwide, including 52 in the United States. The firm is a recognized leader in insurance and reinsurance brokerage, risk management, consulting, actuarial and human resources consulting, and related services.

Johnson & Higgins reached its first billion-dollar revenue year in 1994, which also marked the fifth consecutive year of record growth in new business. Although its recent success is reason to celebrate, the firm is taking nothing for granted. Energized by the changes facing the insurance industry worldwide, J&H is working harder than ever to create the new products, services, and technologies clients need in this constantly shifting environment.

The backbone of J&H's client service strategy is an all-encompassing program called the J&H Quality Initiative. One important facet of the program is the formation of broker teams, each of which specializes in specific industries. The team approach enables J&H to provide each client with broad expertise and tailored service. In this way, J&H can give clients what they want and value, continually monitor and analyze data, and advise clients on ways to control costs and streamline operations.

In recent years, J&H has had outstanding success in integrating communications with its worldwide network of insurance brokers, known as UNISON, the leading insurance brokerage network in the world. The firm believes access to world markets is essential in an era when more and more companies want global protection. Throughout the 1990s, Johnson & Higgins has continued to set records in sales and revenues and to establish new standards for service to its clients.

J&H of Georgia was established in 1956 through the acquisition of a leading local agency owned by Beverly M. DuBose. DuBose was elected a director of J&H and served in the Atlanta office until his retirement in 1981. Albert S. McGhee became the second director of Johnson & Higgins to head the Atlanta office, located in the 191 Building in downtown Atlanta.

J&H's staff operates on the team concept, with local, regional, and corporate support. The Atlanta office, along with its partner offices in Charlotte, North Carolina, Greenville, South Carolina, Nashville, Tennessee, Birmingham, Alabama, and Jacksonville, Florida, are positioning themselves for the challenges of the 21st century.

# INVESCO

INVESCO PLC is one of the world's largest investment management firms. Assets under management were $75 billion as of June 30, 1994. The company manages retirement plans for large pension funds and for tax-exempt organizations around the world. Additionally, the company offers a wide variety of mutual funds for investors in the United States and overseas. Its investment products include equity, fixed-income, and balanced accounts; multiple asset portfolios; stable value assets; and real estate. All products are managed in a conservative, highly disciplined manner.

INVESCO Capital Management, headquartered in Atlanta, is the largest of the company's subsidiaries. In 1978, several INVESCO employees bought the firm from the Citizens and Southern National Bank and became independent. From a base of approximately $500 million in 1978, the company has grown to nearly $34 billion in assets under management today, and it serves some 450 clients. The original leadership remains active in the Atlanta firm and is credited with INVESCO's highly successful record. The investment philosophy the founders created continues to guide client portfolios two decades later.

Charles W. Brady, a founder of INVESCO Capital Management, an Atlanta native, and a graduate of Georgia Tech, is chairman of the London-based parent company. Several of the company's other global partners are also natives of Atlanta and graduates of Emory, the University of Georgia, and Georgia State University.

A key to the company's success is its diversification of its product and client base. INVESCO PLC is composed of specialty companies, each with a defined role within the company and each with its own record of success. INVESCO Capital Management (Atlanta and Coral Gables) invests with a core, value orientation; INVESCO Management and Research (Boston) uses a quantitative approach; INVESCO Trust Company (Denver) has a growth orientation. Stable Value products are provided by PRIMCO in Louisville, and real estate investment management is offered by INVESCO Realty Advisors (Dallas). The company's efforts in the rapidly growing defined contribution arena are handled by INVESCO Retirement Plan Services in Atlanta. INVESCO Funds Group (Denver) is the mutual fund company, and INVESCO Services (Atlanta) distributes the company's products through third parties.

Overseas, the company's investment professionals follow the same conservative approach in their offices in London, Paris, Prague, Moscow, Luxembourg, Jersey, Tokyo, Hong Kong, and Taipei.

INVESCO is positioned today with people, products, and resources to expand its existing business to become the world's premier global investment management company. INVESCO stock is traded on the New York and London stock exchanges.

# REGENT PARTNERS

Regent Partners, founded and headquartered in Atlanta, Georgia, since 1983, has grown to be one of the nation's most versatile and active real estate firms. Although the company's experience stretches to projects with international boundaries, its strongest presence is in the Southeast, especially Atlanta.

As a wholly owned subsidiary of Philipp Holzmann USA, the firm is highly capitalized with over $200 million in assets and extensive resources through its parent and sister companies.

In Atlanta, the firm is best known for its revitalization of the 1,000,000-square-foot Tower Place complex in Buckhead. Between 1993 and 1995, Regent Partners redeveloped the 30-story office tower and 221-room Wyndham Garden Hotel and added a 165,000-square-foot dining and entertainment center, transforming the 25-acre complex into one of the most comprehensive of its kind in the U.S. Additional office, retail, entertainment, and residential components are planned for the project.

Regent Partners is also involved in a number of other projects in the Atlanta area that demonstrate its versatility and expertise. Bluegrass Place, in North Atlanta, is a 500-acre industrial, retail, and office community with potential for 5 million square feet of space. Another project, Riverwood, in Northwest Atlanta, is a 25-acre mixed-use complex with potential for 1.5 million square feet of office space. In addition, the firm is responsible for the Centennial Gateway Pavilion in downtown Atlanta, a corporate marketing and hospitality center for the 1996 Olympics that will be converted into a hotel and parking facility following the Olympics.

Staffed by skilled real estate professionals who possess high degrees of expertise, integrity, and accountability, Regent Partners has earned an enviable reputation in the real estate industry. Conscientious and responsive service to its clients is enhanced by the financial resources of the organization and the diversity of expertise that the company offers.

*Tower Place—the new heart of Buckhead*

Fleet Capital is a leading national secured corporate lender serving customers throughout the United States in a range of industries. Offering loans from $5 million to $300 million, Fleet Capital assists customers with refinancing, restructuring, and recapitalization; growth; leveraged buyouts; acquisitions; turnarounds; and capital expenditure financing. Fleet Capital is a subsidiary of the Fleet Financial Group, an $81 billion banking entity that ranks 10th in the U.S.

Headquartered in Hartford, Connecticut, Fleet Capital operates a network of offices within five geographic regions of the country and has been serving corporate borrowing needs for over 80 years. In addition, through its International Services Group, Fleet Capital lends internationally to foreign subsidiaries of its U.S. customers. For all customers, Fleet Capital aims to provide creative financial solutions that satisfy unique requirements.

Recognizing the vitality, diversity, and charm of Atlanta, Fleet Capital has made a commitment to investing in the city's future. Based in Atlanta are Fleet Capital's Southern Group headquarters, the office of company president Irwin Teich, the headquarters of the company's International Services Group, and the Corporate Appraisal Department. Fleet Capital's Atlanta office employs over 50 seasoned professionals dedicated to providing superior customer service by developing a comprehensive understanding of customers' businesses, markets, and industries.

In the greater Atlanta area, Fleet Capital lends to manufacturers, wholesalers, distributors, retailers, and selected service businesses. By providing a source of capital for middle-market companies, Fleet Capital is contributing to the growth of the Atlanta business community. And by providing support to financial intermediaries who are based in Atlanta, such as members of the investment banking community and buying groups, as well as CPAs, financing becomes possible for their customers worldwide.

To further support the Atlanta community, Fleet Capital is involved in annual fund drives for the Scottish Rite Children's Hospital and is a member of both the Atlanta and the Cobb County Chambers of Commerce. In addition, Fleet Capital employees support many charitable organizations, including Meals on Wheels, United Way, House Next Door, Hands on Atlanta, Atlanta's Children's Shelter, and Habitat for Humanity.

Courtesy of Fleet Capital

*From left, Irwin Teich, president, and Ferrell Coppedge, executive vice president and Southern Group manager, of Fleet Capital Corporation*

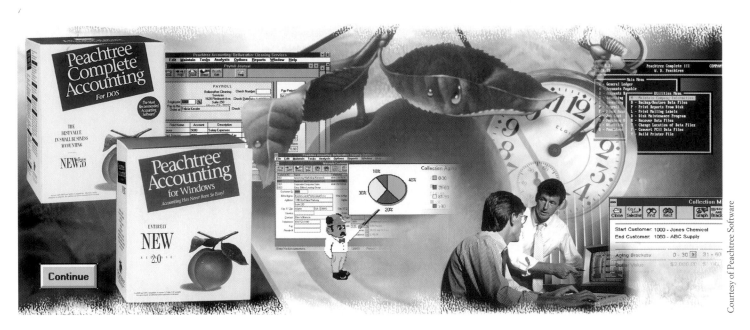

Peachtree Software, the nation's leading small business accounting software company, has deep roots in Atlanta. It has grown from a small retail computer store founded in 1976 to a multimillion-dollar software publisher of award-winning small business accounting systems.

Peachtree was the first company to provide low-cost, off-the-shelf accounting systems for microcomputers; the first to offer PC-DOS accounting systems; the first to provide accounting software for the Apple Macintosh and CD-ROM; and the first to market a Windows-based accounting system.

### FIRST BUSINESS SOFTWARE FOR THE PC
Peachtree Software's breakthrough occurred in 1980, when IBM selected the firm to produce a high-end accounting system for the then top-secret IBM PC. The new system was called the Peachtree Business Accounting Series, and it set the precedent for Peachtree products that followed.

Changes came in 1981 as the newly created accounting system started shipping. The company was acquired by Management Science America (MSA), which is operating today as Dun and Bradstreet Software.

Under MSA ownership, Peachtree built brand recognition and expanded its line of accounting software to the home, education, and business markets.

### CREATING A NEW MARKET
In 1986, more change took place. The firm entered a new market for low-cost, high-end accounting products for small to medium-sized businesses by bundling the individual modules of the Peachtree Business Accounting Series into one product and lowering the price from $5,000 to $199. As a result, business blossomed. Growth continued under the new ownership of Intelligent Systems.

When Intelligent Systems took over Peachtree, Bill Goodhew, a former MSA vice president, became Peachtree's president and CEO. The company was clearly marked for success, as Goodhew confidently targeted new distribution channels, cut overhead and manufacturing costs, and streamlined the product. In 1988, with the help of a group of investors, Goodhew and Peachtree management purchased Peachtree from Intelligent Systems. Intelligent Systems retained a 16 percent ownership.

Under Goodhew's direction, Peachtree

*Peachtree Software has evolved into a mission-critical tool for successful small businesses.*

concentrated its energy on the small business accounting market. This focus has enabled Peachtree to carve out a successful niche.

### ACQUISITION PROMISES NEW SERVICES
With today's highly competitive business environment, companies need all the management help they can get. In an effort to offer additional products and services for its customers, Peachtree Software was acquired in 1994 by Automatic Data Processing, Inc. (ADP), the nation's largest provider of computerized transaction processing and information services and synonymous with payroll processing.

Commenting on the acquisition, Goodhew notes, "The combined offerings of Peachtree and ADP enable us to deliver complete financial transaction and human resource solutions. Our partnership with ADP enables us to connect seamlessly with ADP's renowned direct-deposit, payroll, and tax-filing services. In the future, additional resources, such as on-line banking, will be accessible

directly from Peachtree programs."

As a result of the company's commitment to quality, value, and its customers, Peachtree products are used by nearly a million businesses worldwide. Peachtree designs software for small to medium-sized businesses that need to manage their accounting in a comprehensive yet inexpensive way.

The Peachtree Software product line is headed up by the award-winning Peachtree Accounting for Windows, recognized as the technology leader in accounting software, and Peachtree Complete Accounting for DOS, a standard-setter for value. For businesses that have outgrown manual systems or

personal finance software, Peachtree First Accounting provides real accounting functionality at an exceptional price.

To back up its products, Peachtree Software has an extensive customer service department, as well as a network of authorized support centers throughout the U.S. to provide customers with local installation as well as support and training options. Starting with 10 employees and growing to more than 240, Peachtree Software knows what is involved in the day-to-day operation of running and expanding a business. "That is why Peachtree Software continues to flourish, launching new and successful products," explains Goodhew.

*Peachtree Software shares its Norcross headquarters with the software development division of parent Automatic Data Processing, Inc.*

# SELIG ENTERPRISES, INC.

Selig Enterprises is a well-known and respected name in the history of modern Atlanta. This commercial real estate firm, founded in 1942 as CMS Realty Company, has played a significant role in metropolitan Atlanta's progress toward national and international status.

The Selig family owns and operates the company and follows a tradition of leadership in business, civic, and cultural endeavors. "We are committed to the growth and prosperity of this region," says S. Stephen Selig III, president. "We believe it is our responsibility to be deeply involved in our community and to promote and support its well-being through contributions of time, energy, and resources. To us, 'community' encompasses business and the arts, as well as the civic, charitable, and social facets of our region."

This commitment is a cornerstone of the company's success, and family ownership is a key to its stability.

Headquartered in Atlanta's midtown area, Selig Enterprises has grown steadily for five decades. CMS founder Ben J. Massell, often called "the father of Atlanta's skyline," helped set the building blocks that have shaped the city of today. It was through his daughter, Caroline Massell Selig, and her husband, Simon S. Selig, Jr., that the Selig family became involved in the company. Their son, S. Stephen Selig III, and their daughter, Cathy Selig, continue their grandfather's and parents' tradition.

Selig Enterprises' extensive and diverse portfolio includes more than 250 properties located throughout Atlanta and other parts of the Southeast. The properties, totaling in excess of 8 million square feet, are divided equally among retail, office, and industrial sites.

Selig provides commercial real estate leasing, development, accounting, administrative, construction, and property man-

*Executive Committee of Selig Enterprises, Inc. (left to right): David E. Witt, Cathy Selig, Robert Riddle, S. Stephen Selig III, and William J. Dawkins*

agement services for its own portfolio and those of its affiliates. The company also owns and operates AAA Parking, which manages over 85 parking facilities located primarily in the metropolitan Atlanta area.

Long-term ownership is one of the company's basic strengths. An equally important factor in Selig's exceptional reputation and growth is its relationship with its tenants, from small start-up businesses and local merchants to Fortune 500 corporations and national retailers. A history of responsive, efficient service is the foundation for ongoing relationships.

"Atlanta is moving into a position of importance among the notable cities of the world," says Stephen Selig. "Selig Enterprises and the Selig family are proud to be both a contributor to and beneficiary of this city's and this region's growth and leadership role."

*Buckhead Triangle, at Peachtree Road, site of major commercial development in Atlanta*

When Piedmont Hospital was founded on August 5, 1905, Atlanta's population was 100,000. Three quarters of a century later, Piedmont has grown along with Atlanta. Phenomenal changes have occurred in medicine, technology, and scientific achievement, and even bigger changes in the delivery of health care are yet to come.

As Piedmont Hospital reflects on the past and anticipates the future, some things have not changed. Its commitment to medical excellence, community responsibility, a tradition of quality, and reasonable costs remains as strong as ever.

Piedmont Hospital was founded by Ludwig Amster, M.D., and his wife, Flora, immigrants from Vienna, Austria, and by Floyd Wilcox McRae, M.D., an Atlanta surgeon. After practicing gastroenterology in New York, Dr. Amster was attracted by the growth and challenge of 1905 Atlanta, where horseless carriages and trolley cars shared dusty red thoroughfares. Dr. and Mrs. Amster leased the Swift House, a 15-room residence, complete with young flowering magnolia trees, on the corner of Capitol Avenue and

Courtesy of Piedmont Hospital

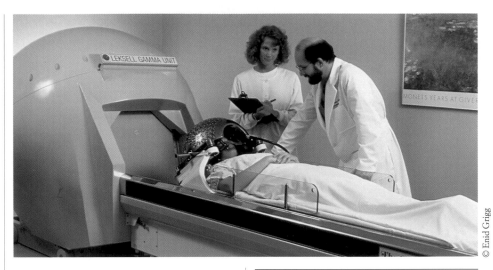

© Enid Grigg

Crumley Avenue, and petitioned for a charter to become a 10-bed sanatorium dedicated to the treatment of gastrointestinal disease. On the northeast side of Atlanta-Fulton County Stadium, at Gate P, stands a group of magnolia trees that once graced the lawn of Piedmont Sanatorium.

In those early years, not unlike today, the growing number of patients required the addition of beds and treatment space. A five-story pavilion was added in 1922, bringing the total number of beds to 132. In 1957, a $5 million, 213-bed facility was opened in what was then considered to be "out of town," on Peachtree Road in Buckhead.

Today, Piedmont Hospital is a private, not-for-profit, 500-bed tertiary-care facility. More than 2,300 employees, 820 physicians who specialize in every category of medicine, and 500 Woman's Auxiliary volunteers make up the Piedmont family. Whether introducing new life in the Maternity and Women's Center or helping older adults remain independent with help from the Sixty Plus program, Piedmont Hospital provides high-quality medical services ranging from outpatient surgery, renal transplantation, and diagnostic procedures to

---

*The family-oriented Maternity Center at Piedmont Hospital offers a complete range of programs for parents, siblings, and grandparents to ensure a highly personal birth experience.*

---

*The Gamma Knife revolutionized neurosurgery by enabling surgeons to destroy some brain tumors that were previously inoperable. Piedmont Hospital has one of 20 Gamma Knife units in the United States.*

---

open-heart surgery, cardiac rehabilitation, and heart disease prevention offered by the Fuqua Heart Center of Atlanta. The Neuroscience Institute's revolutionary Gamma Knife is used to treat inoperable tumors and vascular conditions in the brain, without an incision. Weekend athletes receive the same major league care as Atlanta's professional sports teams from Piedmont's sports medicine specialists/orthopedists, while patients in need of joint replacements can avail themselves of the expertise of physicians and staff at the Reconstructive Joint Center of Atlanta. Oncology services not only are comprehensive but offer personalized care for cancer patients. The 24-hour Emergency Department is equipped and staffed to handle even major trauma.

Piedmont Hospital was founded as a specialty hospital in an era when specialists were rare. Drs. Amster and McRae were considered "ahead of their time," and they wanted the best for their patients. That philosophy has not changed.

What is changing is the way health care is accessed and delivered. The revolution in health care now in full swing is driving hospitals to make health care accessible to the greatest number of people in the most cost-efficient manner. Piedmont Hospital is no exception.

In 1993, Piedmont Medical Center opened the Women's Center of Piedmont Hospital in the Atlanta suburb of Peachtree City to provide physician's office care in obstetrics and gynecology. In 1994, the Piedmont Hospital Specialty Clinic opened adjacent to the Women's Center, offering area residents access to physicians on staff at Piedmont Hospital in specialties ranging from cardiology to urology.

In 1994, in order to compete in an ever-challenging health-care environment, Piedmont Hospital became a founding partner in PROMINA Health System, a not-for-profit health alliance consisting of Piedmont Medical Center, PROMINA Gwinnett Health System, and PROMINA Northwest Health System. The alliance was formed in order to provide broader geographic coverage and health services to surrounding communities.

In 1995, unprecedented growth took

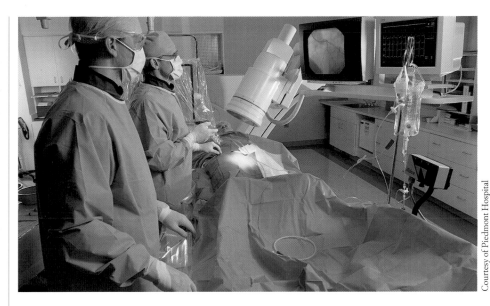

place as Piedmont Medical Center began the development of a 100-bed hospital in Fayette County, south of Atlanta; and Piedmont Medical Care Foundation, a subsidiary of Piedmont Medical Center, Inc., broke ground for two primary-care facilities in the suburban communities of Vinings and Sandy Springs.

*A cardiac catheterization in progress in the Fuqua Heart Center of Atlanta at Piedmont Hospital*

These and other plans for expansion will enable Piedmont Medical Center to thrive well into the next century as a leader in the delivery of quality, cost-efficient health care.

*Piedmont Hospital in Buckhead*

New Year's Day 1953 saw the birth of one of Atlanta's most valued institutions—The Emory Clinic. Today, what began as a 17-member clinical practice plan for Emory University medical faculty is the linchpin of a wide-ranging and comprehensive health system with satellites and affiliates throughout metropolitan Atlanta, the state of Georgia, and the Southeast.

With more than 750 physicians whose specialties range from primary care to the most sophisticated surgical and diagnostic techniques, The Emory Clinic serves as the gateway to the Emory University System of Health Care. Along with the clinic, the other well-respected institutions comprising the system include Emory University Hospital, Crawford Long Hospital of Emory University, and Wesley Woods Geriatric Center at Emory University.

Through affiliations with the Veterans Affairs Medical Center, Grady Memorial Hospital, and other health-care providers, Emory System physicians are currently responsible for more than 3,000 hospital beds, 2 million in- and outpatient visits, and almost half a million emergency visits in the state each year. Fully 25 percent of Georgia's health-care professionals received their education and training at Emory University, which also has schools of nursing and public health.

In 1913, the Atlanta College of Physicians and Surgeons and the Atlanta School of Medicine merged to become Atlanta Medical College. Two years later, the medical school completed yet another merger—this time with the nascent Emory University, created when Emory College moved 50 miles west from Oxford, Georgia, to Atlanta.

Emory University School of Medicine's early days coincided with tremendous strides in the practice of surgery and the prevention of surgical infection. Students first trained at Grady Memorial Hospital and later at Emory University Hospital, which served for years as the only private hospital in DeKalb, Gwinnett, Rockdale, Newton, and Henry counties.

From the beginning, the medical school attracted many of the nation's top physicians, and it continues that stellar tradition today. From the pioneering procedure angioplasty, a now-standard technique in cardiac care, to the development

Courtesy of Emory University System of Health Care

*U.S. News and World Report has consistently named Emory University Hospital one of America's best health-care centers.*

*Emory has attracted some of the nation's top physicians and has set a standard of care in Atlanta, the state, and beyond.*

of microelectrode-guided pallidotomy, a state-of-the-art surgical treatment for patients with Parkinson's disease, Emory physicians have set a standard of care for Atlanta, the state, and beyond.

Consequently, the magazine *U.S. News and World Report* has named Emory University Hospital one of America's best health-care centers for nearly a decade. The magazine cited Emory's strengths in cardiology, ophthalmology, urology, and neurology in naming the hospital to its annual list.

Not content to rest on past and present laurels, however, the Emory University System of Health Care is committed to the goal of seeing its Winship Cancer Center become Georgia's first National Cancer Institute-designated Comprehensive Cancer Center. Granted to a select group of institutions, NCI designation represents the best in cancer research, treatment, and patient care the nation has to offer.

The Emory University System of Health Care is now applying its excellent reputation in research and specialty care to primary health care. From pediatric and geriatric medicine to obstetrics and preventive care, Emory doctors are now available at satellite offices throughout the Atlanta metropolitan area. Additionally, the system's teleconsulting services put Georgia doctors and their patients as close to Emory expertise as the nearest telephone.

These same telephone lines will soon enable Emory doctors to do even more. Currently under way are initiatives in telemedicine, a new fiber-optic, computer-driven technology that will eventually allow Emory physicians to view patients for consultation or diagnosis without the patient ever leaving his or her doctor's office.

The Emory System continues to build on its prominence in specialty care by consolidating several of its most utilized specialties—cardiology,

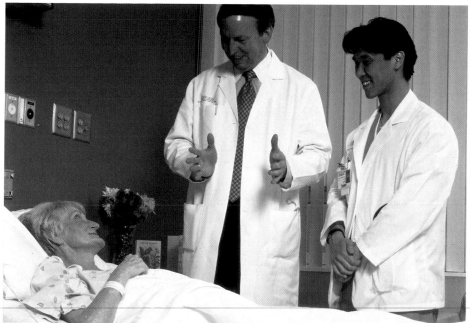

*The Emory Clinic, which began in 1953 with 17 members, now has more than 750 physicians and is the linchpin of the Emory University System of Health Care.*

cancer, transplantation, and women's care among them—into easily accessible interdisciplinary centers that offer patients a full spectrum of care.

The Emory Heart Center has served as a model for this approach. Termed a "center without walls," the Heart Center unifies all cardiac services and activities under one umbrella with a primary emphasis on quality and compassionate care and a secondary goal of cost-effectiveness. The

center's activities extend to numerous community wellness and prevention programs.

Past, present, and future, the Emory University System of Health Care has been and will be commited to the health and well-being of the community and the patients it serves through a multipronged approach that emphasizes quality patient care, research, and teaching.

# BLUE CROSS AND BLUE SHIELD OF GEORGIA

The state's largest health insurer, Blue Cross and Blue Shield of Georgia, has grown from its origin as Georgia's first provider of prepaid health insurance to a company intent on enhancing the quality and cost of health care for more than 1.2 million Georgians.

The strong relationship between Blue Cross and Blue Shield of Georgia and the medical and business communities can be traced to its founding. The company's original Georgia presence dates back to 1937, when the Atlanta Blue Cross Plan was founded with a $5,000 loan from five local hospitals. The company, called the United Hospitals Service Association of Atlanta, was formed by an act of the Georgia General Assembly with the goal of providing prepaid hospital care. The original office, which housed seven employees, was in downtown Atlanta. At the time, the company offered one contract: a 90-cent-per-month plan that covered one person. The Atlanta Blue Shield Plan, designed to cover physician charges, issued its first contract in 1954.

Blue Cross and Blue Shield of Georgia's roots are also tied to the Savannah Plan and the Columbus Plan. The Savannah Plan was founded in 1939 as the Savannah Hospital Service Association. The Columbus Blue Cross Plan was founded in 1946. The two plans merged in 1966 to form Blue Cross and Blue Shield of Georgia/Columbus. The Columbus and Atlanta organizations merged in 1985 to form Blue Cross and Blue Shield of Georgia.

Nationally, the forerunner of the Blue Cross Plan was a prepaid hospital program started in 1929 at Baylor University in Texas. Just two months after the 1929 stock market crash, Justin Ford Kimball negotiated a 50-cent-per-month plan with Baylor Hospital in Dallas, assuring each participant care for 21 days in a semiprivate room. During the Great Depression, citizens began using the Baylor prepayment program to serve group customers. The Blue Cross plans developed as a nonprofit association designed to handle administrative details for these programs.

The success of Blue Cross plans created a demand for a program to cover physician expenses. The Blue Shield symbol, inspired by the U.S. Army's

medical insignia, was first used in 1939 to promote a plan to pay for individual physician services. The Blue Shield name and symbol were adopted by a national nonprofit association in 1948. The Blue Cross and Blue Shield associations merged in 1975.

On a national and state level, Blue Cross and Blue Shield has undergone tremendous changes in its approach to business. The traditional concept of health insurance was that companies paid claims as they received them, according to the benefit levels within a customer's policy. Today, Blue Cross and Blue Shield plans typically offer a mix of traditional indemnity products and newer coordinated care products, designed to maximize quality, cost, and access to health care. The heart and objective of Blue Cross and Blue Shield of Georgia's long-term strategic plan is to be the leader in coordinated care in Georgia.

The centerpiece for the company's long-term strategy is the development of Community Health Partnership Networks (CHPNs), which integrate the financing and delivery of health care in local communities throughout the state. CHPNs are partnerships between Blue Cross and Blue Shield of Georgia, physicians, hospitals, and others. CHPNs are jointly owned and governed and are designed to provide community solutions to community health-care needs.

Blue Cross and Blue Shield of Georgia's first CHPN became operational in Atlanta on January 1, 1995. The network includes more than 500 of metropolitan Atlanta's leading personal physicians. Blue Cross and Blue Shield of Georgia has established CHPNs in Columbus, Savannah, Rome, Augusta, and Athens and is in the process of establishing these networks throughout the state.

Blue Cross and Blue Shield of Georgia's coordinated care products include BlueChoice Healthcare Plan, a health maintenance organization (HMO) product featuring prepaid coverage and preventive care, underwritten by HMO Georgia, Inc., a wholly owned subsidiary of Blue Cross and Blue Shield of Georgia;

BlueChoice Option, a point-of-service product, also underwritten by HMO Georgia, that allows members to choose between BlueChoice Healthcare Plan network providers and out-of-network providers; and BlueChoice PPO, a preferred provider organization.

The mission of Blue Cross and Blue Shield of Georgia—to provide access to affordable health care for as many Georgians as possible—is characterized by the company's efforts to create high-quality health care that is affordably priced and supported by excellent customer service.

PROFILES IN EXCELLENCE

South Fulton Medical Center (SFMC) is a not-for-profit regional provider of preventive, curative, and life-enhancing services. Positioned at the forefront of the country's health-care providers, the medical center combines the latest in improvement techniques, information systems, and technology to create a sophisticated approach to delivering medical services. SFMC's goal is to consistently provide better patient outcomes and higher patient satisfaction while offering services at competitive rates.

These efforts have not gone unnoticed. In 1994, SFMC was recognized as one of the top 100 hospitals in the country in the HCIA/Mercer Benchmarks for Success Survey, in which the facility also received an honorable mention in 1995 for sustaining outstanding performance over time. In addition, SFMC was named to the official Hospital Support Network for the 1996 Olympics.

SFMC has more than 500 primary-care physicians and specialists throughout the south metro area. Among the many services the center provides are a Health Info Hotline, staffed by registered nurses; two breast health centers; a primary-care center; a family-focused child-birth environment, where more than 1,900 babies are born each year, as well as a Level II neonatal nursery; a rehab center dedicated to inpatient physical rehabilitation and independence; and oncology, cardiology, and surgical services. Managed-care clients benefit from the center's wellness and prevention programs.

South Fulton Medical Center also reaches out to the community by providing preventive care services, free screenings for cardiovascular disease, diabetes, and cancer, and wellness seminars.

South Fulton Medical Center demonstrates the importance of finding innovative ways to deliver superior quality health care in a cost-effective manner. The hospital's strong commitment to quality, technology, wellness, and community involvement positions SFMC as a leading health-care provider in south metro Atlanta.

It started out as a six-bed unit operating out of leased space in an Atlanta hospital in 1975. Today, Shepherd Center is a private, not-for-profit 100-bed specialty hospital that provides a comprehensive continuum of care for people with spinal cord injuries, acquired brain injuries, multiple sclerosis, other neurological disorders, and urological problems.

The impetus for the creation of the center was James Shepherd, who suffered a spinal cord injury in a body-surfing accident. Following his rehabilitation in Colorado, James, his parents, Harold and Alana Shepherd, and friends Clark Harrison and David Webb were determined to develop a top-notch spinal cord injury center that would serve Georgia and the rest of the Southeast. Through hard work and successful fund-raising, and with the support of Dr. David F. Apple, Jr., Shepherd's first medical director, they made their dream come true.

In 1982, Shepherd Spinal Center opened as a free-standing 40-bed facility on Peachtree Road adjacent to Piedmont Hospital. It soon achieved national recognition by being designated a model center for spinal cord injury care. The number of beds was doubled in 1985 to include an eight-bed intensive care unit.

Another milestone was reached in 1992 with the opening of The Billi Marcus Building, a $23 million facility that more than doubled the center's size. The building houses the ProMotion Fitness Center, fully accessible to people with disabilities; the ABI Unit, created in 1995 to serve people with acquired brain injuries; and outpatient services. In addition to clinics for gynecology, urology, bracing, seating, and mobility, the outpatient area houses the Multiple Sclerosis Center, established in 1991 and designated an official MS center by the National Multiple Sclerosis Society-Georgia Chapter.

With this expansion of services, Shepherd Spinal Center changed its name in 1995 to Shepherd Center.

Today, Shepherd continues to be recognized for helping people with catastrophic injuries return to active recreational, educational, and occupational lifestyles. A powerful advocate for people with disabilities, Shepherd is the founding sponsor of the 1996 Atlanta Paralympic Games.

*Courtesy of Shepherd Center*

*Pictured in front of Shepherd Center, a specialty hospital in Buckhead, are (from left to right) Gary Ulicny, CEO; David Apple, Jr., M.D., Medical Director; James Shepherd, Chairman of the Board; and Alana Shepherd, Secretary of the Board.*

# SOLVAY PHARMACEUTICALS INC.

Solvay Pharmaceuticals Inc., whose corporate headquarters are located in the Atlanta suburb of Marietta, has a tradition of developing and marketing products that reflect the latest advances in pharmacological science. In today's uncertain market and with the emergence of managed health care, Solvay Pharmaceuticals is committed to implementing strategies to meet future health-care needs.

Over the years, the Solvay name has come to stand internationally for scientific innovation, vision, and integrity. The company is grounded in a heritage of research and fresh thinking, dating to 1863, when Belgian scientist Ernest Solvay started the business. Recognizing the importance of fundamental research, he founded a series of conferences on physics in Brussels attended by such leading scientists as Albert Einstein, Max Planck, Marie

Curie, and Ernest Rutherford. Because Solvay passed along his commitment to innovative scientific discovery, the firm, Solvay S.A., quickly became world renowned for its pioneering research.

In 1986, a milestone of strategic importance occurred when Reid-Rowell, a southeastern United States company known for quality therapeutic products in obstetrics, gynecology, and gastroenterology, became part of the Solvay S.A. group of companies. The transaction brought with it a reputable, established product line, a vigorous and talented workforce, and a determination to make Solvay Pharmaceuticals, as the company was renamed, the supplier of choice for selected therapies.

Solvay Pharmaceuticals' commitment to basic research is bolstered by the considerable contributions of the other mem-

ber companies of Solvay S.A.'s Human Health group, which together reinforce the belief that innovation is the key to growth. Since 1988, research and development expenditures have grown dramatically. The Human Health Business Group of companies of Solvay S.A., including Solvay Pharmaceuticals, reinvests 16 percent of every sales dollar in research and development.

The firm's corporate commitment to research and development is an important part of Solvay Pharmaceuticals' continuing strategy to market innovative products that respond to a broad range of human health needs. Membership in Solvay S.A's Human Health group augments the talents of Solvay Pharmaceuticals' professionals by providing access to over 1,000 researchers employed by the firm's two sister companies—Solvay

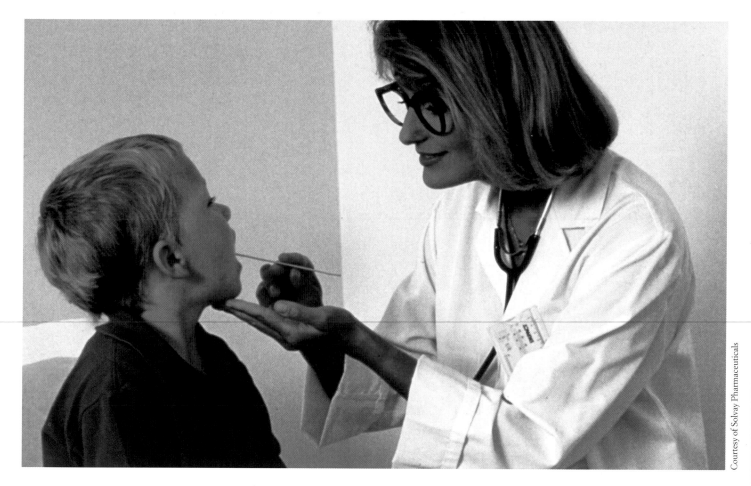

Pharma Deutschland GmbH (Germany) and Solvay Duphar B.V. (The Netherlands).

By focusing its efforts in selected therapeutic areas compatible with the firm's global strategy, Solvay Pharmaceuticals can deliver quality products that meet specific clinical needs of physicians and their patients.

Therapeutic products in the gastroenterology field, for example, include ROWASA®, for the treatment of ulcerative colitis; CREON®, for the treatment of pancreatic enzyme insufficiency; and DUPHALAC®, a colon-specific and non-systemic laxative. In the women's health area, Solvay Pharmaceuticals produces ESTRATAB® and ESTRATEST®, for menopausal symptoms, and Advanced Formula ZENATE®, a prenatal multivitamin/mineral supplement tablet. Products for the central nervous system include LUVOX®, for the treatment of obsessive compulsive disorder, and LITHOBID®, a slow-release tablet for manic-depressive illness. The company is continually making strategic additions to its product line

to ensure dynamic growth and to meet patient needs. In addition to continuing research in traditional specialties, Solvay Pharmaceuticals has committed substantial resources to product development.

Central to Solvay Pharmaceuticals' operations is the belief that no product, however revolutionary, can be a success without superior customer support. As a result, the sales and marketing departments work side by side with research and development teams. The sales staff is knowledgeable, motivated, and committed to customer service. The sales staff also stays up-to-date by continuously augmenting its training. Field sales managed care account executives quickly receive instruction and training to answer their customers' questions.

As a service to physicians, Solvay Pharmaceuticals has participated through the years in a wide variety of continuing education programs for patients and healthcare professionals. Today, this commitment to service is reflected in the firm's regional professional services associates

(PSAs). These specialists are a resource for practitioners, providing awareness of medical developments and issues related to Solvay Pharmaceuticals' products and therapeutic concerns.

*Conseil de Physique Solvay 1911*

PSAs also work with professionals to encourage them to present and publish work in relevant therapeutic areas of interest and make these professionals aware of research support and various company educational and assistance programs.

Through the firm's Health Economics

Department, the costs and consequences of Solvay Pharmaceuticals' products and services are identified, measured, and compared to aid customers in determining their value in the treatment and prevention of disease.

Quality service means responding to inquiries with complete, prompt information about products and relevant therapeutic areas. Each month the company receives over 1,000 requests for information. Skilled researchers, called medical information specialists, respond to each request, usually within 24 hours, with accurate, comprehensive, and balanced scientific information.

Solvay Pharmaceuticals supports its focus on service with an ongoing investment in state-of-the-art facilities, information, technology, and equipment. This commitment starts in the laboratory and continues in the company's Baudette, Minnesota, manufacturing plant, where production activities are concentrated in a modern 115,000-square-foot facility that includes high-speed, automated processing and packaging machinery, enabling the firm to quadruple its production capacity in recent years and to respond promptly to changing production needs.

Driven by Solvay Pharmaceuticals' commitment to customer support, the Minnesota facility fills 95 percent of its orders the same day. And upgrades to the information management systems continue to benefit both customers and patients. By improving its data-processing equipment and enhancing the management information services staff, the firm is positioned to provide both scientific and marketing personnel with timely access to the information they need.

While science gives Solvay Pharmaceuticals its strength, it is the firm's employees who give the company its confidence, depth, and competitive edge. Not only do they have vision, but they also understand the power of science and innovation and the importance of being attentive to customers' needs. Teamwork, self-discipline, and pride in accomplishment are important to these talented and highly motivated professionals.

Solvay Pharmaceuticals is dedicated to being a responsible supplier of high-quality therapeutic products, to supporting the basic objectives of an improved health-care system, and to responding successfully to changes driven by managed health care. As a service to indigent patients, the company also provides products for individuals without insurance coverage who are unable to afford pharmaceutical therapies.

The company plans to continue to master the challenges posed by an uncertain market while continuing to implement strategies designed to meet future health-care needs.

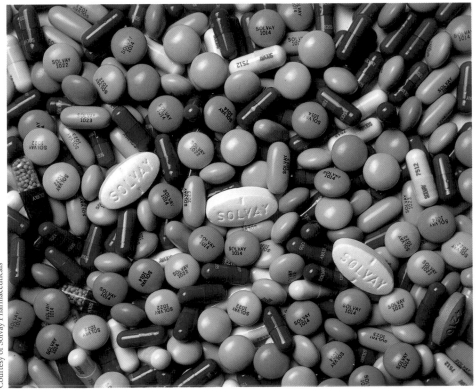

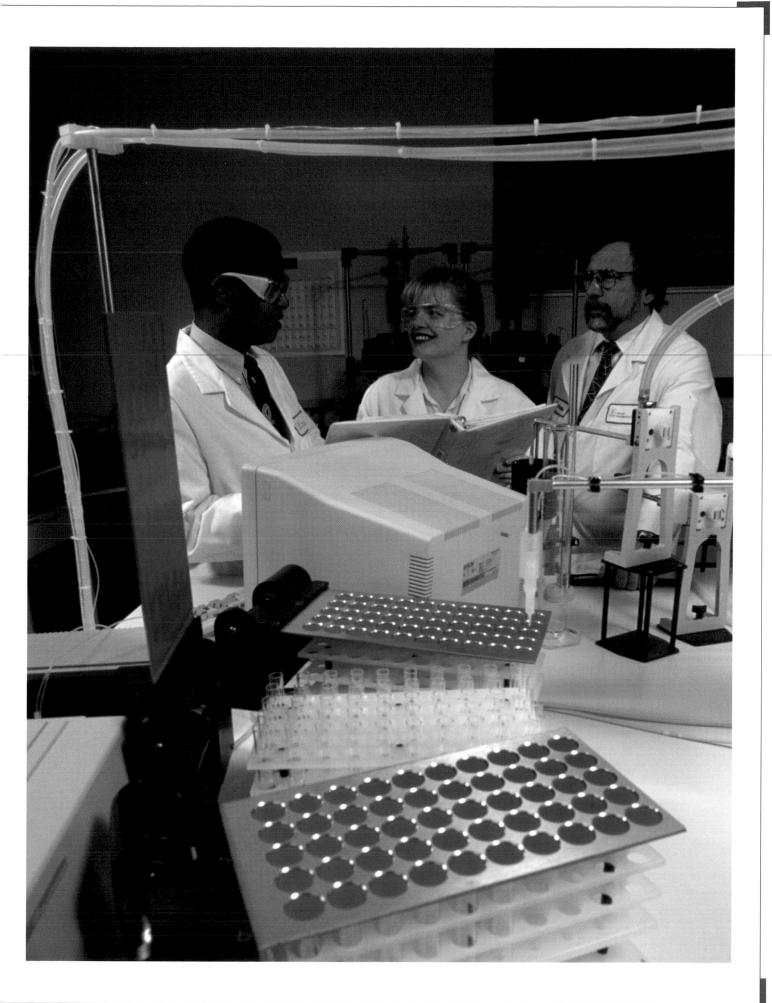

PROFILES IN EXCELLENCE

*Courtesy of DeKalb Medical Center*

The mission of DeKalb Medical Center is to contribute to the well-being and the quality of life of those it serves by providing comprehensive health and wellness services in partnership with its physician practices.

DeKalb Medical Center has been providing comprehensive health and wellness services to the community since it first opened in 1961 as a small 200-bed general hospital. Today, the medical center is a private, not-for-profit 523-bed facility with approximately 2,000 employees, 450 volunteers, and a medical staff of more than 800 physicians representing some 40 medical specialties.

Located in Decatur, just minutes from downtown Atlanta, the medical center is governed by DeKalb Medical Center, Inc., and its parent corporation, DeKalb Regional Healthcare System. It is accredited by the Joint Commission on the Accreditation of Healthcare Organizations and

serves approximately 20,000 inpatients and more than 200,000 emergency patients and outpatients each year.

DeKalb Medical Center is recognized as a leader in progressive medicine at the forefront of major advances in diagnosis, treatment, and prevention. Its skilled healthcare professionals, supported by leading-edge technology, are among its greatest assets.

Over the years, DeKalb Medical Center has developed several centers of excellence, including a 24-hour emergency center with a trauma triage center, chest pain emergency services, and sexual assault treatment facilities. An extensive array of wellness and health promotion programs are offered through the medical center's Wellness Center, which was the first of its kind in the Southeast when it opened in 1985. DeKalb Medical Center's new Outpatient Surgery Center was the first in Atlanta to be fully equipped with

fixed-video surgery capabilities, transforming the medical center's surgical facilities into one of the area's premier programs.

The medical center's TenderCare Maternity Services offer a family-centered approach to maternity care, featuring new and attractive maternity suites, a state-of-the-art neonatal intensive care unit, specialized perinatology services for high-risk pregnancies, and obstetrical education classes for the whole family.

Other specialized programs include the Charles B. Eberhart Cancer Center, which offers comprehensive diagnostic, treatment, and support services to cancer patients and their families, including an extensive network of support groups. DeKalb Medical Center also offers comprehensive cardiology and critical care services, as well as a full array of rehabilitation, occupational health, and mental health programs.

In 1994, DeKalb Medical Center's parent company acquired Decatur Hospital, a 120-bed downtown Decatur facility whose specialties include outpatient surgery, behavioral care (substance abuse), ophthalmology, and podiatry. As part of the same healthcare system, the two facilities are able to consolidate services for direct savings, as well as enhance opportunities to receive managed-care contracts.

Another important event that occurred in 1994 was the opening of DeKalb Medical Center at Hillandale, the first phase of a planned second campus located in Lithonia, in south DeKalb County. The 42,000-square-foot facility includes an outpatient diagnostic center offering imaging, laboratory, rehabilitation, and wellness services, as well as private physician offices.

Other satellite facilities include a network of more than 10 community-based primary-care centers designed to make healthcare more convenient and accessible to residents. Three FamilyCare Centers, located in Decatur, Tucker, and South DeKalb, provide care for minor emergencies and illnesses.

DeKalb Medical Center maintains a high level of community involvement through a wide range of free services and programs such as its physician referral service, speakers' bureau, and ongoing health screenings and health promotion events. In addition, the medical center participates in community outreach programs that include the DeKalb Medical Society's Physicians' Care Clinic, the DeKalb County Teen Pregnancy Task Force, the DeKalb Rape Crisis Center, and the medical center's own AIDS Education Task Force.

DeKalb Medical Center's goal or "vision" is to be the leading provider of high-value heathcare services for its patients and others it serves by being the provider of choice, the employer of choice, and the most clinically effective and cost-efficient healthcare system.

DeKalb Medical Center expects to attain its mission and vision by embracing the following values: accountability—to take initiative and ownership in clinical, economic, and ethical decision-making to provide appropriate service to its patients; collaboration—to provide service in an atmosphere of cooperation, mutual respect, and trust; continual improvement—to consistently strive to achieve higher levels of service; dignity—to provide service by treating patients, families, co-workers, and all others with care, courtesy, and respect; diversity—to recognize each other's unique backgrounds, experiences, and viewpoints when providing service; and innovation—to support and encourage creativity, learning, and change in order to continually improve service.

# MANUFACTURING AND DISTRIBUTION

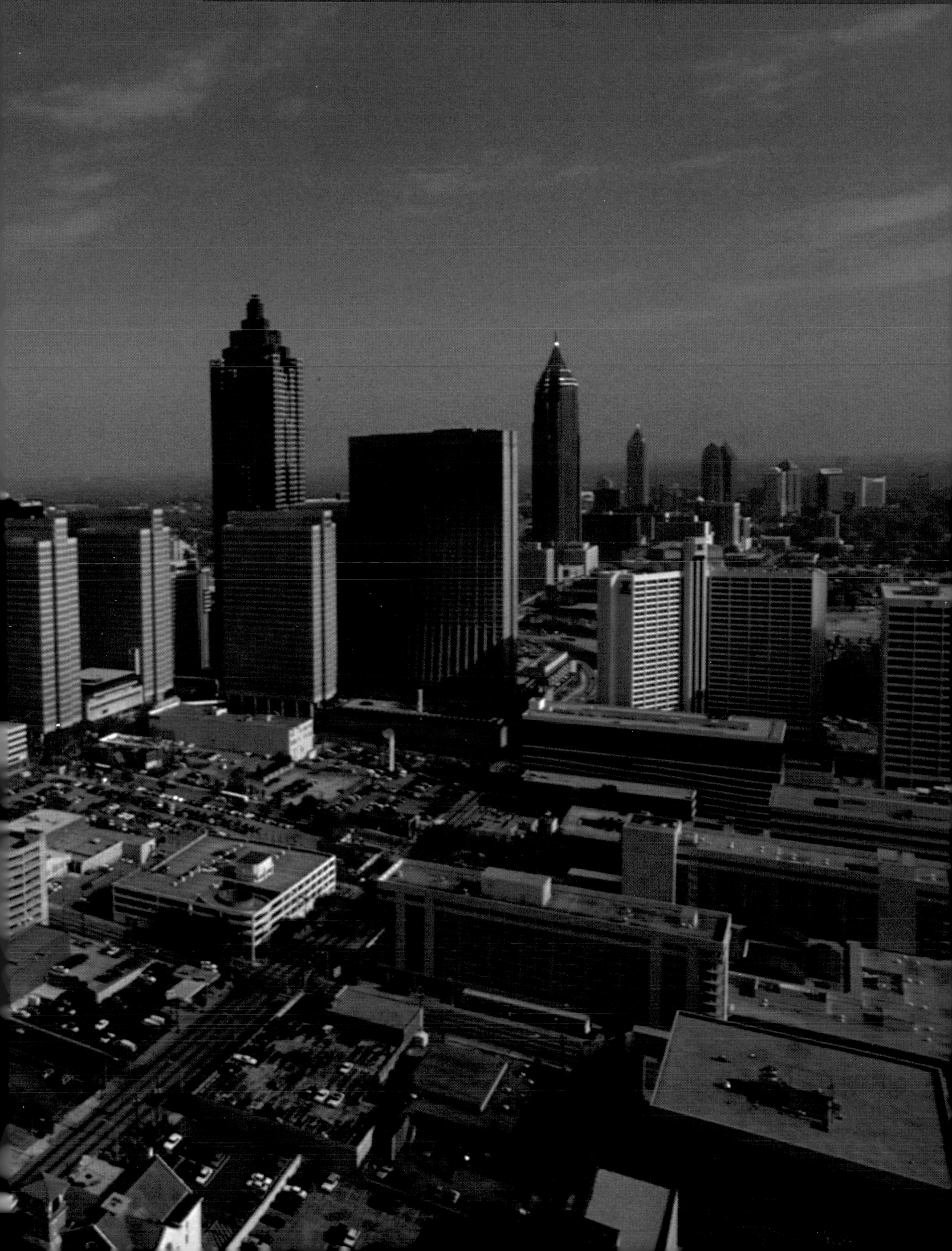

# CIBA VISION

Given Atlanta's rise to prominence as one of the world's truly international cities, it should come as no surprise that a number of the world's most innovative companies have chosen to make Atlanta their home. Counted among that select group is CIBA Vision, which maintains its worldwide headquarters in the northern suburb of Duluth. From this location, CIBA Vision pursues its global mission: "To be the worldwide leader in providing quality eye care products and services which best satisfy our customers' needs."

The Duluth facility also serves as the worldwide and U.S. headquarters for the Optics businesses and for CIBA Vision Ophthalmics U.S. The 70-acre site includes an administration building, research and development laboratories, and a distribution center. Encompassing nearly 500,000 square feet, the four-building complex houses a workforce of 700 who serve as the corporate nerve center for approximately 6,000 employees throughout 40 countries in Asia, Africa, Europe, Australia, and North and South America.

A few miles south of Duluth, the Amwiler manufacturing site serves as a major production center for CIBA Vision contact lenses marketed worldwide. This facility is an important element in the company's execution of efficient, high-volume production of contact lenses.

In the tradition of its centuries-old parent corporation, the Swiss-based biological and chemical group Ciba-Geigy, Limited, CIBA Vision has already achieved a position of both respect and leadership in the international marketplace for contact lenses, lens care products, and ophthalmic pharmaceuticals. Established in 1980 as a diversification effort of Ciba's U.S. Pharmaceuticals Division, the company was the 26th entrant in the crowded field of soft contact lens manufacturers. By 1992, CIBA Vision had emerged as the number-two supplier of contact lenses and lens care products worldwide. This rapid rise is directly attributable to the three cornerstones of CIBA Vision's business: technical innovation, geographic expansion, and aggressive business building through strategic acquisitions.

Initially, it was CIBA Vision's technical strengths that provided its entree into the contact lens market. In 1981 the firm introduced the industry's first tinted soft lens. Quick to recognize the opportunities presented by tinted lenses, the company threw its resources behind the development of a lens that would enhance the wearer's natural eye color.

The result was Softcolors, which was introduced with great success in 1984. These revolutionary lenses were the first example of the rapid product development curve that has provided CIBA Vision with its competitive advantage. As its position in the market grew, the company pursued expansion via acquisition with the purchase in 1985 of American Optical Company's contact lens and lens care product line.

During the past 10 years, CIBA Vision has continued to grow. In 1988 the company was quick to capitalize on the expanding market for disposable contact lenses with its NewVues product. In 1990 CIBA Vision Ophthalmics was formed to serve the ophthalmic pharmaceuticals market. That year the company also introduced the Focus product line, the first entry in a rapidly expanding line of lenses designed for planned replacement. In 1994 CIBA Vision extended its position in over-the-counter lens care products with the introduction of QuickCARE, the industry's first five-minute lens care system. Later that year, the company acquired the entire ophthalmic pharmaceuticals line of Johnson & Johnson's IOLAB Corporation.

The CIBA Vision that has emerged from this growth and change is a very different company than the one that was started 16 years ago. With worldwide sales approaching $1 billion and more than 2,000 employees statewide, the company continues to follow a strategy of relying on ingenuity and business acumen to meet the challenges of the 1990s and beyond. As Dr. Glen Bradley, CEO of the CIBA Vision Group, puts it, "The contact lens industry will undergo many changes between now and the year 2000. At CIBA Vision, we intend to be an agent for that change where it benefits our customers."

Courtesy of CIBA Vision

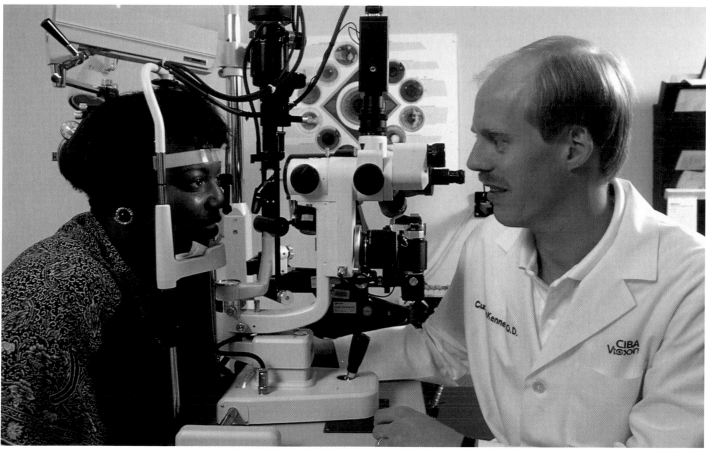

PROFILES IN EXCELLENCE

# THE COCA-COLA COMPANY

Atlanta and The Coca-Cola Company share much more than mere geography.

Both Atlanta and The Coca-Cola Company were born of modest beginnings—one a simple soda fountain concoction, the other a stop on a southern train line.

Both grew from those modest beginnings to unimagined heights, defying those who said they couldn't get bigger or better. While Atlanta rose from the ashes of war to become an international hub, Coca-Cola crossed international lines to become the favorite soft drink in virtually all of the nearly 200 countries where it is now available.

Both have become stewards of the world's most admired global symbols, with Atlanta hosting the world's premier sporting event—the Olympic Games—and The Coca-Cola Company serving as the steward of the world's best-known and most-admired brand, Coca-Cola.

Both reflect an inspiring spirit of optimism. More than a century after its creation just miles from where the headquarters stand today, The Coca-Cola Company not only still calls Atlanta

*The company's "Reaching Out" program helps employees, retirees, and their families give back to the community. Here, volunteers help renovate a local community center.*

home, but its leaders and its employees support their local community with more pride than ever.

And looking ahead, both Atlanta and The Coca-Cola Company remain more focused on their futures than on their pasts. No longer content to be just an "international city," Atlanta is working now to become a model international city. Never content with the success of its past, The Coca-Cola Company is working each day to make Coca-Cola more distinctive and more relevant to more people around the world.

© Ed C. Thompson

Courtesy of The Coca-Cola Company

*Each year, nearly 1 million people visit The World of Coca-Cola, a three-story museum featuring memorabilia, soda fountains of the past and future, and advertising from throughout the company's history.*

# METRIC CONSTRUCTORS, INC.

Committed to clients' needs, experienced, and financially strong, Metric Constructors, Inc., is one of the most diverse and firmly established construction services companies in the Atlanta area. An affiliate of the worldwide J. A. Jones Construction Company, whose building experience in Atlanta dates back to the 1930s, Metric offers a full range of commercial, institutional, and industrial services across the Southeast.

Working closely with a cadre of strong local subcontractors and suppliers, the craftsmen of Metric have built much of the Atlanta skyline—Georgia-Pacific headquarters, the Peachtree Plaza Hotel, the Marriott Marquis, One Peachtree Center, and 40 buildings in the Peachtree Center Complex. For the

*Atlanta History Center*

1996 Olympic Games, Metric built the Wolf Creek shooting complex, which involved development of the 100-acre site and construction of the buildings for shooting events.

Metric offers its clients a comprehensive array of services second to none in the construction industry. The company provides construction management, program management, and turnkey design/build services to clients that represent many of the nation's Fortune 500 companies, leading developers, utilities, and municipalities. The company's Southeast Division operates primarily in Georgia, Alabama, and Mississippi, where it provides expertise on the following diverse projects:

- Retail centers and malls
- Office buildings
- Hotels and motels
- Colleges and schools
- Medical and retirement facilities
- Distribution and manufacturing facilities
- Multi-family housing

Metric's Multi-Family Group offers the competitive pricing of a small builder, backed by the safety and clout

*Interior of Chateau Elan*

of a top-ranked general contractor. This combination is unparalleled in the construction industry. Metric's Interiors Group creates distinctive environments of any size, and its warehouse/industrial work features the economic advantages of self-performed activities while offering experience in design/build and the coordination of complex mechanization and equipment installation.

Under the direction of James C. Taylor, the division is currently ranked by the *Atlanta Business Chronicle* as one of the Atlanta area's top five general contractors. Other divisions within the company provide service to the energy, heavy civil, and marine markets. Complementing this experience is Metric's ability to perform numerous in-plant services, including maintenance, repairs, retrofit, and equipment installation and erection.

Metric has a wealth of experience, capabilities, and professional manpower resources to provide its clients with high-quality construction projects on schedule and within budget. Metric also draws on the resources of its parent firm, Philipp Holzmann AG of Frankfurt, Germany, one of the largest and most respected engineering and construction organizations in the world, and on its operating subsidiaries, representing more than 400 years of construction services. With a $2 billion bonding credit with Aetna Life & Casualty, Metric consistently receives the highest credit and financial ratings, as well as excellent references from a broad base of financial institutions.

Beyond being a high-quality builder of the physical structures of Atlanta, Metric is making a difference in Atlanta's communities by contributing money and donating time and materials to worthy causes. The company's employees also give their time and money to a wide variety of charities in the areas in which they work and live. On the job or off, the team of Metric Constructors is committed to Atlanta's *Vision for the New Millennium.*

*One Peachtree Center*

# KIMBERLY-CLARK

In 1872, Kimberly-Clark's founders committed their new company to the principles of quality, service, and fair dealing. Today, this commitment remains unchanged. As a global manufacturer of consumer, paper, and health-care products, Kimberly-Clark has come to represent excellence in many highly competitive markets.

From the introduction of Kotex feminine pads and Kleenex facial tissue in the 1920s to the more recent debut of such products as Huggies disposable diapers and Pull-Ups training pants, Kimberly-Clark has remained at the forefront of technology and product innovation.

Kimberly-Clark is a Fortune 500 company with its world headquarters in Dallas, Texas. Its consumer product businesses are based in Neenah, Wisconsin, and its nonconsumer products businesses are located in Roswell, Georgia, just north of Atlanta. World-wide, the company employs 43,000 people, has manufacturing operations in 27 countries, and markets its products in 150.

The company's operations in the Atlanta area—home to 1,100 employees—have been a key component of Kimberly-Clark's success. Opened in 1980, the Roswell office and research facility is headquarters for a number of major business units—Technical Paper, Neenah Paper, the Pulp and Newsprint Sector, the Service and Industrial Sector, the Professional Health Care Sector, and the Nonwovens Sector.

The Roswell facility also has established Kimberly-Clark as a key player in the Atlanta business community, both as a well-regarded employer and as a generous contributor to charitable efforts. Kimberly-Clark is a major supporter of United Way and of the Atlanta Union Mission and other human services agencies. The company also contributes to organizations that meet cultural and educational needs, such as the Woodruff Arts Center, Emory University, and Spelman College. In support of the 1996 Summer Olympics, Kimberly-Clark became an employer in the Olympic Job Opportunities Program for athletes in training and a corporate contributor to Centennial Olympic Park. The corporation's commitment extends to employees, who enjoy an on-site health-care and exercise facility, educational support for themselves and their children, and recognition of their community involvement.

During the 1990s, Kimberly-Clark's vision is to be recognized as one of the best companies in the world. To achieve this goal, the company seeks to employ the best people, produce and sell the best products, and provide the best returns to its stockholders.

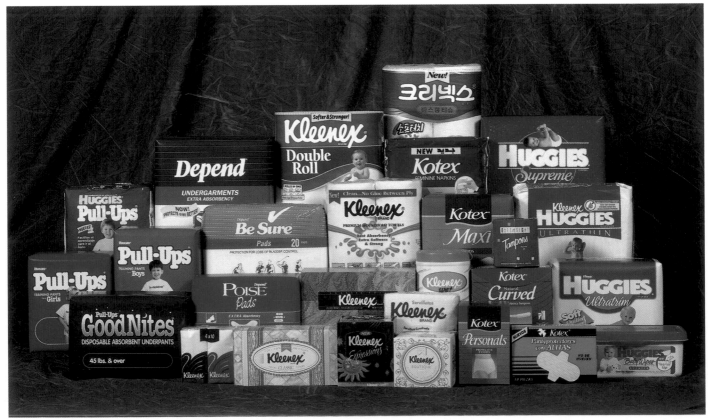

# SCIENTIFIC GAMES INC.

When the Georgia Lottery Corporation needed to find a company to print, warehouse, and distribute its tickets to kick off the state's instant lottery, it did not have to look far. Scientific Games Inc., the world's leading full-service supplier of instant lottery tickets, systems, and consulting services, is headquartered just north of Atlanta in a state-of-the-art 185,000-square-foot facility. As a result of the firm's excellent reputation, it was awarded a five-year contract.

Scientific Games has a rich history, dating back to 1973, when the company was established. In 1974, the firm sold and delivered its first shipment of instant lottery "scratch-off" tickets—25 million—to the Massachusetts State Lottery. These tickets represented the first such tickets in the U.S. market. In 1977, Scientific Games introduced the first secure tickets manufactured by a computer-controlled, ink-jet imaging process, which remains the industry standard. The firm also introduced the lottery industry's first instant lottery ticket that is both secure and fully recyclable.

In addition to lottery consulting and startup services, Scientific Games can provide market research, strategic marketing, cooperative services programs, instant game management computer software and hardware, automated bar code validation systems, commercial instant games, and pull-tab games.

Since 1974, Scientific Games has supplied instant game tickets for about 65 lotteries worldwide and has delivered more than 45 billion instant game tickets. The company also supplies computerized hardware and/or software for the instant ticket accounting systems for 30 lotteries worldwide.

Scientific Games, which has annual revenues of about $150 million, employs nearly 800 people in its three printing facilities, located in Alpharetta, Georgia, Gilroy, California, and Albert Lea, Minnesota. The three plants have the capacity to print about 14 billion tickets per year for both the public and private sector.

The firm's stated objective is "to provide premium lottery products and services to a global marketplace as well as to support these products with high-integrity, environmental sensitivity, and technical excellence."

Courtesy of Scientific Games Inc.

Lotus Development Corporation, a subsidiary of IBM Corporation, offers high-quality software products and support services that reflect the company's unique understanding of the new ways in which individuals and businesses must work together to achieve success. Lotus's innovative approach is evident in a new class of applications that enables information to be accessed and communicated in ways never before possible, both within and beyond organizational boundaries.

Lotus provides a comprehensive offering of award-winning desktop and communications products for the DOS, Windows, OS/2, Macintosh, and UNIX environments that are easy to use and easy to use together. Key products include Lotus Notes™, cc:Mail™, SmartSuite®, NotesSuite™, 1-2-3® spreadsheet, Word Pro™ word processor, Freelance® presentation graphics, Approach® database, and Organizer™ personal information manager. The company markets its products in more than 80 countries, and 44 percent of Lotus's 1994 revenue was generated outside the U.S. Lotus sells its products through dealers and chains representing approximately 6,000 stores and through value-added resellers. Customers may also purchase directly from Lotus.

The Lotus Word Processing Division, founded in 1982 as Samna Corporation and acquired by Lotus Development Corporation in 1990, is headquartered in Atlanta. This division develops and markets word processing programs for all standard business graphical environments, such as Microsoft Windows® and IBM OS/2®. Lotus markets its word processor to the microcomputer spectrum—from small businesses seeking high-quality word processing systems to Fortune 1000 companies, government agencies, and legal firms. Key products developed by the Lotus Word Processing Division include Lotus Word Pro for Windows 3.1, Windows 95, and OS/2 Warp.

Lotus Word Pro is a new word processor that helps teams of individuals work together more effectively by streamlining the process of creating, reviewing, and editing shared documents. Word Pro is also a key product in Lotus SmartSuite, the complete suite of desktop applications for users who work alone or collaborate in teams. In addition, the Lotus Word Processing Division supports the Lotus SmarText® electronic publishing tool.

In addition to software development and manufacturing, Lotus provides businesses with additional support services.

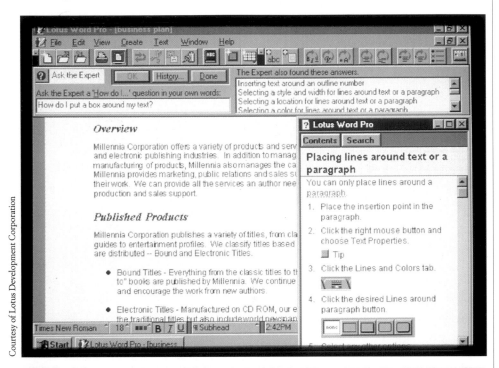

*Courtesy of Lotus Development Corporation*

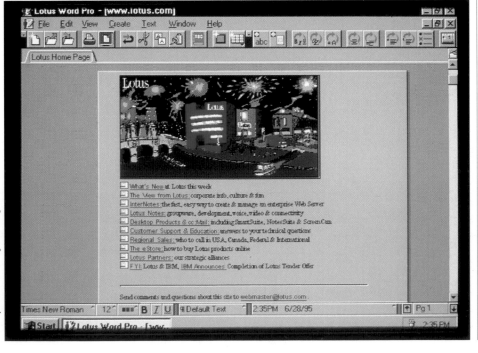

*Courtesy of Lotus Development Corporation*

Lotus's award-winning customer support and service organization offers an array of support options that help customers achieve maximum value from Lotus products. The Lotus Business Partners Program offers a variety of benefits designed to equip, enable, and train the growing community of 10,000 partners who offer products and services based on Lotus technologies. Lotus Consulting Services, founded in 1990, is a worldwide professional services organization that provides strategic business and technology services to Lotus's major commercial and government accounts. Lotus Education is a worldwide organization dedicated to providing consistent, high-quality training and education programs to users of Lotus Notes, cc:Mail, and the full range of Lotus Desktop products.

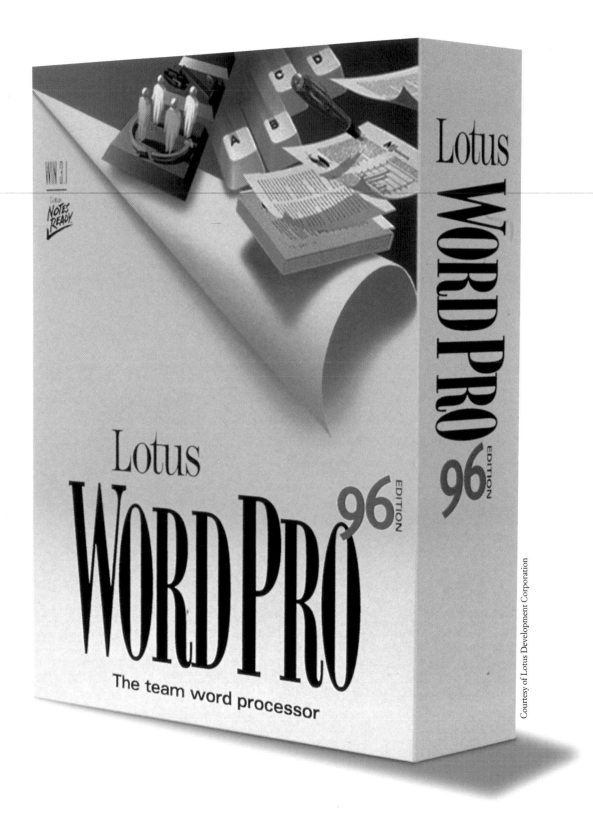

Courtesy of Lotus Development Corporation

PROFILES IN EXCELLENCE

# SANDERSON INDUSTRIES, INC.

Sanderson Industries is one of the major contract manufacturers of stamped metal products and related assemblies in the Southeast. Minority-owned and operated, it is headed by founder and Chief Executive Officer Walter Sanderson and his son, Rory Sanderson, who is president.

The firm supplies stamped metal components for both passenger and commercial vehicles, computers, typewriters, copier equipment, golf carts, and other leisure vehicles. Ford, G.M. Saturn, Yamaha, AT&T, and IBM are just some of its clients. Sanderson ships its merchandise all over the U.S. as well as to Mexico and Canada. The firm is becoming more international as it is entering the South American and European markets.

In addition to its high-volume manufacturing abilities, the company is a full-service supplier, complete with a CAD engineering office that is capable of providing rapid documentation on designs and feasibility agendas.

The automotive industry is Sanderson's biggest customer and Ford, for which it services all of its assembly plants, its largest client. Ford's Hapeville, Georgia, plant alone receives about 5 million parts a year.

The firm's relationship with Ford goes back 30 years to when the company was first founded in Chicago in 1965. In 1989, Sanderson Industries received Ford's prestigious Q1 Quality Achievement Award. Currently, it has contracts with Ford worth more than $10 million annually.

With 1995 sales approaching $20 million, Walter Sanderson attributes his firm's success and growth to the philosophy of never-ending improvement. He explains, "This philosophy is a way of doing business at Sanderson Industries. A further overview can be achieved by examination of our product and service enhancements resulting from our 'continuous improvement management system' (CIMS). Our short-range goal is to increase sales by 15 to 20 percent per year and to grow to $25 million in sales by 1997. At the same time, these achievements will be supported by consistent quality and service improvements to our customers while continuing to strengthen our operational and management teams. We presently have a comprehensive training program for all employees and thereby a reinforcement to the never-ending improvement philosophy."

The firm is especially known for its ability to improve quality through the application of statistical methods that focus on defect prevention rather than detection. By reducing the need for redundant testing, inspection, product rework, and material scrappage, productivity and quality are increased. Sanderson notes, "It is our belief that today's highly competitive markets and ever-changing demands for quality and service are signs of a progressive move toward world competition. Our commitment to

our customers and ourselves is to produce products that not only meet all the requirements of our customers, but exceed them. Our goals are high, and our intentions are clear—to develop the best-quality parts available today."

Sanderson got his start in the industry at the age of 10 when he swept floors on a Fulton, Missouri, machine shop. By the time he was 12, he had more responsibility and earned $12 a week, which was $2 more than his dad earned from two jobs. Sanderson studied mechanical art at Lincoln University in Jefferson City, Missouri, and worked at several manufacturing facilities after graduation until he opened his own plant in Chicago in 1965 with $25,000 in savings. The company made speakers and other parts for the radio and TV industry. By the end of his first year, the firm had sales of $450,000 and 12 employees. By 1968, the company purchased a larger facility and began producing more parts for the telephone industry as well as parts for Ford's plant in Chicago Heights. The firm was also chosen to produce parts for the National Accelerator Laboratory, now known as Fermilab.

The firm needed additional space again in 1983 because of its growth, at which point Sanderson decided to relocate to another state. After meeting Mayor Maynard Jackson and being courted by officials of the Atlanta Economic Development Corporation, Sanderson chose to relocate to Atlanta in 1985. "Atlanta offered us the best deal and incentives," explains Sanderson. He adds, "The enterprise zone at Atlanta Industrial Park gave us tax relief for the first five years, and our location off of I-285 is good for trucking. Also, I do not miss the weather in Chicago."

The Atlanta facility, which ships 150 to 200 million parts per year, is located in a 70,000-square-foot building and employs 120 people. "Our press room capabilities range from 38- to 1,000-ton presses, producing over 130 different parts. To maintain and repair our production tooling, we have a staff of expert tool and die makers and a well-equipped tool shop. Hav-

ing these facilities in our plant helps to ensure minimum production time loss because of die repairs. We produce most of our own assembly tools/fixtures and design and build many of our smaller dies," says Sanderson.

The CEO is also proud that his company

uses the latest techniques in computerized electronic releases, advance shipping notices, and bar code labels and supports just-in-time delivery systems. He notes, "It is our motto that when our customers need fast deliveries, . . . Quality Service Is Our Business."

Georgia-Pacific Corporation has experienced tremendous growth since it was founded in 1927 by 24-year-old Owen Cheatham in Augusta, Georgia, as a wholesaler of hardwood lumber and called the Georgia Hardwood Lumber Company. Now one of the world's largest forest products companies, Georgia-Pacific—known as "The Growth Company"—is a major manufacturer and the leading distributor of building products, industrial wood products, pulp, paper, packaging, paperboard, commercial and consumer tissue, and chemicals used for papermaking and the production of building products. In addition to employing approximately 47,000 people and operating more than 350 plants, mills, distribution centers, and facilities throughout the United States, Georgia-Pacific manages more than 6 million acres of forestland in North America.

After its founding in Georgia, the company moved its headquarters to Olympia, Washington, in 1953 and then to Portland, Oregon, in 1954, where it remained until relocating to Atlanta in 1982. When the company moved into its newly constructed downtown headquarters, the architecturally distinctive Georgia-Pacific Center at 133 Peachtree Street, the Atlanta metro area had a population of about 2 million people and the company's annual sales were about $5 billion. Since that time, the Atlanta area has grown into the commercial hub of the Southeast with a population of nearly 3 million residents and Georgia-Pacific's annual sales have grown to more than $12.7 billion.

Atlanta was the choice of the company's leadership because of the city's excellent quality of life, reliable transportation network, and pro-business environment, as well as the South's abundant and available timber supply and the quality of the workforce.

Courtesy of Georgia-Pacific Corporation

Since relocating to Atlanta, a milestone in the company's growth occurred in 1990 when Georgia-Pacific acquired the assets of Great Northern Nekoosa Corporation, making the company one of the world's largest pulp and paper manufacturers. Today, Georgia-Pacific's focus under the leadership of A. D. "Pete" Correll, chairman and chief executive officer, is a vision "to be the best at everything we do." Embraced by all employees, this vision is based on the belief that to remain a successful competitor, Georgia-Pacific must be the low-cost producer of the highest-quality forest products available. A safe workplace for employees, protection of the environment, conservation of resources, and management of sustainable forests for the future are also key principles of the company's operations throughout North America.

As evidenced by the more than 3,000 people employed by Georgia-Pacific in the metro Atlanta area, the company is made up of employees who are involved and active in their hometowns across the nation. In fact, local community involvement and contributions are a hallmark of Georgia-Pacific. Employees are encouraged to commit their time to serve as volunteers for local social service or cultural organizations. For example, a 300-strong Olympics force is supporting the Atlanta Centennial Olympic Games through committed voluntarism.

Since 1954, the Georgia-Pacific Foundation has awarded more than $10 million in college scholarships nationally. The firm's matching gift program encourages personnel to lend financial support to educational and medical institutions, cultural organizations, and public television and radio. In addition to being one of Atlanta's leading United Way supporters and top annual contributors, the company and its employees have a history of providing paper and building products and assistance to those in need in the wake of natural disasters both near and far.

Atlanta's cultural community also benefits from the company's presence. Corporate headquarters is the site of the High Museum of Folk Art and Photography, and the company sponsors "Art at the Heart," a semi-annual series of lunchtime music, theater, and dance performances in downtown Atlanta.

The company also is active in advancing downtown through involved and committed leadership. Georgia-Pacific was instrumental in inner city redevelopment through the formation of its Project HOPE, which stands for Housing People Economically. Believing that home ownership is key to the development of community pride and essential to upgrading local neighborhoods, Georgia-Pacific committed $2 million to this nonprofit project, which has focused on building or renovating homes in a six-block area in West Atlanta for purchase by low-income families.

Since its emergence on the downtown skyline, "The Growth Company" has made an indelible impression on Atlanta. It is committed to maintaining a strong and beneficial relationship with its headquarters city.

PROFILES IN EXCELLENCE

Since opening for business in November 1992, America's Favorite Chicken Company (AFC) has grown explosively. It is now the world's second-largest quick-service chicken company, thanks to aggressive franchise expansion and an equally aggressive commitment to the neighborhoods and communities it serves.

AFC, the parent company of Popeyes Chicken & Biscuits and Churchs Chicken, opens at least one new restaurant every day, has more than 2,400 restaurants around the world, posts systemwide sales of more than $1.5 billion, and ranks as one of Atlanta's 10 largest privately held companies. In addition, according to a report from Robinson-Humphrey, AFC has more than doubled shareholder value since its inception.

AFC's impressive growth is aided by a $110 million investment in information technology systems, which has significantly improved restaurant operations and profitability, as well as improved the performance of all employees.

At the same time, AFC is pursuing a highly focused strategy of community support and service aimed at creating economic opportunity in its markets. This includes initiatives to recruit minority franchisees and to create jobs with career growth potential for community residents. With a pledge to build 200 homes worldwide, it also includes the largest corporate commitment ever to Habitat for Humanity.

According to Frank Belatti, chairman and chief executive officer of AFC, "We believe we have an obligation both to our communities and to our business. If we can stimulate genuine economic expansion and opportunity in a community, then in all likelihood we can enhance our own position in that market and make ourselves stronger in the process.

"To that end," says Belatti, "we manage this company under a philosophy that requires us to ask ourselves constantly whether we are doing the most effective job possible of deploying our corporate resources to generate a fair return on current investments and to create economic and human opportunity in the markets we are privileged to serve."

So far, the philosophy is working. This year, more than 500 million customers will visit AFC's restaurants—Churchs, for its southern-style chicken and value-priced side dishes, and Popeyes, for its New Orleans-style spicy and mildly seasoned chicken and signature side items, such as Cajun rice and red beans and rice. Although the menu items for both chains are time-tested winners, AFC's product research and development team never rests in its continual search for new and exciting menu items.

The company continues to expand, both domestically and internationally, at a breathtaking pace. While the number grows annually, AFC secures about 700 new franchise agreements each year. This rate has enabled the company to realize its central mission of being recognized throughout the restaurant industry as the "FRANCHISOR OF CHOICE" for interested franchise and investment partners.

AFC is committed to new business expansion. In addition to a variety of traditional, free-standing restaurant designs, AFC is pioneering innovative and cost-effective alternatives, such as placing restaurants inside other retail establishments like convenience stores, grocery stores, or travel centers. AFC also unveiled a comprehensive, fresh new look for its restaurants, including everything from the logo and exterior image to signage, menu boards, dining room layout, and uniforms.

While AFC's roots are in the southern United States, it is enjoying strong growth internationally. The company's International Division has secured agreements to develop restaurants in El Salvador, Vietnam, Jordan, Mexico, the People's Republic of China, Thailand, Oman, Korea, and the United Arab Emirates. As of 1995, AFC had restaurants in 47 countries and U.S. territories.

"I believe AFC can be a model of private sector initiatives and a positive force here in our Atlanta home, within our nation and our world during this Olympics, and for generations to come. I also believe that we can create greater opportunities for our communities and our franchise partners and our employees by celebrating our differeces and our individual entrepreneurship," says Belatti.

*AFC's commitment to build 200 homes for Habitat for Humanity builds dreams and momentum with each groundbreaking ceremony.*

*A newly designed Churchs Chicken, featuring contemporary menu items, serves as a beacon for customers both old and new.*

*Popeyes Chicken and Biscuits sports a new sleek design that attracts customers with its bright color scheme and fresh new look.*

PROFILES IN EXCELLENCE

# RICH'S

When people from around the globe come to Atlanta, they are often searching for the true southern experience—one that blends the genteel past with the promise of the future. At the center of the South is Atlanta's hometown store with a true southern birthright—RICH'S.

Rich's heritage dates back to the dream of a young immigrant who came to this country in the mid-1800s to seek his fame and fortune. Morris Rich saw in Atlanta an opportunity—an opportunity for a war-torn town to rebuild from the ashes. In 1867, a southern tradition was born when the first M. Rich and Brothers store opened its doors.

Even then, Atlanta was the fastest-growing city in the New South, and Rich's happily expanded to meet the needs of the flourishing city. Rich's has been a part of and a partner with the people of Atlanta during all of the store's more than 125 years of doing business. At times when farmers lost their markets for cotton, Rich's accepted the crops in exchange for merchandise. Walter Rich considered this to be a sound business practice. Rich's and the community it served were so intertwined that the *Saturday Evening Post* once referred to Rich's as the "Store That Married a City."

In the 1950s and 1960s, Rich's management saw the opportunity to expand to the suburbs, where Atlanta's population was booming. Rich's Lenox Square store was opened during that time and is now the company's flagship. Situated in affluent Buckhead, the strip where the mall is located represents the financial epicenter of North Atlanta.

Rich's operates 12 stores in metropolitan Atlanta. It also has stores in Augusta and Savannah, Georgia; Birmingham, Alabama; and Greenville and Columbia, South Carolina.

In 1976, Rich's was pursued by and then joined forces with Federated Department Stores, one of the strongest merchandising and buying organizations in the nation. In 1995, Federated designated Rich's the corporate headquarters for its Rich's/Lazarus/Goldsmith's division, creating the fourth-largest department store organization in the country.

*Courtesy of Rich's*

*The Rich's clock has made its mark on Atlanta history.*

*Rich's does fashion southern style.*

From its Atlanta headquarters, the Rich's/Lazarus/Goldsmith's division operates 75 stores in 9 states and 25 cities.

Rich's is an enthusiastic supporter of all that happens in Atlanta. Rich's Partners in Time, an established volunteer force of employees, has given 85,740 hours to 967 community projects in six short years.

Rich's is born-and-bred southern, just like grits on the breakfast table, kudzu on the roadside, and the drawl that flows like the Chattahoochee River. Rich's is southern style.

In London, it's Harrod's; in New York City, it's Bloomingdales; in Paris, it's Galeries Lafayette; and in Atlanta, it's definitely Rich's.

*Shopping in the New South*

Since opening its doors in 1962, the Best Western American Hotel (formerly known as the Atlanta Americana Hotel) has consistently offered its guests comfort, convenience, and reasonable rates. Located in the heart of downtown Atlanta on Spring Street and International Boulevard, the hotel and its president, Dr. Marvin C. Goldstein, have a rich and fascinating history.

When Dr. Goldstein, a world-renowned orthodontist, businessman, and community activist, and his late brother, Dr. Irving Goldstein, along with other investors decided to build the Americana Hotel, they played an important role in the city's emerging civil rights movement.

According to Goldstein, a native Atlantan, "In 1962, when the Milwaukee Braves moved to Atlanta, there was no public hotel that permitted African-Americans. In speaking to Mayor Ivan Allen, I vowed to open the hotel as an integrated facility, despite receiving bomb threats. Even

© Lipofsky

before its completion, Dr. King was using the hotel for private meetings."

It was the first hotel to be built in downtown in more than 40 years, and many Atlantans thought of the hotel as "Goldstein's folly," since it was not being built near the Civic Center. But Goldstein proved his critics wrong. The hotel was a success from the day it opened.

Today, the hotel is near everything, including the World Congress Center, the Georgia Dome, the OMNI, Inforum, the merchandise marts, Peachtree Center, and MARTA. Because of its convenient location and amenities, 80 percent of the rooms are being reserved by the Atlanta Committee for the Olympic Games to house VIPs during the Games.

In addition to the hotel's 321 oversized guest rooms, there is parking for 200 cars; a large, outdoor swimming pool (the first in downtown Atlanta); a fitness center; 18 suites; and three penthouse suites, including the Imperial penthouse, complete with two bedrooms, a sauna, and rooftop balcony. A complimentary continental breakfast and evening hors d'oeuvres are available on the concierge level. A 500-person ballroom and 14 meeting rooms provide ample space for conventions, company parties, banquets, and weddings. A cocktail lounge and two restaurants serve food for all occasions.

The hotel's target customers are business travelers and conventioneers. An active participant in the Atlanta Convention and Visitors Bureau, the hotel estimates that between 50 and 60 percent of its bookings are conventioneers.

In an effort to get help with the hotel's promotion and reservations, Goldstein signed up with Best Western in 1989. He notes, "I became affiliated with Best Western because of its national and international reservation service. It is the largest group of independently owned hotels. Best Western had the name, the standards, and the reservation system we needed."

Goldstein attributes his hotel's longevity to its location, personalized service, and dollar value. "We are the only full-service, moderately priced downtown hotel with luxury-type rooms," he notes.

Dr. Goldstein has been an active leader in the city, the dental profession, the Jewish community, and the civil rights movement. He integrated his dental practice in the 1950s and became known as "the dentist to the civil rights movement." He has been chief of staff for many years at the Sam Massell Dental Clinic and is vice chairman of the board and a founding trustee of the Dr. Martin Luther King, Jr., Center for Non-Violent Social Change; a member of the Georgia Historical Trust Commission; past president of the Atlanta Jewish Federation, Ahavath Achim Synagogue, the Atlanta Men's Organization for Rehabilitation and Training, B'nai B'rith of Atlanta, the American Dental Fraternity Council, Atlanta Technion, the Georgia Society of Orthodontists, and the University of Michigan Club of Atlanta, to name just a few of his leadership positions. In addition, he is a founder and former chairman of the United Service Organization (USO) of Atlanta and on the board of UNICEF. He is past chairman of the Mayor's Human Resource Bank, on which he still serves, and was appointed by Governor Zell Miller to the Governor's Commission on the Holocaust.

Dr. Goldstein's humanitarian work has not gone unnoticed. He has received numerous awards and honors for his hard work. For example, the Medical College of Georgia, where Goldstein is a professor of orthodontics, named its orthodontics complex the Dr. Marvin C. Goldstein Orthodontics Treatment Center in his honor. He has received the Volunteer of the Year Award from a local TV station and, most recently, was selected to have his portrait included on the Centennial Olympic Wall.

PROFILES IN EXCELLENCE

# CHICK-FIL-A, INC.

While 1996 will be remembered as the year Atlanta hosted the Centennial Olympic Games, it also marks the 50th anniversary of restaurant business success for S. Truett Cathy, founder of Chick-fil-A, Inc.

Today, Chick-fil-A is one of the largest privately held restaurant chains and the third-largest quick-service chicken restaurant company in the nation.

Working 36 consecutive hours is unheard of today, but a half-century ago it was not an uncommon practice for Cathy, who is now Atlanta's longest-standing restaurateur. It all started in 1946, one year after the end of World War II, when Cathy opened his 24-hour restaurant, the Dwarf Grill (later renamed the Dwarf House). His 50 years in the restaurant business give Cathy the distinction of being Atlanta's restaurateur with the most years of continuous service.

As if working long stints in the early days wasn't enough, Cathy wanted to be accessible to the hourly operations of his first food establishment, so he set himself up with a room in a boardinghouse literally footsteps away. Committed to the notion

*S. Truett Cathy, Founder and Chairman of Chick-fil-A, Inc., at "The Home of Chick-fil-A," his landmark resturant, the Dwarf House, in the Atlanta suburb of Hapeville*

that "Good Food Is Good Health" and "Food Is the Staff of Life—Therefore, Make It Good," Cathy took his tiny restaurant of 4 tables and 10 stools that was built with used nails, wood, and equipment and patiently grew his profits from day one . . . May 23, 1946, when sales were $58.20.

Today, Cathy is credited with pioneering in-mall fast food, but many people don't realize his Dwarf House was situated in the Atlanta suburb of Hapeville on US 41, which is equivalent to modern-day Interstate 75/85. Many a night Cathy found himself pacing the busy highway wondering when another customer would stop. A recognized restaurant institution today, the Dwarf House, which maintains the integrity it had in 1946 with its timeless wait staff—some of whom have 25 to over 40 years of service—draws faithful local patrons, tourists, and a celebrity or two looking for a glimpse of yesteryear at the

site of the invention of the boneless breast of chicken sandwich.

In 1967, Cathy further introduced his innovative quick-service concept when he opened his first mall restaurant at Atlanta's Greenbriar Mall. The 384-square-foot operation led to Cathy's pioneering of in-mall fast food.

Now that original Chick-fil-A® Chicken Sandwich can be found in 650 restaurants in 34 states and Canada. Not just in

*"We Didn't Invent the Chicken, Just the Chicken Sandwich."*SM *Invented over 30 years ago, the original Chick-fil-A Chicken Sandwich, with the Chick-fil-A Chargrilled Chicken Club Sandwich and the Chick-fil-A Chargrilled Chicken Sandwich*

Courtesy of Chick-fil-A, Inc.

*Having pioneered in-mall fast food, Chick-fil-A restaurants now number over 650 locations in malls, free-standing units, drive-through outlets, Chick-fil-A Dwarf House full-service restaurants, and licensed operations on college campuses, hospitals, and business and industrial sites.*

Courtesy of Chick-fil-A, Inc.

malls or on highways like old US 41, loyal patrons are now discovering Chick-fil-A "good food" through licensees in such settings as college campuses, hospitals, and business and industry locations; in satellite restaurants in high-traffic areas during peak lunch hours; as well as in supermarkets.

Sales in 1994 reached a record $451 million (the 1995 projection was over $500 million), representing a systemwide increase of 13.84 percent and marking the 27th year of consecutive sales increases for the chain since the first mall restaurant opened. Chick-fil-A is pursuing international growth, highlighted by its announcement of plans to expand throughout Southern Africa, starting in Durban, South Africa, in 1996. With the momentum of 50 years of business success that began with 25-cent BLT sandwiches and 5-cent coffee, Chick-fil-A is striving to reach $1 billion in systemwide sales by the year 2000, while also aiming to attain its corporate mission "to be America's best quick-service restaurant at satisfying every customer."

Cathy attributes his company's success and consistency to its purpose, mission, principles, products, and people. The

Corporate Purpose statement, erected in stone outside the South Fulton County corporate headquarters, reads, "To glorify God by being a faithful steward of all that is entrusted to us, and to have a positive influence on all who come in contact with Chick-fil-A."

Chick-fil-A's team spirit is so strong in large part because of Cathy's support of his employees. Since 1973, the company has awarded restaurant employees more than $11 million in $1,000 scholarships. These employees were honored in 1995 with the dedication of a large sculpture called "Climb with Care and Confidence," which can be found in the heart of downtown Atlanta. Cathy's WinShape Centre® Foundation, established in 1984, each year awards 20 to 30 $16,000 scholarships that are funded jointly by the foundation and Berry College to students wishing to attend the Rome, Georgia, college.

Cathy also established the WinShape Foster Care® program, which currently maintains nine foster homes and Camp WinShape®, a summer camp that enrolled over 1,500 campers in the summer of 1995. To heighten awareness of and to add benefits to its WinShape Foster Care program, Chick-fil-A committed to the sponsorship of its first major sports event, the *Chick-fil-A Charity Championship*, an LPGA-sanctioned tournament, which donated $170,000 to WinShape in 1995.

Courtesy of Chick-fil-A, Inc.

*The "Climb with Care and Confidence" sculpture was accepted by Mayor Bill Campbell for the City of Atlanta from Chick-fil-A, Inc., in commemoration of its 10,000th scholarship. The 23-foot-high sculpture was unveiled on October 23, 1995, as a dramatic entryway for the downtown Fairlie-Poplar District on Atlanta's Peachtree Street across from Woodruff Park.*

Looking toward Chick-fil-A's future growth, the restaurateur, who has spent more than two-thirds of his 74 years in the food business, notes, "Not even God can change the past, but He can do a lot of wonderful things about the future if we'll let Him."

Courtesy of Chick-fil-A, Inc.

*The original "Dwarf Grill" (later renamed Dwarf House), which opened its doors on May 23, 1946, with first-day sales of $58.20, gave rise to the Chick-fil-A chain, which projects sales of $1 billion by the year 2000.*

# Old Fashion Foods, Inc.

Old Fashion Foods, Inc., is the largest independent food-service and full-line vending company in the state of Georgia. The firm's focus on freshness, quality, convenience, and customer satisfaction has made Old Fashion Foods a leader in the food-service industry.

When Sheldon Smith purchased the Old Fashion Sandwich Company in 1965, the company was basically a wholesale sandwich firm. It had five employees, and its clients were service stations and convenience stores. Under Smith's leadership, the business expanded and the name was shortened to Old Fashion Foods.

According to Smith, "The primary factor setting us apart is a spirit of commitment and the will to win. It is our goal to bring the finest and freshest food service to the workforce." Since his company is determined to remain on the leading edge of the food-service industry, Old Fashion Foods has consistently expanded its products and services to satisfy the needs of the changing marketplace. This has resulted in new services, such as coffee and bottled water delivery, and limited-menu cafeterias featuring hot buffet-style foods, soups, salads, and custom-made deli sandwiches.

Customers of Old Fashion Foods consume over 10,000 meals daily from 3,000 vending machines and from cafeterias in over 300 locations in hospitals, universities, and businesses. Approximately 6,000 sandwiches, salads, and entrees are prepared each day to meet growing customer demand. Corporate operations, food production, and distribution are handled from the corporate office, dietary center, warehouse, and service center, which are in Austell, Georgia. There is also a branch office in Rome, Georgia.

Today, Old Fashion Foods has over 30 years of experience and 150 employees who are committed to customer satisfaction. Smith notes, "Our employees realize that customers are their main business, and customer service is first and foremost in their minds."

# BILTMORE SUITES/BILTMORE PEACHTREE HOTEL

The Biltmore Suites offers its visitors a historic setting, a great midtown location with cityscape views, 72 beautifully renovated suites, as well as special amenities and a varied rate structure for individuals, corporations, and groups. For longer stays, private and corporate leases are available.

Built in 1924 and recently restored to its former grandeur and charm, the Biltmore Suites has a Georgian architectural design with columned entrances, vaulted archways, and limestone details. The rooms include such special features as 10-foot ceilings, crown moldings, exposed brick walls and hardwood floors, glass block detailing, skylights, ceiling fans, and private balconies and terraces overlooking a garden courtyard.

Other amenities include fully equipped kitchens, baths, and living rooms, shuttle service, a coin-operated laundry, cable TV with HBO, state-of-the-art fire, smoke, and sprinkler systems, an on-site notary public, covered parking, and complimentary continental breakfast.

As a home away from home, the Biltmore Suites has studios, one- and two-bedroom suites, and two-bedroom jacuzzi suites, which have a marble jacuzzi in the master bedroom as well as a living room, a kitchen, and two baths. Jacuzzi rooms, which have king-size beds and marble jacuzzi tubs but no kitchen or shower, are also available, as well as dramatic, tri-level penthouses with marble jacuzzis that overlook the city. A small facility is also available for meetings or receptions.

For those visitors who want a downtown location, the Biltmore Peachtree Hotel is ideal. The European-style hotel emphasizes its smaller size, "old-world ambience," and individual service. It is a secure haven for the business traveler who seeks comfort and relaxation at a reasonable rate.

The hotel's convenient location is close to the Georgia Dome, the World Congress Center, the famous Fox theater, as well as many other venues. MARTA bus and rail service are also nearby.

With 94 spacious, traditionally furnished rooms, the Biltmore Peachtree Hotel also offers complimentary continental breakfast, meeting rooms, cable TV with HBO, a notary public, a fully equipped microwave kitchen, and hotel parking, to name just a few amenities.

Either hotel will make a visit to Atlanta very enjoyable.

When Pano Karatassos opened one of Atlanta's first true fine-dining restaurants (Pano's & Paul's) in Atlanta in 1979 along with executive chef/partner Paul Albrecht, the city was exposed to classic Continental/American cuisine with service previously not experienced in the region.

Today, the restaurants in the Buckhead Life Restaurant Group (BLRG) offer a variety of cuisines and surroundings. In addition to Pano's & Paul's, the BLRG owns 103 West, the Buckhead Diner, Chops, Pricci, Veni Vidi Vici, the Atlanta Fish Market, Pano's Food Shop, the Buckhead Bread Company & Corner Cafe, and NAVA.

The consistency, quality, and specialty designs of these restaurants have brought national and international attention to Atlanta's dining scene. And, as a result of BLRG's success, other talented chefs and restaurant companies have been attracted to Atlanta, causing the city's dining reputation to be viewed with a new respect.

Equally impressive is the Buckhead Life Restaurant Group's commitment to its community, which is unparalleled in the independent restaurant industry. Karatassos and his team have raised over $1 million for the hunger cause alone and contribute time, money, and resources to many other charitable, civic, and cultural causes. They are very involved in the feeding, the fun, and the essence of life in Atlanta.

# RESIDENCE INN BY MARRIOTT

Being away from home, especially for extended periods of time, is not always easy. In an effort to provide travelers with more comfortable surroundings, the Marriott Corporation acquired Residence Inn in 1987. Residence Inn combines the features of a traditional hotel with the comforts of home. With 177 properties nationwide (seven in Atlanta), Residence Inn is considered the leader in extended-stay lodging.

Residence Inn targets business travelers who stay five nights or longer. The typical guest is relocating, on temporary assignment, or attending a training program. Rates are based on length of stay and are close to those for a room in a moderately priced hotel. Residence Inn guests enjoy a family-type atmosphere, as well as rooms that are 50 percent larger than most standard guest rooms.

Accommodations include studio suites and a bi-level penthouse suite. Each suite has a fully equipped kitchen, a living room area, and a private outside entrance. Most rooms also have fireplaces.

The Atlanta Perimeter West Residence Inn is typical of the chain's properties. The inn features an outdoor heated swimming pool and whirlpool spa surrounded by beautiful landscaping.

There is also an area where guests can play racket sports, basketball, and volleyball. Other amenities include complimentary continental breakfast daily, an evening social hour, a free daily newspaper, a grocery shopping service, and daily maid service.

It is the company's mission to "exceed the expectations of every guest, every day, every stay." By offering spacious rooms, reasonable rates, and friendly employees, Residence Inn expects to continue to prosper in the 1990s.

*Residence Inn, "home away from home"*

© Thomas J. McKenzie

# HOLIDAY INN WORLDWIDE

Holiday Inn Worldwide, the hotel division of Bass PLC of the United Kingdom and one of the world's leading hotel companies, has come a long way since the first Holiday Inn opened in the early 1950s. What began as the dream of a forward-thinking pioneer in the industry has become a global conglomerate composed of more than 2,000 hotels, offering business and leisure travelers a wealth of product choices in more than 60 countries and territories around the world.

Holiday Inn is the world's largest single hotel brand and features a wide variety of hotel types and sites, ranging from mid-rises to high-rises in the center of cities, in suburban office parks, and at roadside locations. Crowne Plaza Hotels and Resorts, also a member of the Holiday Inn Worldwide family, offer superb amenities and customer service in metropolitan and resort locations worldwide.

The first Holiday Inn hotel was opened in 1952 by an American entrepreneur named Kemmons Wilson in Memphis, Tennessee. Children stayed free, and it had a swimming pool, air conditioning, and a restaurant on the property. Telephones, ice, and free parking were standard.

Wilson was a pioneer in the franchise business, offering investors the opportunity to purchase the rights to the Holiday Inn name and to build and operate the hotels themselves. His attention to quality control and customer service eventually would make Holiday Inn the best-known hotel brand in the world.

Holiday Inn hotels were built as the U.S. interstate highway system grew across America. The familiar green Holiday Inn sign meant comfort, quality, consistency, and value to millions of postwar travelers. By the end of the 1950s, there were 100 Holiday Inn hotels in the U.S.; by 1964, 500 hotels; and by 1968, 1,000 hotels. International expansion was next. Holiday Inn opened its first hotel in Europe in 1968 and its first in Asia in 1973.

The mid-to-late 1970s brought fierce competition for business and leisure travelers. Other major hotel brands—even those outside the middle market—began aggressive discounting and started offering increased amenities to attract business.

At about the same time, Bass PLC of the United Kingdom was looking for opportunities to expand outside the

*Holiday Inn Roswell (below) and Holiday Inn Select Atlanta-Decatur Hotel & Conference Plaza (right)*

PROFILES IN EXCELLENCE

brewing business. Holiday Inn offered Bass several advantages, not the least being its remarkable name recognition. The acquisition was completed in February 1990, and within a matter of months Bass moved the corporate headquarters of Holiday Inn Worldwide from Memphis to the growing international city of Atlanta.

Of the more than 2,000 Holiday Inn Worldwide hotels today, approximately 94 percent are owned and managed by independent franchise operators. Holiday Inn Worldwide offers a variety of products to meet the diverse needs of midmarket customers, who represent over 70 percent of all room nights sold around the world.

Holiday Inn offers two brands: the traditional **Holiday Inn**®, the mainstay of the system, well known to generations of travelers and the largest single hotel brand in the world; and **Crowne Plaza Hotels and Resorts**, offering superb amenities and customer service in major cities and resort locations worldwide.

Holiday Inn hotels continue to dominate the midmarket spectrum in lodging, offering clean, safe, and dependable accommodations and customer service to millions of travelers each year.

In many towns and cities across America, the local Holiday Inn is the focal point for business meetings, social events, holiday dining, and family and association get-togethers. Around the globe, Holiday Inn hotels embrace the local culture in dining and customer service, while maintaining the strict standards of operation common to all Holiday Inn franchises. To maintain product quality and customer service standards, 20 to 25 percent of the Holiday Inn Worldwide system undergoes extensive renovation each year.

In the early 1990s, the company expanded beyond its conventional product line of full-service Holiday Inn hotels to offer **Holiday Inn Express**®, properties that provide Holiday Inn comfort and value without conventional three-meal dining service. Favored by "road warrior" business travelers who do not require full-service lodging and by families en route to vacation destinations, the Holiday Inn Express line of hotels is the fastest growing of Holiday Inn Worldwide's products. By mid-1995, there were more than 325 Holiday Inn Express hotels worldwide, and more than 500 total Holiday Inn Express hotels are expected to be in operation by the late 1990s.

In similar fashion, in Europe and South Africa, **Holiday Inn Garden Court**ᔆᴹ hotels combine the value and standards of Holiday Inn with the flavor and ambience of the local markets these properties serve. Many feature bistro or cafe-style restaurants, offering a casual dining alternative for guests and local businesses.

Targeted to meet the needs of the family vacation market, **Holiday Inn SunSpree**® Resorts feature comfortable, full-service lodging "for kids of all ages" in preferred family leisure locations. Most resorts feature a mascot for the children, carrying out a theme that helps the wide variety of children's activities programs "come alive." Another feature common to all Holiday Inn SunSpree Resorts is the "marketessan," a combination deli and convenience store, offering competitively priced food, beverages, and other items typically needed by travelers.

As part of its new branding strategy announced in 1994, Holiday Inn Worldwide introduced **Holiday Inn Select**ˢᴹ, a hotel designed specifically to meet the needs and demands of the business traveler. All guest rooms in Holiday Inn Select hotels feature voice mail and data port connections, an iron and ironing board, a coffee maker, and large, well-lit work areas. Extensive meeting facilities and on-site meeting planners and business services also are available. Holiday Inn Worldwide expects to have more than 175 Holiday Inn Select hotels open by the end of the decade.

**Holiday Inn Hotel & Suites,** a product for the traveler on an extended stay or seeking more spacious accommodations for work or leisure, also was launched in 1994. Featuring separate guest rooms and living and kitchen areas,

*Holiday Inn Worldwide Data Center, in Alpharetta*

Holiday Inn Hotel & Suites properties also offer the convenience and flexibility of a full-service hotel, so that conventional guest rooms, restaurants, meeting services, and leisure facilities are available.

Introduced by Holiday Inn in the early 1980s, **Crowne Plaza Hotels and Resorts** was established as a separate brand in the Americas in 1994 because of its superior market recognition among business travelers. Properties outside the Americas continue to operate under the Holiday Inn Crowne Plaza name. Under either sign, however, these properties offer the finest in guest amenities and customer service, including elegant dining options, on-site business and meeting services, and extensive leisure facilities. With locations as diverse as Berlin, New York, Bangkok, and Istanbul—no matter where a traveler's plans may take them— it is likely a Crowne Plaza will be waiting.

For years, Holidex®, the company's global 24-hour reservation system, has led the industry in service and innovation. Constantly upgrading and enhancing its information capability, Holidex processes millions of reservations each year—generating more than 200,000 room nights per day and 75 million room nights annually.

Holiday Inn Worldwide reservation centers around the world handle 28 million calls each year, or in excess of 75,000 calls per day. A significant part of the value delivered by Holiday Inn Worldwide to its franchisees, Holidex generates nearly a third of all room night sales for independent Holiday Inn owners and operators worldwide.

Taking but another innovative step in technology and guest service, in mid-1995, Holiday Inn Worldwide announced the start of its own home page on the World Wide Web on the Internet, making it the first hotel company to offer live Internet booking capability. The company's Internet venture opened the doors to yet another generation of services, featuring virtual reality tours, high-quality imagery, a travel trivia game, and direct access to the Holiday Inn Worldwide reservation information network.

Over the years, the look, variety, and geographic diversity of hotels bearing the Holiday Inn name have evolved, in some ways, dramatically. But the founding principles of customer service, quality, and value initiated in 1952 have remained unchanged.

*Crowne Plaza Ravinia, in Atlanta*

Atlanta-based United Parcel Service, a global delivery company with 1994 revenues of $19.6 billion, is proud to serve as the official international express courier and package delivery company of the 1996 Summer Olympic Games. Supporting all 197 national Olympic teams, UPS will provide exclusive service to all Olympic venues, including the Olympic Village, and entertainment, hospitality, and media areas.

It is not surprising that UPS took on such an important task since the firm has as its advertising theme "Moving at the speed of business." This message reinforces the company's strong presence in the business-to-business arena.

UPS serves more than 1.3 million shippers a day with a network of 315,000 employees around the globe who move almost 12 million parcels and documents daily. More than 3 billion parcels and documents are delivered annually throughout the U.S. and

to more than 200 countries and territories. UPS's delivery fleet is among the world's largest with 130,000 vehicles, including more than 200 jet aircraft. The air fleet is augmented by 300 chartered aircraft to provide continuous service to 400 airports in the U.S. and to more than 200 airports overseas.

Through an aggressive strategy of acquisitions and service partner agreements, UPS has established a worldwide package distribution network. With same-, one-, two-, and three-day guaranteed delivery services in the U.S. and a choice of international services, the company has the broadest range of distribution options of any integrated air and ground carrier.

UPS announced its Worldwide Express Plus service in August 1995, which guarantees overnight delivery to most metropolitan U.S. areas by 8 A.M. from major business centers in Europe, Asia, Canada, Mexico, and Puerto Rico.

Earlier in the year, the company

launched UPS SonicAir service, an international next-flight-out service from the U.S. to international business destinations in more than 183 countries and territories.

In the U.S., UPS also offers its Early A.M. service, which guarantees delivery as early as 8 A.M. to most metropolitan areas and complements the company's popular UPS Next Day Air service, which guarantees delivery by 10:30 A.M.

While speed is important to customers, quality service is mandatory. In 1995, for the 12th year in a row, UPS was the most admired company in its industry and for the second consecutive year made the overall top-10 list in *Fortune* magazine's annual survey of America's most admired corporations. The magazine recognized UPS for such attributes as innovativeness, ability to attract and keep talented people, financial soundness, and community and environmental responsibility. In addition, UPS placed among the top-10 brands in the sixth annual 1995 EquiTrend brand quality survey conducted by Total Research of Princeton, New Jersey. The survey ranked consumer confidence in 200 name brands.

UPS's commitment to the environment is indisputable. Its air fleet is on schedule to meet or exceed the strictest federal noise standards, and the firm's Boeing 757 aircraft sport the "Quiet Freighter" designation. On the ground, the company operates about 1,000 alternative-fuel vehicles in North America.

When UPS relocated its headquarters from Greenwich, Connecticut, to north Atlanta in 1992, it took great care during construction to preserve the beautiful trees growing near the complex, and engineers installed an underground sediment filtration system to keep a natural

Courtesy of United Parcel Service, Inc.

*UPS's main air hub is located in Louisville, Kentucky.*

stream flowing across the heavily wooded site and under the middle portion of the office complex. In addition, an elaborate pumping system was used to create scenic waterfalls around the building.

Although UPS has come a long way since its founding as a messenger company in 1907 in Seattle, Washington, one aspect of the business has not changed: its commitment to community service. UPS Chairman and CEO Kent C. (Oz) Nelson led the 1995 fund-raising effort for the Atlanta United Way campaign. In 1994, UPS employees contributed a record amount, more than $27 million, to the United Way, and UPS added another $6.9 million. In 1995, the UPS Foundation provided nearly $15.6 million in grants to more than 300 charitable and other service organizations. UPS people take pride in the fact that the company and their co-workers help improve the well-being of the communities in which they live and work.

*Top: Cindy Gentry is a UPS employee and an Olympic hopeful in trap shooting. She resides in Stone Mountain, Georgia. Bottom: UPS guarantees overnight delivery to most major metropolitan U.S. areas by 8 A.M. from major business centers in Europe, Asia, Canada, Mexico, and Puerto Rico.*

Courtesy of United Parcel Service, Inc.

Courtesy of United Parcel Service, Inc.

# THE HOME DEPOT

Customers were enticed with $1 bills and the promise of a phenomenal shopping experience when The Home Depot opened its first store, in Atlanta, in 1978. Since then, the company has grown at a spectacular rate, and do-it-yourself warehouse-style stores are now scattered across North America, from the tip of Florida to the shores of Lake Ontario and west to the Pacific Ocean.

The Home Depot story began with a vision and investor support of $2 million. Bernie Marcus and Arthur Blank, who found themselves out of work after being fired by another retailer, settled on Atlanta as the test site to launch their dream. Their mission was simple: offer thousands of home improvement products at everyday low prices and give the customer expert one-on-one advice. The three original Atlanta stores were the springboard for what is today the largest do-it-yourself warehouse business in North America.

By the end of 1995, the familiar orange and white logo sat atop 18 stores in the Atlanta metropolitan area and more than 400 other locations across the United States and Canada, and approximately 80,000 associates were serving and teaching customers.

The Home Depot has thrived in part because of its progressive corporate culture, which emphasizes that every employee should have a say in the company. Experienced associates are hired and management is decentralized, along with decision making.

"We know that one person can make a difference," stresses Marcus, chief executive officer and chairman of the board. "It doesn't matter where our associates work in our company, they can make a difference."

The Home Depot has grown to be among the country's 20 largest retailers, according to *Fortune* magazine, which in 1995, for the second year in a row, named the company America's most admired retailer.

"We are not just a big store with thousands of products," says Blank, president and chief operating officer. "A store is only as good as its associates because they are the ones who help make things happen for our customers. We strongly believe in building relationships and giving that extra special attention to shoppers. People thrive when they know they have accomplished a task, whether it is simple or nearly impossible. We want people to feel good about shopping in our stores."

Both men frequently refer to the rise of The Home Depot as a "Cinderella story," from humble beginnings to a company that posts record earnings year after year. At the end of 1994, the company recorded gross sales of more than $12.4 billion.

Associates like to say that "good things happen when Home Depot comes to town" because it sums up the community involvement behind the familiar orange apron. The company's progressive culture includes a budget for philanthropic causes that is directed back to the communities Home Depot serves. Its organized force of volunteers, called Team Depot, focuses on affordable housing, "at-risk" youth, and the environment.

Team Depot volunteers in Atlanta help build low-income housing for organizations like Habitat for Humanity, and the "Christmas in April" program has volunteers repairing homes for the elderly, the disabled, and the poor. The company also has committed funding and resources to the Atlanta Project, a program dedicated to bettering low-income areas through the broad participation of both residents and volunteers.

In 1992, the company signed on as a Centennial Olympic Games Partner and in 1994 announced its sponsorship of the

*Kevin Braunskill is fast on his feet in the aisles of The Home Depot and the track where he runs.*

Paralympic Games, which will follow the Summer Games in Atlanta. The Home Depot also is at the forefront of a program to help pave Centennial Olympic Park in downtown Atlanta with engraved bricks.

"We will always be grateful to the folks who gave us our start in Atlanta," says Marcus. "Had it not been for the overwhelming and enthusiastic support, none of our spectacular national success would have been possible."

OLYMPIC JOB OPPORTUNITIES PROGRAM
As one of the world's fastest humans, Kevin Braunskill runs everywhere—to retrieve merchandise, to help a customer, to catch a phone, and to chase his Olympic dream.

Braunskill is a Home Depot associate from the crack of dawn to midday, when he trades his orange apron for running shorts and heads to the track at DeKalb College to check his time in the 200-meter dash.

He is one of nearly 100 athletes hired by The Home Depot as part of the Olympic Job Opportunities Program (OJOP). Coordinated through the U.S. Olympic Committee, the program pays athletes full-time salaries and benefits for part-time work. The athletes say the greatest reward of the program is that it allows them time off to train and compete.

"This is a great fit for me," Braunskill says, "because it's very flexible and has allowed me to travel and train. I can stockpile my hours one week and go off and train the next."

The Home Depot is the largest corporate sponsor of the program, not just for the Atlanta Games, but for all

*The Home Depot culture is about assisting customers in the stores and helping the communities in which the company serves.*

time. The company embraces the ideals of the Games and the level of intense commitment.

"The desire to be the very best, to reward and encourage teamwork, individual initiative, and perseverance and to extend a helping hand to all are the foundation of The Home Depot culture," says Arthur Blank, president and chief operating officer.

The athletes represent nearly all Olympic sports, from track and field to team handball to boxing. Some are gold medalists, some are not. But all share the common goal of being the best they can be, both on the playing field and off.

PROFILES IN EXCELLENCE

# CADMUS MARKETING SERVICES

Atlanta-based Cadmus Marketing Services is a vertically integrated marketing and print communications services company with over 25 years' experience. Founded in 1970 as American Graphics, Cadmus Marketing Services was a privately held company until it was acquired by Cadmus Communications Corporation in 1986.

Fredda McDonald, president of Cadmus Marketing Services, says, "Recently Cadmus Communications has been undergoing a corporate unification process focused on aligning its printing, publishing, and marketing companies more closely under the Cadmus banner. To strengthen this bond and better reflect our relationship with Cadmus, we have changed our name to Cadmus Marketing Services. The foundation laid by American Graphics is well established, and we've put into place a strategic plan that positions us to offer a very broad array of leading-edge services and capabilities to our clients."

"As an operating division of Cadmus Communications and by effecting a close working relationship with our sister companies under the Cadmus umbrella, our position as an outsourcing partner to our clients is optimized," notes McDonald, who adds, "We fully intend to capitalize on this opportunity to offer our clients a much broader range of capabilities, including interactive media, direct marketing, and catalog publishing. These services complement our current capabilities and solidify our position as a promotional printing and marketing specialist to our clients."

The core competencies of Cadmus Marketing Services cluster in three categories that include identifying customers' needs, designing solutions, and providing world-class implementation. A diverse mixture of state-of-the-art technologies and creative talents are offered that ultimately enable clients to view Cadmus as a single-source supplier for

their marketing and print communication needs. Cadmus Marketing Services is well equipped to handle everything from creative development to the most complicated front-end prepress needs, from database management to print-on-demand digital solutions, as well as customized fulfillment of the final product to any location around the world.

"For a number of years we have been developing an increased specialization in products and processes," explains Bob Kinsey, executive vice president and chief operating officer of Cadmus Marketing Services. "As a result of these efforts, we are able to supply more focused and higher value-added services to our clients. We are rapidly bettering our competencies to achieve continuing improvement in four key areas—lead-time reduction, quality advancement,

*Cadmus Marketing Services' facility at 2300 Defoor Hills Road, in Atlanta*

*Executive Vice President and COO Bob Kinsey*

and efficiency and service response. In concert with these changes, we are developing and enhancing systems and processes to link our manufacturing operations, thus enabling a fast and easy interchange of work with our clients."

As well as a commitment to excellence in the business arena, Cadmus Marketing Services has a strong commitment to the communities it serves. In addition to supporting the nonprofit organization founded by the firm's employees, the Foundation for Challenged Youth, Cadmus Marketing Services provides volunteer manpower and financial resources to other worthy causes, including, to name just a few, the Atlanta Care Center, the Georgia Special Olympics, the Atlanta Alliance on Developmental Disabilities, the Calvary Children's Home, and the Atlanta Steinway Society.

*President Fredda McDonald*

*Executive Vice President and COO Bob Kinsey*

Courtesy of Cadmus Marketing Services

Courtesy of Cadmus Marketing Services

# THRASHER TRUCKING, INC.

When Atlanta native Michael Thrasher received his business administration degree from Clark Atlanta University in 1983, he knew he wanted to be successful. He began his career with the Frito-Lay Company after college as a marketing and sales representative, but it wasn't until he left the firm to establish his own company, Thrasher Trucking, Inc., in 1987, that Thrasher started to realize his dream.

Thrasher chose the dump-truck business since he had been exposed to it through an uncle and saw that it could be a one-man operation with growth potential. He made an investment in a truck and drove it himself for two and a half years before buying a second truck, which enabled him to work with the Alabama Department of Transportation and then in Darlington County, South Carolina, cleaning up after Hurricane Hugo.

Thrasher, who is the seventh of nine children, subsequently returned to Atlanta, worked out of his home, bought a third truck, and employed two other drivers. By 1990, he had four trucks and four drivers and had moved his business, which specializes in hauling, light grading, and site-preparation work, into an office.

By 1995, the company had grown into 21 full-time and three part-time employees and 16 trucks and trailers; all together, Thrasher has about 20 different pieces of equipment. Gross revenues in 1994 were $1.4 million and were expected to reach over $2 million in 1995.

Thrasher attributes his success to the fact that "I give good service to my customers for the prices I bid to them, while still making a profit. I am reliable, keep up my equipment, and communicate with my customers both in the field and on the administrative side. I get new business through word of mouth, advertising in the *Yellow Pages*, networking, and referrals, since in the construction industry, your name travels fast."

He counts as some of his clients major private developers, municipalities, and highway and airport developers. For example, he has done hauling for such projects as the Olympic Stadium and Aquatic Center, Concourse E at Hartsfield International Airport, water treatment plants for the City of Atlanta, and the demolition of the Spring Street Viaduct. Thrasher had the "haul away and disposable" contract on the demolition of the Rich's department store building.

Thrasher's firm also sells stone, sand, fill-dirt, and gravel for construction purposes. While his short-term goal is to expand the grading part of the company for larger site-preparation jobs, his long-term dream is to become an Atlanta developer.

Atlanta-based LongHorn Steaks Inc. is the pioneer of "cowboy cuisine" in America. Described as "the great American dream come true," LongHorn was founded in Atlanta by Chairman of the Board George McKerrow, Jr., in 1981 on a shoe-string budget with only one employee.

Less than a decade later, LongHorn Steaks Inc. had grossed $41 million in revenues and was consistently named to *Restaurant Business*'s annual "U.S. Top 50 Growth Chains" list and *Restaurants & Institutions'* prestigious "R&I 400" listing. By its 15th anniversary, the thriving public company had grown to 60 company-owned and 10 franchised restaurants in nine states and had 4,500 employees. Its healthy financial results, proven concept, and strong employee/management infrastructure continue to enable the company to move forward successfully. As the company expands into new markets, the importance of being considered "the employer of choice" in the industry and the value of a positive work environment remain key.

Under the direction of company president and CEO Dick Rivera, and his executive team, LongHorn's long-term plans for expansion are "very aggressive," with a move toward more joint-venture partnerships and acquisitions. No matter how quickly LongHorn expands, however, Rivera and his team vow not to change the company's proven formula for success—giving the LongHorn guest the most satisfying experience possible through enthusiastic, efficient service. Satisfied guests who become repeat visitors are a priority at LongHorn, according to Rivera.

Modeled on the traditional Texas steakhouse, LongHorn Steakhouse restaurants offer casual, full-service dining in a spirited and colorful atmosphere. LongHorn's signature item is fresh, hand-cut USDA-Choice beef comple-mented by a variety of menu items like award-winning Pacific Northwest Salmon, Canadian baby back ribs, pork chops, chicken, and much more. Boasting a bodacious Texas spirit, guests can consistently count on being served great food by the friendliest people around. To guarantee the flavor, freshness, and quality of its beef, the company established its own meat company to supply all of the LongHorn Steakhouse restaurants.

Since its inception, LongHorn's leadership has taken "what we like and know how to do best and put all of our resources behind it." The result has made LongHorn a highly regarded national player in the restaurant industry. The folks at LongHorn Steakhouse restaurants throughout the U.S. can attest to the company's success, a success that has been due to . . . the vision and dedication of LongHorn's executive team . . . the loyalty and teamwork of the company's employees . . . and the support of the hundreds of thousands of guests who keep coming back for more.

Courtesy of LongHorn Steaks Inc.

# THE KROGER COMPANY

At Kroger Food Stores, people make the difference—the people who shop at the over 80 metro Atlanta stores and the more than 12,000 employees who work there.

A strong presence in Georgia since 1937, the Kroger Company and its management have made a commitment to Atlanta and its people. Employee and company involvement in community projects targeting children's health, wellness, and education gives the organization a dynamic presence.

The Atlanta-area Kroger stores support the ongoing Children's Challenge program, for which an event is held each October that includes Kroger Company vendors. In addition, funds are raised for the program through golf tournaments, hot dog sales, bowling tournaments, car washes, and other special events sponsored for and by Kroger employees. Store customers, employees, and vendors all contribute through a variety of other activities throughout the year. The money raised is then distributed to several children's hospitals and charities.

Through community Partners in Education programs, individual Kroger stores have joined with schools in providing youngsters with support and activities, including store tours and sponsorship of special events. One major way Kroger has contributed to its school partners is through the establishment of mini-markets or mini-Kroger stores within schools. These facilities help students learn about budgets, sizes, weights, and geography and acquire other skills. Typically, the mini-store is placed in a spare classroom, closet, or end hallway and comes equipped with a cash register, real money, produce, and shelves of product. A curriculum has been developed to guide teachers and students through real-life

*Children's health, wellness, and education are the targets of Kroger's philanthropy.*

Kroger situations, such as taking inventory, making signs, and merchandising.

"Earning for Learning," which allows schools to earn computers and cash by collecting Kroger receipts, has been in place since 1988. Including the school year ending May 1995, the company has given away over 7,500 computers and other educational resources through this program.

Each holiday season Kroger stores participate in food drives through which they contribute tons of food to the Atlanta Food Bank. In addition, stores help out during food drives to help those in need in their communities. Kroger also is a major sponsor of Atlanta's premier holiday events, including Art of the Season, benefiting Scottish Rite Children's Medical Center, and the Festival of Trees, benefiting Egleston Children's Hospital. "Our employees care about the community," says Paul Smith, president of the Atlanta Marketing Area. "The activities each store orchestrates for community involvement are a reflection of our employees' dedication to their neighborhoods."

*Kroger's "Earning for Learning" program has provided over 7,500 free computers to schools that save grocery receipts.*

But community involvement is just one of the areas in which the Kroger Company has made a statement in Atlanta and Georgia. Kroger is the largest U.S. grocery store chain in the nation, has dominant market share in Atlanta, and is a leader in the Atlanta market in introducing new concepts and products.

The company has truly taken the concept of one-stop shopping to the ultimate. Many of the stores have full-service bank branches, as well as other services such as

Courtesy of the Kroger Company

Kroger stores promise shoppers quality, variety, and excellent customer service.

Western Union windows, fax machines and copiers, driver's license renewal offices, facilities where customers can purchase money orders and postage stamps, cleaners, and shoe repair shops, not to mention gourmet food sections, bakeries, and coffee shops. In addition to delis and bakeries, Kroger is partnering with various food franchises to lease space so it can provide additional options in prepared foods for its customers.

Kroger built the first combination food store and pharmacy, in Snellville, Georgia, in 1980. Almost all its stores now have pharmacies where customers can fill prescriptions while they shop. In 1995, Kroger opened its first 24-hour pharmacy in the Atlanta area, and it plans to open others to serve all areas of the city. These pharmacies will operate as all Kroger metro Atlanta stores do—24 hours a day, 364 days a year. They will close only on Christmas Day.

Another innovative concept Kroger offers in metro Atlanta is its "Citi-Center" stores. There are currently four in metro Atlanta, three in the inner city and another in a suburban area. Each of these stores has smaller shops around its perimeter, which is attractive to small business owners because it offers them an opportunity to operate with lower overhead in a safe environment. In addition, each store has a

*Citi-Center stores, like this one in Atlanta's Cascade neighborhood, provide one-stop shopping for Kroger customers.*

large community room that can be used by civic organizations, schools, and groups such as Literacy Action and as places in which to immunize children.

Kroger continues to lead the way in the expanded grocery business. It has nutrition departments for the health-conscious customer, gourmet chef shops for customers looking for something tempting for their palates, sections that sell kosher foods, and even video departments, which also rent Sega games, VCRs, and books on audio. The first Kroger Cooking School was opened in 1995, and there are plans to operate other such schools in communities throughout metro Atlanta. These will offer a showcase for Kroger's own chefs, as well as chefs from Atlanta restaurants and their vendors.

In many ways the Kroger stores of today are very different from the original

store that opened in Cincinnati, Ohio, in 1883. Barney Kroger was hired to manage that store for the Imperial Tea Company.

While that one small store continued to grow and more stores were opened, many Kroger Company philosophies and traditions were being established—the attention to quality, responsiveness to customers' needs, and commitment to providing a wide variety of products and services.

Barney Kroger put his stores at the leading edge of the grocery business. Kroger's was one of the first grocery stores to advertise regularly in newspapers (1884), the first grocery company to operate its own bakeries (1901), and the first to put meats and groceries under the same roof (1904).

As his company grew, Kroger did not forget the people who made his business possible. Examples of his concern for others are evident throughout the firm's history, including the company's donation of 300 loaves of bread per week to feed the poor during the severe winter of 1905.

While the early Kroger stores were indeed different from the modern one-stop stores of today, there were similarities. Barney Kroger's philosophy of helping people and providing high-quality goods and services is very much in evidence in the Kroger Food Stores of the 1990s.

Courtesy of the Kroger Company

# ATLANTA MARKET CENTER

One world, one marketplace. For hundreds of thousands of retailers from throughout the U.S. and around the globe, the Atlanta Market Center is the preferred product source .

Housed in an integrated campus encompassing the Atlanta Merchandise Mart, Gift Mart, and Apparel Mart, the Atlanta Market Center—America's most complete wholesale environment—offers an extraordinary array of home furnishings, home textiles, floorcovering, and gift, apparel, and sporting products from the world's top manufacturers. Merchandise exchanged from vendor to retailer at the Atlanta Market Center finds its way

onto store shelves—and into consumer shopping bags—in every U.S. state and more than 50 countries worldwide.

Buyers and sellers come together in markets conducted at the Center throughout the year. In addition, hundreds of meetings are staged annually in the Center's facilities, which host some of the city's most prestigious conferences and conventions.

Long a powerful engine in the city's convention business, the Atlanta Market Center casts an imposing mark on Atlanta's downtown skyline. It is the fulfillment of visionary architect-developer John Portman's continuing efforts to

secure Atlanta's position as an international wholesale trade destination. The Center's history dates to 1962, when the Merchandise Mart opened to establish Atlanta's immediate presence as a dominant regional market. In the succeeding three decades, the Atlanta Market Center's role has evolved from regional to national to international, and with the evolution have come meteoric expansions of product categories and corresponding buyer base growth.

As Atlanta's international business growth continues, the Atlanta Market Center will play an increasingly pivotal role in serving the world's retailing communities.

© Aerial Innovations

From the airport to downtown to beautiful Lake Lanier, there's a Renaissance hotel or resort in Atlanta that has exactly what you're looking for.

At Hartsfield Atlanta International Airport, the **Renaissance Atlanta Hotel–Concourse** is a AAA Four-Diamond hotel featuring 387 spacious rooms surrounding a soaring atrium, along with 28 meeting rooms, including 11 conference suites, private banquet suites, and a grand ballroom for 1,200. Twenty-four-hour room service is available to pamper guests, as well as a completely equipped health club and indoor and outdoor pools.

Also in the airport vicinity is the **Renaissance Atlanta Hotel–Airport**, just minutes from downtown and one block from the Georgia International Convention Center. The hotel features 496 spacious rooms, an outstanding restaurant, in-room dining, and a private Club Floor. The 23 meeting rooms, executive boardrooms, and hospitality suites accommodate 10 to 600.

The European-designed **Renaissance Atlanta Hotel–Downtown** is convenient to the business district and in the center of the city's exciting attractions. It is the only hotel in the city that features a spectacular view of Atlanta from atop the 25th floor. The property offers 504 beautifully appointed guest rooms, fantastic dining, a private Club Level with 47 VIP rooms, an array of boardrooms and conference rooms, and a grand ballroom and business center.

Forty-five minutes north of downtown Atlanta is the **Renaissance PineIsle Resort**. Overlooking Lake Lanier, this AAA Four-Diamond resort features water sports, fishing, outdoor and enclosed tennis, indoor and outdoor swimming, horseback riding, and a picturesque 18-hole championship golf course. When business is the focus, 20 meeting rooms and seven outdoor function

Courtesy of Renaissance Hotels and Resorts

areas accommodate up to 400. Visitors can relax in one of 250 guest rooms, including 28 spa rooms with hot tubs on private patios.

The **Renaissance Waverly Hotel**, in Northwest Atlanta's Galleria shopping and office complex, is 10 minutes from downtown and 25 minutes from the airport. A spectacular 14-story atrium is surrounded by 521 spacious guest rooms and 24 suites. The meeting facilities include an executive boardroom and a grand ballroom for up to 3,000. The Waverly is connected to the Galleria Mall and the 280,000-square-foot Cobb Galleria Convention Centre, so guests can shop, meet, and dine without ever stepping outside.

If you've ever stayed at a Renaissance hotel or resort before, you know all about Renaissance's commitment to providing you with a hotel experience you'll never forget. If you haven't stayed at a Renaissance hotel or resort,

sit back and relax: the capable staff will take care of everything.

The Renaissance's professional staff members are expertly trained to cater to your every need, and they're ready to provide you with all that's necessary to make your visit to Atlanta—and the Renaissance hotel—truly memorable.

It's Renaissance's pride and dedication to quality service in each of the 75 Renaissance hotels and resorts throughout the world that keep guests coming back again and again and again.

Superb amenities. Excellent dining. Luxurious rooms. Impeccable service. And so much more. Whether you're visiting Atlanta for work, pleasure, or both, Renaissance truly is a name you can be comfortable with.

For reservations or information about any of the five Atlanta Renaissance Hotels and Resorts, or for information about Renaissance Hotels and Resorts worldwide, call **1-800-HOTELS-1.**

# JIM ELLIS AUTO DEALERSHIPS

In 1971, Jim Ellis and his wife, Billie, took the biggest financial plunge of their lives to establish their own automobile dealership. They sold all their assets, used all their savings, cashed in Billie's retirement fund from 15 years of service at Georgia Tech, and borrowed the balance to set up Jim Ellis Volkswagen.

Through the years, the Ellises purchased additional franchises: Northlake Porsche-Audi, Mazda in Marietta, Mazda in Atlanta, Chevrolet-Geo in Chamblee, and Volkswagen-Audi in Marietta.

Over the years, the Ellis formula for success has resulted in numerous accolades, including number-one national sales rankings for Jim Ellis Volkswagen, Jim Ellis Audi, and Jim Ellis Mazda. The dealerships have been recognized and honored with National Excellence Awards for parts and service and are recognized throughout metro Atlanta for dependability and integrity. Today, after 24 years of sustained growth, Ellis has four dealerships with nine franchises and employs 364 people, including members of the Ellis family.

Jim Ellis has a history of making something out of limited resources. He held a variety of jobs from childhood—farm work; milk, paper, and laundry routes; construction work; and concessions at Grant Park. Ellis served in the Army, was captain of the football team at West Georgia College, and worked his way through Georgia State University, earning a B.B.A. degree in 1957.

From the beginning, the Ellises' commitment to excellence and service has been expressed in their business and in their community. Their volunteer efforts on behalf of auto industry associations and generous support of numerous charities have elevated the name "Jim Ellis" to national prominence.

Slim and aristocratic, The Grand's graceful silhouette at Fourteenth Street rises 53 stories above the prime midtown business thoroughfare along historic Peachtree Street, adjacent to the Woodruff Arts Center, the cultural heart of this city of almost 3 million.

Opened in 1992, The Grand is the first multi-use building of its kind in the South. With its neoclassic architectural design of imported rose granite, the 53-story tower features 20 stories of luxury hotel with 244 rooms and suites, four restaurants and lounges, and a private health club, 23 stories of fashionable condominium residences, including a three-story penthouse, and 10 stories of premier office and retail space. The Grand caters to the knowledgeable traveler, one who appreciates the amenities of grand European hotels with contemporary American conveniences.

The environment of The Grand can be described as warm, blissful, and elegant, yet decidedly unstuffy. Clients experience a wonderful sense of residency, luxurious comfort, and privacy. In-room dining is available 24 hours a day.

All rooms, individually decorated and tastefully appointed, feature marbled bathrooms with European fixtures, hair dryers, robes, remote-control cable televisions, and in-room movies. The suites, with their spacious living rooms, original art work, and complete wet bars, offer every thoughtful amenity for entertainment, business, or just relaxation.

Chefs of The Grand satisfy even the most discerning appetites and palates in a variety of dining experiences and settings, from gourmet to casual.

Versatile conference and board meeting facilities and services at The Grand are designed to accommodate business and executive groups from six to 600.

Vistas and convenience are other important assets of The Grand, whose corporate neighbors include AT&T, IBM, and BellSouth. The panorama from the hotel offers incomparable views of Atlanta's skyline, the Centennial Olympic Ring and venues, and the downtown area. Proximity to the interstate as well as to Hartsfield International Airport, only 20 minutes away, gives The Grand an extraordinary degree of convenience.

The Grand has received many of the highest accolades in the hospitality industry, including praise in the Zagat Survey, which in 1995 named The Grand "The most elegant place to stay in Atlanta."

Courtesy of The Grand Hotel Atlanta

# AARON RENTS, INC.

Aaron Rents, Inc., was launched in 1955 by Charles Loudermilk with a $500 loan and an order for 300 folding chairs. Today, after 40 years of growth, the firm has become the nation's leading furniture rental and sales company with 1995 net earnings of $11.3 million and revenues of $228.9 million.

Throughout its 40-year history, Aaron Rents has expanded not only the number and locations of its stores but its concept as well. In addition to renting furniture, in the 1960s the product line was increased to include large outdoor tents; in 1965, the company began operating its first furniture sales store; and in 1967, it opened the first store outside Atlanta, in Baltimore. Aaron Rents' manufacturing division debuted in 1971 with the acquisition of MacTavish Furniture Industries; the convention furnishings division was created in 1980; and the firm went public in 1982.

Aaron's Rental Purchase franchise program was launched in 1992 and has proven to be a great success. Systemwide revenues in 1995 for the Rental Purchase division, which has 122 units (96 company-operated stores and 26 franchise stores) were $88.2 million, a 68 percent increase over the previous year. To provide products for the Rental Purchase stores, the firm opened two new distribution centers.

The franchise program received national recognition when it placed first in *Entrepreneur* magazine's Annual Franchise 500 in appliance/furniture rental and sales, and it ranked second in the Annual Franchise Gold 100, sponsored by *Success* magazine and Ernst & Young.

Commenting on the division's success, Loudermilk notes, "The quality of our franchising is attracting a high caliber of owners, including independent retailers, rental operators, and other successful entrepreneurs. In addition, the company arranged a new inventory financing program with a major bank for existing franchisees as well as to attract new franchisees."

The company's core rental business, the Aaron Rents' Rent-to-Rent division, with 107 stores, also produced increased revenues (12 percent) of $153.1 million for 1995 and is undergoing an expansion program that includes plans to open six stores in 1996.

The Convention Services division is looking forward to a surge of rentals for the 1996 Olympic Games.

Loudermilk attributes the success of Aaron Rents to "our people's commitment to excellence—providing customer service unequaled in our industry. The people of Aaron Rents are our greatest resource and our most valuable asset. Their dedicated, quality work creates the revenue, the customer satisfaction, and the success of Aaron Rents."

Courtesy of Aaron Rents, Inc.

# ARC Security, Inc.

Anyone traveling through Atlanta's Hartsfield International Airport, as well as other airports in several states, has come in contact with employees of ARC Security, Inc.

The company's history began in 1967 when Alfred (Fred) R. Chouinard established a security guard business as a sole proprietor. He saw a need for positive baggage claim security at the Atlanta airport and in 1969 was awarded a contract from Delta Air Lines to match baggage claim tickets at the exit doors. At this time the firm had a staff of 20 employees. The service of predeparture screening was added in 1970, and the number of employees grew to 150.

Because of the firm's growth, it was incorporated in the State of Georgia in 1971 with the name ARC Security, Inc. From its small beginnings, the company has grown into a substantial provider of security services, ranging from airport security, predeparture screening security, baggage claim security, and parking lot security, for the entire aviation industry.

While growing in many states in the aviation security field, ARC also diversified into the standard commercial security guard business and has expanded into six states, where it offers consistently high-quality services. The company's expansion and success have been due mainly to its excellent reputation and the unique procedures that it has developed in the areas of training, supervision, quality assurance, and corporate support.

ARC Security is led by its owner and chairman of the board, Fred Chouinard, who has more than 30 years of experience in the security industry. From the beginning of his career in Chicago to when he relocated to Atlanta and established his own business, Chouinard has developed a tough, fiscally sound business format for both selling and managing his business.

The fair and loyal traits he has displayed to his clients have led him to be a highly respected businessman in the community and with his client base. He has been known to roll back his billing rate when a client was suffering financially, which proved to be a sound decision in the long run. As a result, his clients have responded with long-term contracts, which is not representative of the industry.

The fair way ARC treats its clients is reflected in how it treats its employees. Chouinard believes that if he manages his employees properly, promotes them internally, and compensates them with higher-than-standard wages and benefits, not only will they make that extra effort to perform their job responsibilities in a very professional manner but their entire deportment and demeanor will be elevated to higher levels. Chouinard has chosen his corporate staff carefully to ensure that his company operates on a foundation of creativity and good communications and responds to client needs in a proactive manner. The company does not allow anything to fester. With the company's unique responsiveness, its high-quality service has remained consistent throughout its years of service.

The old adage that "the customer is always right" has helped in the growth of ARC. Associated services were started because clients convinced Chouinard over the years that because of his style, he would be a natural success in other business services they needed.

This happened when the firm was developing and starting its ground-handling operations for airlines in New York and Pennsylvania. As a result, the company now provides such services as pushing and pulling airplanes, loading and unloading airplanes, cleaning the cabins, and deicing the planes. Another request for providing cabin cleaning services at Atlanta Hartsfield Airport from a major airline has led the firm to possess the best reputation as a cabin cleaner in the entire system of the airline.

Chouinard's contract bus company, Appoloosa Transport Company, Inc., was started in the same manner. Clients requested that the firm bid on their busing needs, and Chouinard was eventually awarded the contracts. Today, the firm provides contract bus services in Atlanta and Dallas and operates a fine charter bus service in the Atlanta metropolitan area.

The success of this firm can be attributed to its management, to the bus drivers' training, which is extremely customer oriented, and to the preventive maintenance systems, which provide the clean, safe, and good operating vehicles that passengers expect from a high-quality operation.

Whichever service the company offers, there is a preselection process and evaluation for potential employees. The following criteria must be met before employment is offered: the applicant must be able to communicate effectively in the English language both in speech and report writing; must possess good physical health; must be well groomed, courteous, and have good interpersonal skills; must pass a drug test; must pass a five-year background test; may not have a criminal record; must be credit worthy; must have good references; and must pass the management interview process.

It is the company's goal to become the best provider of security, airline services, and bus transportation in the United States. Also, ARC Security, Inc., plans to ensure the integrity of its reputation, through its hiring philosophy, training of personnel, promotion and career mindedness of its employees, and loyalty to its customer base.

Atlanta has been the base for Cox Enterprises for more than half of its nearly 100 years in business. The company began in 1898 in Dayton, Ohio, where Gov. James M. Cox acquired his first newspaper. In 1939, the governor acquired *The Atlanta Journal* along with WSB Radio. And a few years later, he put the South's first television station and FM radio station on the air, WSB-TV and WSB-FM.

Today, Cox Enterprises, headquartered in Atlanta, is one of the largest media companies in the country. Cox has four subsidiaries, all of which are leaders in their industries: Cox Newspapers, publicly held Cox Communications, Cox Broadcasting, and Manheim Auctions. Cox also has investments in related businesses and new media technology.

In addition to *The Atlanta Journal-Constitution* and WSB Radio and TV, Atlanta has become home to several other operations that represent the four Cox subsidiaries.

Outside Atlanta, Cox businesses can be found coast to coast as well as in Hawaii and Canada. The company also has investments and partnerships in other parts of the world.

Of Cox's more than 38,000 employees in this country and Canada, almost one-quarter call Atlanta home—more than any other city in which a Cox business operates.

At Cox, diversity among employees is a strength. One of the company's guiding principles is that to best serve its communities—to truly understand their perspectives and concerns—Cox workforces need to reflect their communities.

Another guiding principle is that the company must embrace technology—and the risks that go with it. This principle was upheld when the company ventured into the radio market in the 1930s and has driven its pursuit of technology since then.

In the 1940s, Cox was a pioneer in the newly emerging field of television. (It's been told that in the late 1940s Gov. Cox looked at the tower of his Dayton TV station and said, "Are you sure this is going to work?")

Cox entered the cable television business in 1962. Today, Cox Communications is a fully integrated, diversified broadband communications company—and one of the largest cable companies in the country.

In 1968, Cox decided to enter the automobile auctions business, which brings together wholesale buyers and sellers of used cars. Less than 30 years later, Manheim Auctions is the world's largest and

Courtesy of Cox Enterprises

highest volume automobile auction company in the world.

Many of Cox's new technological developments have originated in Atlanta.

Cox is finding new ways to leverage its newspapers' expertise in information gathering and distribution and to apply that expertise to new technology. Among the company's pioneering activities is Access Atlanta, an online, interactive service provided by *The Atlanta Journal-Constitution*.

Thousands of Access Atlanta subscribers are not only getting the news of the day electronically, but are accessing the newspaper's library, up-to-the-minute global, national, and state wire service reports, e-mail, the Internet (and,

through the Internet, the World Wide Web), and much more.

In addition, with a number of Cox businesses developing Web sites, the company is exploring innovative ways to expand business opportunities on the Internet.

Another example of a new undertaking in which Cox is leveraging its expertise is a pay-per-call telephone information service Cox is pioneering in Atlanta and other markets.

At Cox, expanding a business goes hand in hand with helping to increase the well-being of the communities it serves.

Cox and its Atlanta employees have given time, energy, and resources to civic and community organizations, the arts,

education, health services activities, and many other causes.

Cox is doing its part to ensure that Atlanta shines during the 1996 Summer Olympic Games. The company actively supported bringing the Games to Atlanta. Cox was there in Tokyo when the announcement was made that Atlanta would be the site for the '96 Games. Daily news coverage of the city's preparations has been a centerpiece ever since.

Just as Atlanta's spirit of a dream brought the Olympics to the city's front door, Cox's spirit of innovation has brought the company to the threshold of its second century. To the next 100 years! To Atlanta!

Advanced Control Systems (ACS) has been conserving the world's energy resources since 1975. It is the oldest privately owned company providing supervisory control and data acquisition (SCADA) systems for electric, gas, and water utilities and industrial companies worldwide. ACS provides products necessary to control the generation, transmission, and distribution of power.

The company's founders, John M. Muench, Peter H. Wu, and Ken W. Murphy, all alumni of Atlanta's Georgia Institute of Technology, led the firm to its present position as the number-one supplier of small- to medium-sized SCADA and distribution management systems in the United States. In fact, the company's first five years of growth were so rapid that *INC.* magazine ranked the firm number 49 in a list of the top 500 companies. More recently, ACS has been selected as one of Atlanta's Fast Tech 50 companies by the *Atlanta Business Chronicle* every year since 1983, when the honor was first bestowed. Today, with over 400 systems delivered, ACS effectively competes with large, multinational corporations.

According to John Muench, chairman and CEO of the company, "We are ranked number one in the United States in product technology, quality, and service. Our customers are secure in knowing that our systems consistently perform and will continue to provide them the tools they need to identify problems and dispatch service in a timely, cost-effective manner."

ACS customers can be divided into five groups: investor-owned utilities, such as Georgia Power; rural electric authorities, such as Cobb EMC in Cobb County, Georgia; municipalities, such as Marietta and Albany, Georgia; federal agencies, such as Southwestern Power Administration in the U.S.; and industrials, such as Amoco and Alcoa. "Municipalities and rural cooperatives are our primary market, making up about 70 percent of our business," observes Muench.

ACS began as a technology-driven company and has allocated approximately 13 percent of its revenue annually to product development or enhancement. The company's technology focus is so pronounced that 19 percent of the employees work in research and development.

"We are the technology leader because we stay abreast of the market requirements," believes Muench. For example, ACS introduced a small microprocessor in 1977 to meet the distinctive needs of rural electric authorities and municipalities, and in 1983 the company debuted a larger master to accommodate larger distribution management systems. ACS systems automate and manage the distribution of electric, gas, and water resources, thereby reducing utilities' costs. According to Muench, "We saved the City of Albany, Georgia, $2.5 million annually since they began using our system to manage their water, energy, and gas usages."

Many of the products delivered by ACS are firsts for the utility industry. For example, when founded, the firm specialized in being a remote terminal unit supplier. As a result of this specialization, ACS introduced the industry's first fully integrated microprocessor-based remote terminal unit. The belief that distribution management systems were products of the future, and required new hardware and software platforms as a foundation for distribution automation, led the company to develop the industry's first distribution management system, the first

*All systems are thoroughly tested and customer-approved at the factory before shipping.*

Courtesy of Advanced Control Systems

*Ken W. Murphy, John M. Muench, and Peter H. Wu, who founded ACS in 1975*

microprocessor master, and the first multi-microprocessor master for larger systems.

The firm's decision to design and develop a UNIX-based product line that could span the entire product spectrum from small systems to very large systems turned out to be wise and profitable. According to Muench, "We saw the vision of the future and it was a move to UNIX-based open systems architecture, which permits computers to talk to each other and eliminates the need to rewrite software. We made a major investment and succeeded in delivering the world's first UNIX-based SCADA system with open architecture in 1991." In 1995, ACS delivered the industry's first open architecture energy management system.

ACS realizes that its development is also driven by product technologies from other industries. The firm's relationship with Hewlett-Packard dates back to 1978, when ACS developed the first HP computer-based master system. Annual meetings with Hewlett-Packard's development team in Cupertino, California, enable ACS to stay far ahead of the product development cycle, resulting in introductions of key system solutions. In January 1992, ACS became a Hewlett-Packard Premier Solution Partner—the highest recognition provided by HP to any of its third-party solution suppliers. This partnership facilitates joint marketing and sales support worldwide.

As for the company's future, Muench says, "We are expanding worldwide in energy management, distribution management, and distribution automation. ACS was the first American-owned company to deliver major distribution management systems to Russia and South Africa. Our goal is to be a world leader."

*ACS's corporate headquarters in Norcross, Georgia*

Courtesy of Advanced Control Systems

Courtesy of Advanced Control Systems

PROFILES IN EXCELLENCE

Atlanta's history has always been tied to transportation. It is a city on wheels, and it keeps on rolling. Terminus, as Atlanta was once called, was the point where several railroads converged. Later, with the opening of the largest and one of the busiest airports in the world, Atlanta became the gateway to the South. Finally, true to form, it became the first city in the southeastern United States to usher in the rapid rail age with the opening of the first MARTA line in 1979.

The Metropolitan Atlanta Rapid Transit Authority, or MARTA, is Atlanta's award-winning bus and rapid transit system. Created in 1965, the eighth-largest transit system in the country carries almost 500,000 passengers a day on 700 buses and 240 rail cars. That means MARTA is responsible for transporting more than 68 million passengers a year—to work, school, social events, conventions, attraction sites, and much more.

It's a job MARTA takes seriously. After all, with 4,000 committed employees and a 30-year history, its roots are firmly established in Atlanta. As such, the Authority operates with an eye on business, civic, and community needs. Programs such as Clean Commute Day, which encourages the use of public transportation to help eliminate air pollution problems, and support of the annual AIDS Walk, the United Way Campaign, and dozens more community activities demonstrate MARTA's dedication to quality of life in metro Atlanta.

As Atlanta's businesses grow, so does MARTA's reputation for service. The system is ever expanding to meet the needs of a growing region. The addition of three new rail stations in June 1996—Buckhead, Medical Center, and Dunwoody—provides better access to healthcare facilities, shopping, and new job opportunities. And MARTA's 150 bus routes are continually adjusted to meet the needs of riders.

Besides providing safe and affordable transportation, MARTA is responsible for spurring private investment. Through design and construction of the transit system's $3 billion infrastructure, many companies—including hundreds of minority and women-owned firms—have benefited from MARTA's contracts and purchases. Corporations build new offices close to MARTA stations, and the linkage between Hartsfield International Airport and MARTA, which can whisk you to downtown Atlanta in just 15 short minutes, is world-renowned.

Courtesy of MARTA

Courtesy of MARTA

Courtesy of MARTA

freeing up parking spaces for customers. Nearly 100 Atlanta-area companies participate in the MARTA Partnership, with the numbers steadily growing every year.

Continually recognized for achievements in safety, design, and community involvement, MARTA is committed to providing safe, reliable, and convenient transportation at an affordable price. Attractive, discounted fares are available to senior citizens, disabled persons, convention groups, businesses, students, and frequent riders.

MARTA is one of the main reasons Atlanta was chosen to host the 1996 Centennial Olympic Games. MARTA's ability to move hundreds of thousands of people safely and efficiently bodes well for the region. MARTA, the Olympic Games Spectator Transportation System, is the first public transit system in the history of the Olympic Games to receive such a designation. The showcasing of state-of-the-art technology and added customer service features during the Games position MARTA as a leader in the transit industry.

MARTA is instrumental in enhancing Atlanta's economical, social, and cultural infrastructure. It is this bond that results in a vibrant economy, and one that continues to grow daily.

New projects include a compressed natural gas (CNG) bus facility, designed to house one of the largest CNG-powered bus fleets in the country. The purchase of low-floor buses is bringing MARTA closer to its goal of 100 percent accessibility by the year 2000. Also by that same year, the North Springs and Sandy Springs stations will be operational on the new North Line.

As the new millennium approaches, MARTA will be there—as a shining example of community investment. For MARTA does more than simply transport people around metro Atlanta. MARTA transports ideas, dreams, and visions for a brighter tomorrow.

Looking at MARTA, it's no wonder Atlanta is a community on the move.

Other customer-oriented services, such as the MARTA Partnership, have become well-sought-after job benefits to downtown workers and others. Through this program, employers underwrite unlimited-ride monthly transit passes—called TransCards—to their employees. Employees arrive at work relaxed and on time, and employers get a business tax deduction while

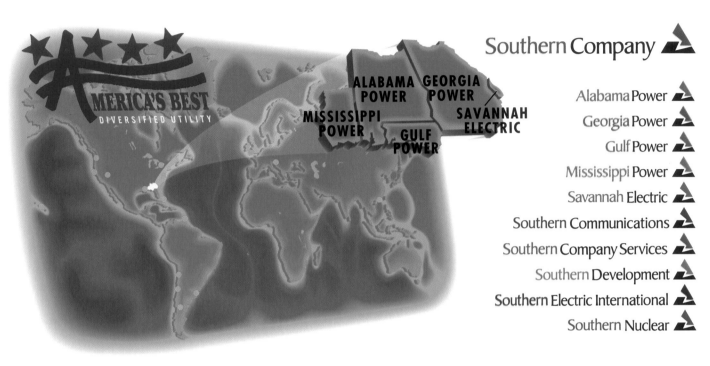

Southern Company

Alabama Power
Georgia Power
Gulf Power
Mississippi Power
Savannah Electric
Southern Communications
Southern Company Services
Southern Development
Southern Electric International
Southern Nuclear

Courtesy of The Southern Company

With annual revenue exceeding $8 billion and assets topping $27 billion, The Southern Company is the parent firm of one of the nation's largest investor-owned electric utility groups. The company—with its headquarters at 270 Peachtree Street—calls downtown Atlanta home. More than 37,000 of the company's shareholders live in Georgia.

The Southern Company's core business is the generation, transmission, and distribution of electricity to more than 3.5 million customers in most of Georgia and Alabama, the panhandle of Florida, and southeastern Mississippi. To serve its 120,000-square-mile territory in those four states, The Southern Company has some 25,000 miles of transmission lines that interconnect the 254 generating units within its system. The operating companies that make up The Southern Company's core business are Georgia Power,

Savannah Electric, Alabama Power, Gulf Power, and Mississippi Power.

The Southern Company—through its Southern Electric International subsidiary—also develops, builds, owns, and operates cogeneration and independent power production facilities throughout the United States and around the world.

Another subsidiary—the Southern Development and Investment Group—develops new business opportunities related to energy products and services.

Southern Communications Services will provide wireless communications services to Southern Company subsidiaries and their customers. It also plans to offer commercial service.

Two other subsidiaries function as internal service companies. Southern Company Services provides Southern Company subsidiaries with engineering, computer, planning, research, and financial and accounting services and support.

Southern Nuclear provides specialized services for The Southern Company's three nuclear power plants.

The Southern Company's current success comes from the company maintaining its financial strength, sharpening its competitive edge, serving a growing area, and taking advantage of global opportunities.

As the scope of change within the electric utility industry continues to grow and competition continues to increase, every action The Southern Company takes is aimed at being America's Best Diversified Utility.SM

With its expertise in what's going on in the marketplace, in regulation, in national trends, and in competition, the company plans to be an energy-solution company that moves quickly. And it's moving in four main areas: its core business, its international electric business, its domestic power generation and power marketing business, and new businesses it decides to enter.

In its core business, The Southern Company is working to maintain and increase its market share through price leadership. While it's not possible to predict the form and extent of competition that regulation might allow over the long term, the company plans to enhance its competitiveness by continuing to drive down cost and improve customer satisfaction.

The company's international electric business—through Southern Electric International—seeks attractive projects with superior financial returns. The world continues to have a great demand for electricity, and the international trend toward privatization also continues. With its expertise and strong performance in building, operating, and maintaining plants— and in running utilities—Southern Electric International is working to take advantage of global growth opportunities.

The Southern Company's domestic power generation business—other than its core business—is also through Southern Electric International. As regulation and competition change and evolve, the company will aggressively seek new markets that provide growth opportunities. While aiming to be the best competitor in the areas served by its core business, The Southern Company also intends to be successful by aggressively competing in other geographic areas and new markets if opened to competition by regulatory changes.

The Southern Company will also explore new energy-related businesses that provide additional growth opportunities. The Public Utility Holding Company Act severely restricts investments outside The Southern Company's core business, but proposed legislation would repeal the act. The other restriction on investments is one The Southern Company places on itself. It plans to get involved only in what it knows how to do—energy-related products and services and other types of utilities.

PROFILES IN EXCELLENCE

# GEORGIA POWER

The Official Power Source of the 1996 Olympic Games

Atlanta—A Vision for the New Millennium

As Atlanta caps the 20th century by hosting the most significant athletic event of the century, Georgia Power is proud to serve as the Official Power Source of the 1996 Olympic Games. When the festivities begin, Georgia Power will be there to light the way for the thousands of athletes, millions of visitors, and billions of television viewers who will take part in the centennial event.

During the Games, Georgia Power will supply an additional 600 megawatts of energy, enough to power 50,000 homes for one year. Georgia Power will also serve as the Official Power Source of the 1996 Paralympic Games.

### A Heritage of Economic Development

From the 1880s, Georgia Power and its predecessor companies were at the heart of Georgia's modernization. Georgia Power's first president, Preston Arkwright, understanding that the well-being of the company was closely tied to the people it served, coined the company's motto, "A Citizen Wherever We Serve." For nearly a century, that belief has formed the basic character of Georgia Power.

In the early 20th century, the emergence of industrialization in an agricultural economy marked the beginning of the New South, linking its economy with a modern power supply. In 1926, several independent power companies merged into the modern-day Georgia Power, establishing a network to deliver dependable, economic power. Georgia Power added electric service to 28 towns and established its Economic Development Department to market the state as a place to locate industries.

Georgia Power established its Community Development Department in 1947. In Atlanta's Carter Presidential Library, a photograph from more than 50 years ago shows the former president as a young man with another Plains businessman installing street signs in their town. The Georgia Power "Better Home Town" program helped pay for the signs.

Today, Georgia Power is targeting portions of metro Atlanta for economic development assistance. The company is

---

## WHO WE ARE

Georgia Power, an investor-owned, tax-paying utility, serves customers in 57,000 of the state's 59,000 square miles, and its 1.67 million customers are in all but six of Georgia's 159 counties. While Georgia Power's common stock is held by The Southern Company, Georgia Power's parent firm, more than 11,000 stockholders own the company's preferred stock.

Georgia Power's net plant investment of approximately $10.7 billion reflects sales of about 70.3 billion kilowatt-hours. Residential customers pay an average of 7.53 cents per kilowatt-hour, and the average annual use is 10,766 kilowatt-hours. One of the state's largest taxpayers, Georgia Power pays taxes to city, county, state, and federal agencies totaling nearly $580 million. Nearly 40 plants across the state generate energy to power Georgia's homes and businesses. Approximately 75 percent of the company's electricity is generated from coal; nuclear sources account for 22 percent, hydro for 3 percent, and oil and gas for approximately 0.2 percent.

---

a strong supporter of President Carter's Atlanta Project and is a sponsor of its Washington Cluster. Operation Legacy—a public-private partnership spearheaded by Georgia Power—is designed to bring high-quality economic development to the state by leveraging Georgia's Olympic connection.

### Competition

Georgia's electric utilities have competed for large customers since 1973. Today, the electric utility industry faces even more competition as federal legislation passed in 1992 opens wholesale markets and allows greater access to the nation's transmission system. Georgia Power's Technology Applications Center near downtown Atlanta sells efficiency by helping customers compete in a growing world market. The center is an industrial testing and educational facility where Georgia Power customers test new electric technologies.

Georgia Power draws upon its entrepreneurial past and experience to position itself as a strong competitor in the emerging markets. The company will continue to provide value and high-quality service to the people, businesses, and industries it serves.

### A Citizen Wherever We Serve

Generations of Georgia Power people have been proud to serve their communities under the motto "A Citizen Wherever We Serve." Hardwired into the state, Georgia Power takes its role as a corporate citizen seriously. The future of Georgia and of Georgia Power depends upon our young people; supporting them continues to be a top priority. In addition to a formal Educational Services section, more than 1,000 company volunteers work with students in their communities as mentors, teachers, and friends.

With its statewide presence and its broad investment in land, Georgia Power is especially concerned with environmental protection. As far back as the 1940s, the company began adding special equipment to its plants to reduce particulate emissions. That concern for the environment is even more evident today in Georgia Power's strategy to sell efficiency by promoting the environmental benefits of electricity. Georgia Power also supports the research and development of environmentally friendly electric technologies, such as electric vehicles and leading-edge manufacturing applications.

Throughout its service territory, the company works to preserve the state's diverse and sometimes unique species of plants and animals. One of the company's goals is to preserve Tallulah Gorge's natural beauty and its unique habitats.

As the new century approaches, Georgia Power looks forward to continuing its partnership with the people of Georgia as it works to preserve the state's natural resources and heritage while working to meet the challenges of a new era.

Headquartered in Atlanta, with local telephone service in nine southeastern states, BellSouth is the largest and fastest-growing of the regional Bell telecommunications companies. With cellular, paging, and mobile data service in the U.S. and 15 foreign countries, BellSouth is also a worldwide leader in wireless telecommunications.

The communications network that BellSouth has developed, maintains, and is continually enhancing is a major factor in the economy and quality of life of Atlanta and the Southeast. That network has enabled the city to grow into a

> *"With 4.5 million customers from Chile to China, BellSouth International is a worldwide leader in telecommunications."*
>
> CHARLES C. MILLER III,
> PRESIDENT,
> BELLSOUTH INTERNATIONAL

world center for computing, banking, telecommunications, cable television, medical technology, home electronics, and other industries, as well as to become the host of the 1996 Centennial Olympic Games.

### BELLSOUTH AND THE 1996 OLYMPICS

The communications demands of the Olympic Games are monumental and unique. Two million spectators will watch the exploits of 11,000 athletes at 41 separate locations in and around Atlanta and in 10 other cities. A total of 15,000 media representatives will report on the events, and 3.5 billion people around the world will see the Games on television. All of the information, words, sounds, and images generated by the Games will be carried on BellSouth's communications network.

Television coverage of over 270 events, totaling at least 3,000 hours of Olympic competition, will be provided by 400 cameras, including 40 mobile units. Live broadcasts from the dozens of remote locations will first be transmitted to the International Broadcast Center in downtown Atlanta and from there by satellite to the world.

To make complete coverage of the

*Courtesy of BellSouth*

*John Clendenin, BellSouth's chairman and CEO, announced that the company would be a sponsor of the 1996 Olympic Games. With him is IZZY, the official mascot of the Games.*

Games available to journalists covering specific events, broadcasts from each venue will be shown live at every other venue. Because BellSouth will transmit the signal in an uncompressed digital format (providing the highest video and audio quality possible), traffic on the fiber-optic cables will reach 100 billion bits per second, a capacity equivalent to 400,000 telephone lines.

To meet the video, voice, and data needs of the 150,000 members of the Olympic family and the millions of visitors, BellSouth is increasing the capability of the network by allocating over $120 million to new optical fiber and equipment; these improvements will ensure network quality and capacity long after the Olympics are over. In the case of cellular phone service, BellSouth Mobility (BMI) will increase its

*BellSouth's clear, reliable, and sophisticated telecommunications network serves more than 20 million customers across nine southeastern states.*

*© Jay Maisel*

Courtesy of BellSouth

*BellSouth is involved in the communities it serves. The proceeds of the BellSouth Golf Classic, a major PGA event sponsored by the company each spring, go to an Atlanta-area children's hospital.*

call-carrying capacity within the Olympic Ring by as much as 700 percent. The entire BMI system will be enhanced by 200 percent. This increased capacity will remain in place after the Olympics, serving current and future customers.

BellSouth is supporting the 1996 Olympics in a number of ways. As an official sponsor, the company is donating $20 million in products and services to the Atlanta Committee for the Olympic Games. Information on the games will be featured in selected BellSouth telephone directories.

### THE POWER OF THE NETWORK

The network that will meet the demands of the 1996 Olympic Games extends throughout nine states: Alabama, Florida, Georgia, Kentucky, Louisiana, Mississippi, North Carolina, South Carolina, and Tennessee. BellSouth serves over 20 million telephone customer lines in those states, the largest customer base of any regional telecommunications provider in the country.

BellSouth's regional network includes about 1.5 million miles of fiber-optic cable, which forms the backbone of some of the world's most sophisticated communications networks. For example, the North Carolina Information Highway, a public-private partnership that includes BellSouth and local telephone companies, is the world's fastest wide-area multimedia communications network.

While the demands of the Olympics provide a dramatic demonstration of the capabilities of the BellSouth network, there are other examples of network utility that have and will continue to provide economic and community benefits to the region. The Georgia Statewide Academic and Medical System, for example, uses two-way, interactive television carried by high-speed telephone lines to provide educational and medical services in every area of the state, eliminating the barriers of time and distance and making scarce resources available to those who need them.

There are similar systems in all of the states served by BellSouth, but the Georgia Statewide Academic and Medical System, with 437 sites, may be the largest distance-learning and telemedicine network in the world. Georgia Governor Zell Miller described it as a revolution in education and health care.

To meet the growing demand for innovative communication services, BellSouth is fast becoming a full-service multimedia company. Alliances such as one with the Walt Disney Company will strengthen BellSouth's ability to provide the content and delivery system for future services. In 1996, the company will test delivery of a range of interactive television services to 12,000 households in the metropolitan Atlanta area.

BellSouth and its partners provide cellular telephone service for more than 3 million customers in 216 U.S. cities. RAM Mobile Data's networks cover 92 percent of the U.S. urban population, providing two-way data communications services for mobile professionals.

BellSouth International has invested over a billion dollars in wireless communications networks, long distance, satellite broadcasting, cable television software, and private network services in more than a dozen countries spanning five continents. In Latin America, Western Europe, the Middle East, and the Asia Pacific region, BellSouth International has brought the latest in telecommunications technology to the most attractive markets in the world.

Courtesy of BellSouth

*A leading provider of cellular technology, BellSouth Mobility markets its convenient wireless services in grocery stores and elsewhere throughout Atlanta and other cities in the Southeast.*

# ATLANTA INTERFAITH BROADCASTERS, INC.

When Rev. John Allen established Atlanta Interfaith Broadcasters, Inc. (AIB), in 1969, he had a mission—to provide good religious television that would enhance and strengthen the local congregation, the basic unit of religious life. This goal was the reverse of the trend at that time, when TV preachers would reach into their viewers' pockets to pay for their TV shows, thereby competing with local congregational life.

According to Rev. Allen, a former engineer on the Polaris missile project and a 1965 graduate of Columbia Seminary in Decatur, "Before AIB, the preponderance of religious television had given religious broadcasters a bad name and had even diminished the stature of religion in our land. Some televangelists flagrantly sought to use this powerful medium to feather their own nests at the expense of the community as a whole. AIB has set out to reverse this trend."

Since 1969, AIB has produced hundreds of public-service programs (such as *Sound of Youth* and *The Midnight Minister*) on Atlanta's radio and TV stations. In 1981, when cable TV was emerging in Atlanta and televangelism was in full flower, AIB was offered a channel. Allen and his wife, O'Lynn,

*Luther Bootle brings a video from the Second Ponce de Leon Baptist Church to Angie Wright at AIB.*

Courtesy of Atlanta Interfaith Broadcasters, Inc.

now AIB's station manager, took the opportunity to turn the tide. Along with a board of representatives from all the major local religious communities, the group set out to establish an interfaith cable TV station that would fly in the face of precedent.

The station is open to all faiths with no favoritism; downplaying of other faiths, solicitations for money from viewers, and disguised fund-raising in the form of selling items at inflated prices are not allowed.

AIB, which is a not-for-profit organization to which tax-deductible contributions can be made, especially emphasizes its interfaith nature. In addition to programming for Christians, there is strong Jewish and some Moslem-oriented programming, and about 30 percent is targeted for African-Americans.

AIB grew with the cable industry and is now the nation's largest local religious cable station. Beginning with 20 hours of programming a week to 3,000 homes, AIB expanded into DeKalb County and later into the suburbs to become a full-time station reaching more than 600,000 homes in a 10-county region. It now uses a regionwide transmitter atop One Peachtree Center to reach cable systems.

Fees for air time sustained a modest $715,695 operating budget in 1995, including 13 full and part-time employees. In the past, AIB's offices and studios were in houses of worship, but in 1995 the organization purchased 1075 Spring Street, where plans are under way to build a state-of-the-art TV studio on the back lot of the property. Special gifts and grants will pay for this addition so the rate structure to the religious community will not have to be increased.

*Rabbi Steven Lebow and Shira Lebow at Temple Kol Emeth on AIB*

# HONEYWELL NETWORK SERVICES

Honeywell Network Services (HNS), located in Norcross, Georgia, is the leading supplier of network consulting, design, implementation, training, and management services for the industrial marketplace. As the global Networking Center of Excellence for Honeywell Incorporated's Industrial Automation and Control Division, HNS specializes in production-related, vendor-independent, turnkey network solutions. Honeywell, Inc., is a 110-year-old Minneapolis, Minnesota-based Fortune 100 corporation and a recognized worldwide leader in the process control marketplace.

HNS focuses its network services offerings primarily on industrial clients in process industries, including pulp and paper, oil and gas, chemical, refining, and food processing. As business needs have evolved, networks have become the critical foundation for the successful operation of enterprises in such industries. Honeywell's background as a leading provider of production control solutions, coupled with an intimate knowledge of communications technologies and their practical application in the production environment, uniquely qualifies HNS to provide the enabling technologies necessary to transfer information between the production environment and the boardroom in a timely and cost-effective manner.

HNS's overall business philosophy focuses on providing high-value solutions that enhance customers' operational and financial performance. This approach combines diverse consulting, design, implementation, training, and management services into a cohesive solution focused on helping customers achieve business success. For example, the professional consulting and design services offered by HNS ensure customer value through an in-depth needs analysis that discovers current and future information requirements. The design process then creates a road map that matches "best-in-class" technology with the client's business needs. Implementation services convey this emphasis on customer value through carefully managed installation, integration, testing, certification, and documentation activities. This value is also extended beyond initial design and implementation activities through high-quality training and ongoing network management services.

The overall goal of Honeywell Network Services is to be a "Partner in Performance" with its clients. This means that HNS operates as a working partner with a significant stake in the competitiveness, innovation, productivity, quality, financial results, and employee satisfaction of its customers. As a network services partner, HNS seeks to team up with its customers to provide the best "delivered customer value" from the immense variety of networking technologies available in the marketplace.

255

As we approach the 21st century, the sharing of information across cultural and economic divides will be more important than ever. AT&T, a global telecommunications company with a significant regional presence in Atlanta, enables people to communicate about the rapid changes in their lives and businesses through its worldwide dominance in network services.

AT&T also works to improve the quality of life in the communities it serves, by investing in education, health and human services, and arts and culture.

AT&T leads the way in an industry that is undergoing dramatic changes. New technology, more flexible regulations, and increased competition have shaped AT&T into a company that flourishes in

*The AT&T Network Control Center in Conyers operates 24 hours a day, every day of the year. Highly trained specialists, using a full array of digital technology and intelligent software systems, monitor the health of the system in the eastern half of the United States and the fiber-optic cable under the Atlantic Ocean and Caribbean Sea.*

the chaotic telecommunications industry, not only by embracing change but also by transforming itself when necessary.

In 1996, the company split into three separate businesses—communications services, equipment, and computers. AT&T knew that three smaller, sharply focused companies could move more quickly in today's fast-paced marketplace.

The AT&T name stays with the communications services group, the part of the business that brings people and information together.

### INFORMATION AT THE SPEED OF LIGHT

Streams of light pulse silently under the streets of Atlanta, carrying personal and business conversations, facsimiles, computer transmissions, and video signals. Tens of thousands of miles of fiber-optic cable crisscross the globe and come together here, in Atlanta, a major telecommunications hub.

AT&T network specialists in Conyers, Georgia, keep an eye on this information highway 24 hours a day, monitoring the health of the system in the eastern half of the United States and the fiber-optic

*AT&T invented the technology that makes speed-of-light communication possible. One pair of optical fibers can carry 64,000 voice conversations. AT&T Bell Laboratories continues to find ways to pack more information on the hair-thin strands.*

cables under the Atlantic Ocean and Caribbean Sea to destinations abroad. On an average business day, close to 200 million calls make lightning-quick journeys through AT&T's worldwide intelligent network.

Voices sound crisp, clear, and close because the network is enhanced with AT&T's True Voice® technology.

The calls reach their destination accurately, reliably, and immediately, delivering information that is vital to AT&T's customers. More than 99.9 percent of all calls are completed on the first try. It takes only two to three seconds for calls to go through, the fastest call setup time in the industry.

If there is trouble on the network, AT&T's intelligent software and digital technology automatically begin finding alternative routes, while highly trained employees fix the problem.

The AT&T Network Control Center in Conyers is part of a triad of network man-

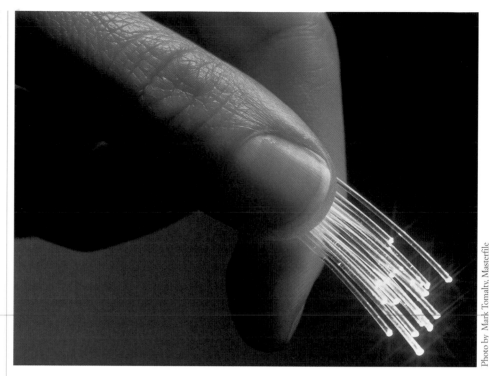

Photo by Mark Tomalty, Masterfile

agement facilities. AT&T has a sister facility in Denver that is responsible for the western half of the U.S. and for the Pacific and Indian Ocean cables to Canada and Mexico. Either center is capable of assuming full network responsibility. The AT&T Network Operations Center in Bedminster, New Jersey, has global network management responsibilities.

## SERVING THE WORLD FROM ATLANTA'S DOORSTEP

AT&T customers can dial direct to hundreds of countries and territories worldwide, and the AT&T network provides access to every country in the world. That's increasingly important in a growing international city like Atlanta, the business capital of the Southeast.

To help businesses in this region and elsewhere communicate with people who speak another language, AT&T established AT&T Language Line Services. Twenty-four hours a day, AT&T interpreters are ready to provide translation services in more than 140 languages. This service is invaluable to those who wish to do business abroad or with those in their community who speak other languages.

© Frank Moscati

*AT&T Language Line Services provides round-the-clock translation assistance in more than 140 languages, making it possible to call an interpreter and communicate with anyone in the world. Shown are Language Line employees (clockwise from lower left) Tien Nguyen, Israel Dominguez, Cons Agbannawag, Claude Constant, Carlos Nascimento, Carrie Tate, Rachel Mosqueda, and Sana Japara.*

### A Vital Partner of the 1996 Olympic Games

AT&T anchored many of its operations in the Atlanta area because of the region's increasing global influence. Chief testament to that influence is the 1996 Olympic Games, hosted by Atlanta.

As a partner in the Centennial Olympic Games, AT&T provided sophisticated switches, fiber-optic cabling, and network services to meet the needs of the world's largest event.

In addition, AT&T made sure that Olympic athletes and their families felt at home. The company spread the warmth of southern hospitality through the AT&T Atlanta Family to Family '96 program, through which hundreds of the athletes' loved ones stayed with local families free of charge.

The welcome mat stretches all the way to Atlanta's Centennial Olympic Park, where AT&T built the first global Olympic Village. This three-story-tall building provided a central gathering place in Atlanta's festival park for all the world's Olympic athletes and their families to meet and share the experience of the Olympic Games.

AT&T extended a welcome to all Olympic Games visitors with a multimedia exhibit of consumer technology in the park. And, for 22 consecutive nights, AT&T brought in popular musicians to entertain the crowds at the 8,500-seat AT&T Olympic Amphitheater.

More than 3,700 AT&T employees also reached out—individually—to keep the Olympic Games running smoothly. They volunteered to deliver uniforms and sports equipment, get the horses in the equestrian competition through U.S. Customs, take tickets, perform administration tasks such as making photocopies and sending faxes, and supplement the security force.

### AT&T Reaches Out to the Community

The successful staging of the Olympic Games required many volunteer hours, and AT&T employees responded generously. That's because they— and the corporation itself—have a long-standing tradition of giving back to their community.

AT&T employees volunteer in local schools, organize fund-raising activities for all kinds of good causes, serve on the boards of nonprofit organizations, build houses for the working poor, coach inner-city sports leagues, and coordinate efforts to help victims of natural disasters.

AT&T volunteers have recruited hundreds of new members and hundreds of thousands of dollars in pledges to support the work of the Metro Atlanta Chamber of Commerce.

AT&T signed on as one of the first corporate partners in the Atlanta Project, a nonprofit initiative of the Carter Center. The company has worked closely with residents in the Carver Cluster in southwest Atlanta, helping with such activities as door-to-door immunization drives and mentoring programs in the neighborhood schools.

AT&T has adopted other schools as well, donating everything from book bags to classroom computers, arranging career seminars, and tutoring students one on one.

### Education Is the Future

AT&T invests in the future. The company has donated millions in grants and equipment to educational institutions in Georgia so they could build computer labs and

© Frank Moscati

*AT&T makes communication possible anywhere, anytime.*

Photo by Shelia Turner

library data networks. AT&T has funded other projects, too, providing mini-grants to local teachers for projects such as butterfly gardens and literary magazines.

AT&T has focused much of its effort on minority students in math and sciences, encouraging them with scholarships and internships. AT&T has nurtured their development with loaned professors from AT&T Bell Laboratories and the engineering staff, as many as two or three a year at the Atlanta University Center.

AT&T has also sponsored High-Tech Month in metro Atlanta, bringing in speakers and exhibits that help consumers and businesspeople stay abreast of the rapidly changing telecommunications industry.

## RECYCLING CAN BE A WAY OF LIFE

AT&T operates the largest private recycling program in the state. All AT&T office waste paper in metro Atlanta winds

up at the company's recycling center in Alpharetta. Local businesses and schools also use the recycling facility.

AT&T ships tons of paper to the Fort Howard Corporation in Savannah, where it is recycled into paper towels, tissues, napkins, and other products. AT&T uses those recycled products in its offices.

AT&T also recycles used toner cartridges, binders, batteries, cardboard

boxes, aluminum cans, glass bottles, and many other items.

## A TRADITION OF BUILDING COMMUNICATION

Providing communications services is AT&T's core business, and it has been since the company was founded in 1885. The lineage stretches even further, to Alexander Graham Bell and his invention of the telephone in 1876.

As parent company of the former Bell System, AT&T provided universal telephone service to virtually everyone in the United States. It also provided international long-distance service.

The shape of AT&T's business continues to change, but the core mission remains the same: AT&T is making it easier to bring people and information together.

*AT&T responds quickly during natural and man-made disasters. In the aftermath of Hurricane Opal, AT&T reopened communications in Destin, Florida, by setting up a satellite dish and trucking in a portable central office.*

Photo by David Lee Hartlage

*Editors, writers, and designers develop stories for Access Atlanta and* The Atlanta Journal-Constitution's *sites on the World Wide Web. On March 10, 1994,* The Atlanta Journal-Constitution *introduced the Access Atlanta on-line service, becoming one of the first newspapers to offer news and information to PC users.*

The *Atlanta Constitution* and the *Atlanta Journal* have occupied unique positions in Atlanta's history. Founded in the early years after the Civil War, both newspapers have kept up a daily dialogue with Atlantans about events that have become history. Bitter rivals from the beginning, each newspaper strived to outdo the other in reporting the news and to stand taller when the city needed a helping hand.

For example, *Constitution* editor Henry Grady established a policy of generosity at the newspaper by sponsoring organizations and civic enterprises (such as the rebuilding of the Young Men's Library and fund-raising for a Confederate Veterans Home) when there was a need; the *Journal* carried fuel and food to Atlantans during a deadly ice storm; and both papers helped start the forerunners of the United Way and the Empty Stocking Fund.

First and foremost, both papers have always been good citizens of the community. The *Atlanta Journal-Constitution* (*AJC*) supports hundreds of charitable causes each year. *AJC* employees sit on numerous boards and action committees, helping to lead the city in its growth, while reaching out to bring all citizens along in these exciting times.

James M. Cox, the statesman and journalist who bought the *Atlanta Journal* in 1939, purchased the *Atlanta Constitution* in 1950 and combined their Sunday editions. The news staffs merged in 1982, but the opinion page staffs still remain separate.

Information is the lifeblood of a democracy, and the *Journal* and the *Con-stitution* have been leaders in reporting the facts and in helping to discern the truth. Starting with "a first-class printing outfit" purchased in New York City in 1883, the *Atlanta Journal* went on to give Atlanta its first radio station in 1922 (WSB) and its first television station in 1948 (WSB-TV).

In 1994, the *AJC* started Access Atlanta, the city's first local news and information service available on personal computer. The on-line service is offered by the *Journal-Constitution* in partnership with Prodigy. Members can access local and national news and information, as well as the latest reports from the world's leading wire services.

Today, the *Journal* and the *Constitution* are the largest of 17 daily newspapers published by Cox Newspapers, a division of Atlanta-based Cox Enterprises, Inc. With the largest news staff in Atlanta (more than 500) and a tradition of leadership in providing news and information, the *Atlanta Journal-Constitution* has won nine Pulitzer prizes. As one of Atlanta's most dependable citizens, the *Journal-Constitution* will continue to offer balanced leadership in all areas of growth. As the *AJC* explores ways to better serve its readers with complete, up-to-date news coverage, it will also maintain its goal of providing a high-quality product for advertisers' messages. While technology is sure to change, the aim of the *AJC* will remain the same: to publish in-depth news accounts, editorials concerned with righting wrongs, colorful sports reports, articles on social events of note, and advertising for valuable goods and services.

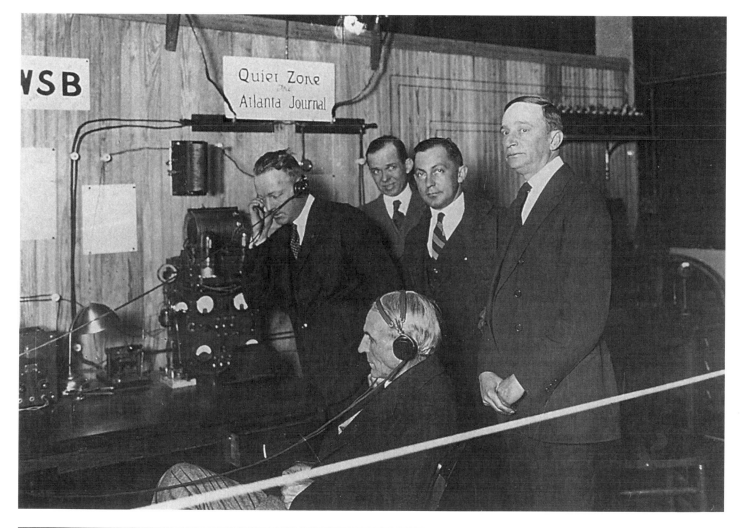

*In April 1922, Henry Ford (seated) listened to radio reception at the* Atlanta Journal's *month-old WSB. The initial broadcast on March 22 was a brief summary of the news from the* Journal.

# MCI COMMUNICATIONS CORPORATION

Atlanta is home to MCI's worldwide business marketing headquarters, MCI's largest operating division. MCI® is one of the world's largest and fastest-growing diversified communications companies, providing consumers, businesses, governments, and educational institutions around the world with a wide range of communications, information, and technology tools.

MCI opened its first Atlanta office in 1983. Since then, the city has been a focal point for MCI's small business sales and service activities through the networkMCI Center for Small Business. In 1992, Atlanta became the home of MCI's national Business Sales and Service Division and the worldwide headquarters for MCI's sales and service to businesses.

Since 1992, the number of MCI employees in Atlanta has tripled to nearly 4,000. With 11 MCI locations, Atlanta continues to be a hub for the company's network and sales operations.

With MCI's call-switching site in Austell, Georgia, the Atlanta area has become a fiber-optic hub for the entire U.S. A significant point in the MCI network for routing calls on the East Coast, Atlanta is more attractive to new businesses in part because of the telecommunications infrastructure MCI has put in place here.

MCI customizes its products, service, and support systems to help its Atlanta customers grow, providing services to such global Atlanta-based companies as Holiday Inn, Equifax, and Georgia Pacific.

## MCI MEANS COMMUNITY INVOLVEMENT
MCI actively contributes to the arts community of Atlanta. A significant supporter of the Woodruff Arts Center, MCI helps bring special events and performances to the city, such as the annual Gospel Christ-

*Atlanta is a critical hub for MCI's 24-hour customer service and technical support to businesses around the world. MCI also offers customer service in many languages, including Spanish, Korean, and Mandarin.*

mas performance. MCI has also been a long-time sponsor of the Georgia Special Olympics, where MCI volunteers oversee the track and field games and provide satellite feed broadcast of the Games to Georgia television stations and CNN. MCI also supports the SciTrek Museum, Hands On Atlanta, the Atlanta Braves Summer Reading Program, and other local organizations.

MCI also connects thousands of viewers nationwide so they can communicate about today's hottest issues via CNN's "Talk Back Live." Broadcast daily from CNN Center, "Talk Back Live" utilizes MCI's videoconferencing, 800 service, and fax capabilities.

Community leader Mike Frost is active in many causes outside his role as a leading account development manager for MCI. Mike went to work for MCI 11 years ago, a year after he was injured in a surfing accident and confined to a wheelchair as a quadriplegic.

An active member of the Atlanta community, Mike is the president of the Jaycettes Foundation. He is currently working to construct a camp for physically and mentally challenged children at the Roosevelt Warm Springs Rehabilitation Center.

Mike is also involved in peer support at Shepherd Center and volunteers at the Tommy Nobis Center in Marietta, helping physically challenged people with career rehabilitation.

Mike has been a national speaker on disability issues, including the annual "Vermont Disabilities Day," where he gave a presentation to Vermont business and state leaders. He serves as a board member for the Georgia Jaycees and is active in other Atlanta community organizations. Mike has been honored by local station WXIA-TV in its annual "Outstanding Volunteers of Atlanta" program.

*As a leading account development manager for MCI, Mike Frost personifies MCI vitality.*

MCI offers an extensive portfolio of communications services, ranging from global long distance to local access, wireless to on-line, and network management to systems integration. Beyond its position as the nation's second-largest long-distance company, MCI offers a wealth of advanced worldwide services through the strength and reach of its global alliances with the BT and News Corporation and North American alliances with Stentor (Canada) and Bannacci (Mexico).

While continuing to grow revenue in the long-distance market, MCI is leveraging its key technology strengths to expand beyond its core business into other rapidly growing markets, such as the Internet, entertainment distribution, and software.

MCI has played a significant role in the creation and growth of the Internet, the world's largest computer network. Always on the leading edge, MCI has launched innovative Internet Web sites, such as marketplaceMCI℠ (secure on-line shopping), the Small Business Center, and @fashion. MCI is also expanding into the entertainment retail market with entertainmentMCI℠. Its first offering, 1-800 MUSIC NOW℠, turns every touch-tone phone and PC with a modem into a virtual music store.

Global, long-distance, and local communications are converging as customers think about their total needs rather than the individual pieces. Commercial boundaries are being redrawn, new technologies are breaking down economic and political barriers, and the global economy is being reshaped around digital information. Opening up opportunity as far as the eye can see, MCI will explore new territory to take Atlanta into the 21st century with the most sophisticated products in the industry.

*MCI's Executive Briefing Center is a state-of-the-art theater used to showcase MCI solutions and value-added products.*

# SIMONS ENGINEERING, INC.

As consulting engineers to industry worldwide, Simons Engineering, Inc., offers its clients a single-source engineering solution. The firm's full-service capabilities and depth of resources provide a benefit that many firms can't match.

The Simons organization was founded in Chicago in 1914 by Venning Simons. In 1944, his son Howard Simons moved to Vancouver, British Columbia, to open the first office of H. A. Simons, Ltd., and from then on the firm experienced rapid growth based on its expertise in the pulp and paper industry. In 1968, Tom Simons succeeded his father as president, continuing a period of expansion and diversification. In 1970, the company purchased Atlanta-based Eastern Engineering, and operations in the United States were begun as Simons-Eastern

Consultants, Inc. In 1994, the name was changed to Simons Engineering, Inc., to more accurately reflect the company's focus. Today, the U.S. operations include offices in Atlanta; Greenville, South Carolina; Minneapolis, Minnesota; and Portland, Maine.

Simons Engineering is headed by President Harry Waterbor. Specializing in the pulp, paper, and forest products industries, Simons has become more diversified over the past five years. While the pulp and paper industries still make up about 60 percent of the firm's business, other areas of specialization include chemicals, food and beverages (especially the baking industry), and general manufacturing. According to Waterbor, "It is unique that we are a private company led by H. A. Simons' president, Tom Simons,

who represents the third generation of his family. Our goal is to continue with diversification in an effort to bring more stability to our business, because the pulp and paper industry is extremely cyclical. In addition, we will continue to advance some high-technology developments."

Simons' approach to the projects it undertakes centers around its project management tools and the communication and applications to make them work effectively. Activities like team building and advanced planning are used at the start of a project to help all project stakeholders understand their goals and responsibilities. Management and design personnel in all disciplines use project control techniques that have evolved over the course of the company's history of over 10,000 significant projects.

*Simons' control system staging and testing facility enables a customer's process control system to be connected to a real-time simulation of the actual process in order to check and debug the system prior to installation.*

To support the project management and controls activities, Simons has made a strong commitment over a number of years to the research and development of design tools; it is estimated that the company spends over $10 million per year on hardware and development. Some of the high-technology advances that have resulted include specialized tools and methods to help minimize the risks inherent in any project.

Several examples illustrate this point.

**Computer-Aided Design.** Simons uses a design software that combines an integrated database with two- or three-dimensional modeling capabilities to generate a variety of construction plans, elevations, sections, perspectives, and materials reports. The database helps ensure design integrity and quality while virtually eliminating interferences. Clients may also "tour" their facilities prior to construction by using the software's three-dimensional "walk-through" capabilities.

**IDEAS™.** This high-fidelity dynamic process simulator integrates process design, control design testing, training, and ongoing process optimization all into one complete plant model. The computer model can operate the plant process, test its functions, and examine "what if" scenarios before the plant is built.

Courtesy of Simons Engineering, Inc.

*Simons' services extend beyond feasibility studies and detailed design. Project team members work through checkout and startup to help ensure that all project goals are met.*

**Control System Staging and Testing.** This "value-added" service is performed at Simons' 5,000-square-foot dedicated facility in Atlanta, where the client's actual process control system is configured and tested prior to installation. By running the control system from a real-time simulation of the client's actual process, bugs can be worked out and maintenance and operations training can be conducted in order to allow a smoother, quicker startup on site.

Waterbor attributes the company's record of over 80 years of success to three main factors: a continuity of management, resulting from three generations of private ownership; a long-term strategy of consistently investing to acquire specialized resources and capabilities; and a continuing dedication to the highest possible standards of integrity, professional ethics, and quality of work.

The company is governed by six basic priorities: do the work right; focus on the customer; use participative management; attract, develop, educate, and train people; take full advantage of available technology; and communicate.

The firm's emphasis on quality has been rewarded with a large number of repeat assignments. To continue this trend, the company implemented the Simons Quality Process (SQP), which is a structured and funded effort directed at continuing improvement in the way the organization offers its services and delivers solutions that meet its clients' needs. The management-led program focuses on improving client satisfaction, employee participation, and company performance.

© Crosby Images

*Communication is a key to any successful project. Simons uses specialized techniques like team building and advanced planning at the beginning of projects to create an atmosphere of openness and cooperation.*

267

King & Spalding was established as a two-lawyer partnership in 1885 by Alexander C. King and Jack J. Spalding. Today, with offices in Atlanta, Washington, D.C., New York, and Houston, King & Spalding has become a nationally recognized law firm with a solid practice throughout the United States and abroad.

Headquartered in downtown Atlanta, the firm provides a vast array of legal services to many high-profile Georgia businesses, including The Coca-Cola Company, Delta Air Lines, Inc., Georgia-Pacific Corporation, and SunTrust Banks, Inc., along with a growing base of national and international clients. King & Spalding counsels corporations, government agencies, and individuals in Europe, the Middle East, the Far East, Mexico, and Latin America.

King & Spalding reflects the traditions and commitments that were instilled by the founding partners. The firm has a long-standing reputation for investing in the community. It was the first law firm in Atlanta to employ a full-time director of community affairs, who coordinates and promotes the firm's community service and pro bono legal activities. In addition, many attorneys are board members, trustees, or volunteers of nonprofit organizations that serve Atlanta and the surrounding region.

King & Spalding encourages public service. Many of the firm's partners served in the public sector before joining the firm or in mid-career and then returned to the partnership. For example, Griffin Bell served as Attorney General of the United States, George Busbee served as Governor of the State of Georgia, William Nelson served as Chief Counsel of the Internal Revenue Service, and Larry Thompson served as U.S. Attorney for the Northern District of Georgia.

Three King & Spalding partners played an integral role in helping to ensure that the city continues to mature as an international hub; they were a part of the team of nine volunteers who were responsible for bringing the 1996 Olympic Games to Atlanta. The firm represents the Atlanta Committee for the Olympic Games as general counsel.

According to Ralph Levy, managing partner, King & Spalding remains unique because "we remain a true partnership—a true 'one-firm firm'—in which commitment to client service and to community is paramount. With all of the changes occurring in the legal profession, we remain convinced that there is no better or more collegial place to practice law than King & Spalding. We celebrate as a symbol of our success the fact that, in our 110-year history, no group of partners has ever left our firm to practice together elsewhere. Service and stability have shaped our professional lives and will guide our future. The generations of partners who preceded us in building a strong institution left a legacy which we hold in trust for future generations."

Levy believes that the firm's longevity and success results from King & Spalding's taking the long view through the years and rewarding behavior contributing to institutional

*Left to right: Managing Partner Ralph Levy converses with Walt Driver, Chilton Varner, and Policy Committee Chairman Clancy Ridley.*

stability. He notes, "We have believed in each other, in the value of the contributions that we make in varied ways to each other's success, and in the value of being involved in important community affairs. We have been fortunate in our ability to attract excellent lawyers to the firm. We have believed in and grown with our clients and benefited by their successes.

"Our firm has gained enormously by Atlanta's emergence as the transportation and financial hub of the Southeast. In addition, King & Spalding has avoided fads that clashed with our culture, but managed necessary changes to fit our tradition and our clients' needs. Our institutionalized checks and balances allow our partners to retain ownership of the direction of the firm."

Levy predicts that the practice in the future will be dominated by clients who want lawyers who listen to and anticipate their needs. Successful firms will be composed of excellent listeners and planners as well as excellent technicians. He explains, "We are creating new reality because the stability of our firm and our strategic objective of enjoying sustained, institutionalized client relationships whenever possible match our clients' present and future needs. We appreciate that our existing clients are our best sources of new business and that our Atlanta roots sustain us."

It was client requests and the desire to provide new opportunities that drove the firm's 1979 decision to open a Washington office, to expand to New York in 1992, and to open a Houston office in 1995. All offices are linked technologically through computer networking, electronic and voice mail, and audio-visual meeting capacity.

According to Levy, "Our past has built a foundation for our future, and we have always been well served by recalling its lessons and focusing on our principles as we confront new challenges."

*Left to right: Governor George Busbee, Larry Thompson, and Judge Griffin Bell*

*Billy Payne, president and CEO of the Committee for the Olympic Games (center), meets with Horace Sibley (left) and Charles Shaffer, Jr. (right).*

# SMITH REAL ESTATE SERVICES, INC.

Atlanta-based Smith Real Estate Services, Inc. (SRES), is a full-service real estate consulting firm that is one of only a few commercial real estate brokerage and consulting firms nationally that are owned by both a woman and a member of a minority group (African-American).

The firm was founded in 1984 by Pamela J. Smith, president and chief executive officer, who holds a bachelor's degree in urban studies from Rutgers University, a master's of public administration from New York University, a master's of science in real estate from Georgia State, and a certificate in real estate development from Massachusetts Institute of Technology, Center for Real Estate.

SRES is dedicated to giving its clients an advantage in the highly volatile and competitive environment of investment real estate. The firm assists a wide range of investors in making successful decisions in the areas of valuation, brokerage, acquisition, development, asset management, and the disposition of real estate assets.

Solutions to problems, no matter how small or complex, are always based on market-derived facts and information. As a result, clients are able to make sound, meaningful investment decisions, which gives them a competitive advantage in the real estate market.

The company's reputation for client satisfaction has become its trademark. Its diverse client base includes the City of Atlanta, the Atlanta Board of Education, Grady Health System, Fulton County Land Department, Metropolitan Atlanta Olympic Games Authority, the Peoplestown Revitalization Corporation, the Housing Authority of the City of Atlanta, and the Atlanta Life Insurance Company, as well as many private investors.

Testaments to the firm's reputation include the facts that 95 percent of SRES's new business is obtained from client referrals and its client base consists mainly of repeat customers. According to Smith, "Total client satisfaction is more than just a slogan, it is a way of doing business and the only real measure of our success. We welcome the opportunity to discuss our clients' real estate needs and are committed to finding creative and effective solutions to the challenging real estate problems they face."

*President and Chief Executive Officer Pamela J. Smith*

# PETERSON DILLARD YOUNG ASSELIN & POWELL

Located in the heart of Atlanta's central business district, Peterson Dillard Young Asselin & Powell offers a comprehensive array of legal services to government bodies, corporations, and individuals throughout the southeastern United States and across the nation.

The firm has carefully assembled a group of attorneys whose areas of expertise complement each other and provide a level of service that exemplifies the best Atlanta has to offer.

Peterson Dillard is a full-service mid-size firm that offers expert legal services in local and state government law, mergers and acquisitions, public and private securities offerings, tax-exempt financing, a wide variety of construction matters, commercial real estate, commercial transactions, zoning, environmental law, and general and complex litigation. The firm's clients include numerous city, county, and state governments, major corporations, regional banks, industrial, commercial, and residential real estate

developers, contractors and sureties, and many of Atlanta's prominent citizens.

The firm's success has also meant growth for Atlanta. When developers sought to expand the horizons of this growing city into the now-thriving Perimeter area, Peterson Dillard pioneered the zoning and land-use efforts. When new health-care facilities, schools, retirement homes, and improvements to the infrastructure were needed, Peterson Dillard prepared and supervised bond issues for city and county governments and private parties. Peterson Dillard has also been instrumental in the growth of business in Atlanta, handling the acquisitions of banks and the development of hotels, multifamily residences, office towers, and conference centers.

The success and diversity that mark the firm's other specialty areas also distinguish its litigation practice. The firm represents various state departments and municipalities in workers' compen-

sation disputes, health-care provider disputes, eminent domain proceedings, and general litigation matters. Peterson Dillard attorneys bring to their clients a wealth of experience in employment, restrictive covenant, condemnation, construction, general business, contract, and securities law, as well as domestic relations litigation and alternative dispute resolution. Additionally, several of the firm's attorneys are certified public accountants or engineers. The experiences of these attorneys enhance the range of legal services the firm offers.

Peterson Dillard's professional commitment to Atlanta translates into a personal commitment from its attorneys, who contribute their time, expertise, and financial resources to the community in which they live and work. From pro bono work to educational advisory committees to support of the arts, Peterson Dillard and its staff are dedicated to Atlanta in all its diversity and all its aspirations.

When Eric J. Lindberg established MSI International (Management Search Inc.) in 1968, his goal was to bring people, companies, and careers together. Today he has not only met that goal but surpassed it. Under Lindberg's leadership as president and CEO, in fiscal year 1995, the firm's revenues were $54 million—14 percent higher than the 1994 figure. Revenues for 1996 are projected to be $67 million.

MSI International's operating divisions, franchises, and subsidiaries provide staffing and human resource consulting services through a network of more than 50 offices throughout the United States and in Europe. Among the services provided are recruitment and placement of executives, health-care professionals, office support personnel, technical engineers, financial professionals, and temporary help.

Lindberg expects the company's future growth to continue at the same rapid pace that has occurred over the past 10 years. From 1985 to 1995, MSI International grew at an average rate of 51 percent per year. For both 1986 and 1987, the firm was named to *Inc.* magazine's annual list of the fastest-growing privately held companies. More than 300 staff employees and several thousand temporaries work for the company. It is not surprising, therefore, that MSI International expects to expand by about 15 offices each year over the next two years and predicts that 1998 figures will reach $120 million.

Lindberg attributes MSI International's success to several key factors. To survive and thrive in this competitive industry, the company goes beyond finding personnel and offers value-added services. "We are a business partner, providing valuable human resource solutions," says Lindberg. "Some of these solutions are outplacement counseling for downsizing clients, updates on employment laws, training for the clients' employees in office automation, and facility staffing."

The fastest-growing segment is Temps & Co./MSI Services, a division of company-owned and franchise offices that provides temporary and permanent employees in the areas of clerical, light industrial, office automation, technical services, and accounting. There are 18 franchise offices with plans to establish 20 more within the next two years.

Lindberg also has responded to personnel needs overseas. SCI Ltd. (Search Consultants International), the international permanent recruiting division established in 1985, has offices in London, Malta, and Cyprus. Additional offices will open in Europe and the Far East.

Lindberg notes, "It's a pleasure to work in a business that provides our clients with their most valuable assets— their people."

Howell Rusk Dodson—Architects (HRD) celebrated its 86th anniversary in 1995, making it one of the oldest major architectural firms in the Southeast. The firm was started in 1909 by Hal Hentz and Neel Reid. Noted architect Philip Shutze joined the firm in 1913 along with Rudolph Adler.

During its early years, the highly respected firm designed many notable and prominent buildings, many of which are considered today to be examples of Atlanta's architectural heritage, such as the C&S main bank building in downtown, the Academy of Medicine building in midtown, and Brookwood Station and the Swan House in Buckhead. Currently, the firm offers a full range of architectural services on multiple building types, including programming, master planning, design, creation of construction documents, contract administration, and construction inspection.

With a staff of more than 40 professionals, of which more than half are licensed architects, HRD focuses on health-care facilities, communications and data-processing centers, professional office buildings, and parking structures. In addition to its staff, HRD maintains a continuing working relationship with leading engineering and specialty consultants for the structural, mechanical, electrical, and civil engineering components of a project. These associations enable HRD to offer a wide range of technical skills and expertise while still maintaining a personal approach with each of its clients. The key to HRD's success for over 86 years is the firm's project approach, which has resulted in repeat clients. HRD's philosophy is to approach every project on a "team basis" in order to achieve effective and positive control.

HRD's main objective is to produce a project that meets the needs and requirements of its clients. To accomplish this goal, HRD believes in communicating with its clients so as to reach a clear understanding of all project goals. This approach, combined with interaction with the client's designated project representatives, ensures not only that a project will have an innovative and creative design solution that adheres to established budgets and satisfies all project schedules, but that it also meets and even surpasses the client's expectations.

Over 95 percent of HRD's projects are for repeat clients, including Egleston Children's Hospital at Emory University, Northside Hospital, Piedmont Hospital, BellSouth Telecommunications, and AT&T. HRD's projects have averaged more than $50 million in construction value per year.

By being dedicated to quality and focusing attention on a client's needs, Howell Rusk Dodson—Architects will continue to be one of the top firms in Atlanta.

Courtesy of Howell Rusk Dodson—Architects

# ERNST & YOUNG

For more than 76 years, Ernst & Young LLP has played a significant role in Atlanta's growth.

Ernst & Young is a leading professional services firm with global resources of 64,000 people in more than 100 countries, including more than 700 people in the Atlanta office. The firm's mission is to be the world's leading integrated professional services firm, committed to continuous improvement in all that it does. Ernst & Young seeks to attract, develop, and retain high-performance people and to deliver the highest-quality work and value-added services in response to its clients' needs and expectations.

The local practice, established in 1919, serves some of the area's largest well-established companies, as well as individual entrepreneurs just starting their businesses. Through industry-specific service groups, Ernst & Young professionals provide a full spectrum of services to its clients, ranging from traditional audit and tax services to litigation support and process improvement consulting.

But Ernst & Young is not only committed to helping its clients achieve their goals; it also is dedicated to the success of the community. Ernst & Young has stepped forth, establishing a long-standing leadership position in numerous civic organizations, as well as local charitable efforts. Whether it's the Chamber of Commerce, the United Way, the Olympic Job Opportunities Program, the Woodruff Arts Center, or the Atlanta Symphony Orchestra, the firm and its people have accepted the responsibility of enriching the city by devoting their time and financial resources.

*Ernst & Young professionals discuss a client meeting.*

*Ernst & Young volunteers help renovate a school during Hands On Atlanta Day.*

*As a national sponsor of the Entrepreneur of the Year program, Ernst & Young honors the outstanding businesspeople and risk-takers in nearly 50 regions across the nation and eight other countries. The Southeast Area program is among the largest and best established and recently produced a national award recipient.*

*International partners (below) create a client service plan.*

Atlanta University Center (AUC), the world's oldest and largest consortium of African-American private institutions of higher education, was established in 1929 to promote and supervise cooperative efforts among its member institutions—Clark Atlanta University, the Interdenominational Theological Center, Morehouse College, Morehouse School of Medicine, Morris Brown College, and Spelman College. The consortium is made up of more than 1,000 faculty members and 13,000 students.

The AUC campuses share several important facilities and services among its members, including the Robert W. Woodruff Library, which houses one of the country's major African-American collections.

In addition to library facilities, AUC institutions share some aspects of security, shuttle service, the Dual Degree Engineering Program, the Radiation Safety Program, the Administrative Data Processing Center, the Career Planning and Placement Center, and classes through cross-registration.

With the approach of the 1996 Olympics, the Atlanta Committee for the Olympic Games (ACOG) made an agreement with AUC that provided approximately $51 million for venue construction and related development. The projects include two field hockey centers at Clark Atlanta University and Morris Brown College, a basketball arena at Morehouse College, and tennis facilities at Spelman College. The Interdenominational Theological Center will be the site of a continuing education center, and the Morehouse School of Medicine will house a sports medicine research center. In addition, Clark Atlanta University will train 500 to 700 students for positions in the Host Broadcast Center.

*The Atlanta University Center family*

With over 5,000 students, **Clark Atlanta University (CAU)** is the largest of the member institutions of the United Negro College Fund and offers comprehensive academic programs leading to bachelor's, master's, and doctoral degrees. Formed in 1988 through the consolidation of Clark College (founded in 1869) and Atlanta University (founded in 1865), Clark Atlanta builds on a distinctive history. In a recent study of more that 3,000 U.S. colleges and universities, Clark Atlanta was cited for the number of African-American graduates it produced in all academic disciplines.

*Living and learning together*

Courtesy of Atlanta University Center

Courtesy of Atlanta University Center

Founded in 1958 through the mutual efforts of four denominations, the **Interdenominational Theological Center (ITC)** is a graduate school of theology and the most comprehensive center of African-American theological education in the world. ITC awards the master of divinity, the master of arts in both church music and Christian education, and the doctor of theology, doctor of pastoral counseling, and double degrees.

Of ITC's current highest enrollment of 411, one-third are women. Its graduates serve the world as bishops, pastors, and college presidents.

**Morehouse College,** founded in 1867, is the nation's only historically black, all-male, liberal arts institution. Morehouse boasts a Phi Beta Kappa chapter and honors and study abroad programs. Among the college's most prominent alumni are the Nobel Prize for Peace laureate Dr. Martin Luther King, Jr., former Secretary of Health and Human Services Louis Sullivan, Centers for Disease Control and Prevention Executive Director David Satcher, Atlanta Mayor Maynard Jackson, and award-winning filmmaker Spike Lee. Morehouse enrolls approximately 3,000 students, representing 42 states and 12 foreign countries.

**Morehouse School of Medicine (MSM)** was founded in 1975 with the mission to matriculate primary-care physicians to serve medically underserved areas and be involved in medical education to serve the same constituencies. It established the first family medicine residency training program in Atlanta and has also developed residency programs in general surgery, internal medicine, psychiatry, and preventive medicine. MSM grants the M.D., Ph.D., and M.P.H. degrees.

**Morris Brown College (MBC),** founded in 1881 by the African Methodist Episcopal Church, is the only college in Georgia founded by African-Americans. MBC has grown to an enrollment of approximately 2,000 students. Through joint programs with Georgia Tech and six other universities throughout America, Morris Brown offers degrees in architec-

*Courtesy of Atlanta University Center*

ture, construction, and industrial design in addition to its regular curriculum, which features a business administration department that has graduated more CPAs than any historically black college or university. MBC has produced many distinguished alumni, including Pulitzer Prize-winning author James Alan McPherson and Atlanta Police Chief Beverly Harvard, the first black woman to serve as chief of police of a major U.S. city.

**Spelman College,** founded in 1881, is not only the largest women's college in Georgia but is one of only two historically African-American colleges for women.

*Stairway to the stars*

With approximately 1,900 students, it is one of the most selective colleges in the South. In September 1992, Spelman was rated the number-one regional, liberal arts college in the South in *U.S. News and World Report*'s annual college issue, "Best College Buys." In addition to providing a comprehensive liberal arts background, the school offers an International Affairs Center, a Women's Research Center, and an independent major.

**The AUC provides not only an education but a future!**

# U.S. ARMY FORCES COMMAND

One of Atlanta's worldwide corporate headquarters is less than a 10K run from Olympic Stadium. Although it has a budget of $4.4 billion, it isn't a Fortune 500 company. What it produces can't be held and admired. But its value is priceless and sometimes taken for granted—the guarantee of freedom for our country and the preservation of the American way of life.

It is called U.S. Army Forces Command (FORSCOM), and its local economic impact is significant. Its 8,000 employees put about $485 million in salaries into the Atlanta economy every year.

Located at Fort McPherson on the boundary of the cities of East Point and Atlanta, FORSCOM headquarters, housed in a 356,000-square-foot complex covering five acres, is the workplace of some 2,000 military and civilian employees. FORSCOM's corporate reach, however, goes far beyond the Atlanta area. It has subsidiaries in 48 states and Puerto Rico, employing nearly 800,000 people—Active Army, Army Reserve, Army National Guard, and Army Civilians—to ensure that the motto "Freedom's Guardian" is more than a goal on the corporate banner. This motto is FORSCOM's pledge that its soldiers will sacrifice, perhaps even at the cost of their lives, to protect freedom wherever and whenever duty calls.

At any particular time, FORSCOM has about 10,000 to 20,000 soldiers working away from their home station. While those locations are often in the far corners of the world, these forces enjoy high visibility and respect wherever they are deployed in support of the country's national security interests.

FORSCOM people have what it takes to get the job done anywhere in the world, and once they arrive, they find solutions, fix problems, and win. Their commanders and leaders are dedicated to meeting a mission statement that would challenge any CEO.

FORSCOM people

- train, sustain, mobilize, and project strategic land military forces worldwide;
- plan for and, on order, execute the land defense of the United States and Canada, including the protection of key assets;
- plan for and, on order, provide military support to civil authorities, assist with disaster relief and emergency response situations, provide support to law enforcement, and help with community improvement;
- plan for and, on order, conduct land force operations in the U.S. Atlantic Command area of responsibility to protect United States national security interests.

FORSCOM also commands the Third U.S. Army, the Army component of U.S. Central Command, which is responsible for Southwest Asia, the Persian Gulf, and the Horn of Africa.

U.S. Army Forces Command is the largest major command in the Department of the Army and comprises the Army component of U.S. Atlantic Command. FORSCOM supervises the training of almost 800,000 active and reserve soldiers to provide a strategic, power-projec-

tion ground force capable of responding rapidly and successfully to crises worldwide.

A significant part of FORSCOM is its Reserve Component forces, outnumbering Active Component forces by two to one. The Army National Guard and Army Reserve provide those soldier-citizens, who are more essential than ever before as U.S. Army Forces Command follows corporate restructuring and downsizing trends that began during the early 1990s.

Part of that Reserve Component is led by a major subordinate command of Forces Command, also headquartered in Atlanta: the U.S. Army Reserve Command (USARC). U.S. Army Reserve forces are prepared to support FORSCOM's combat power by providing specialists in such technical skills as medical treatment, civil affairs, engineering, construction, transportation, maintenance, and supply.

And, when they are federalized, U.S. Army National Guard units within the continental United States are incorporated as combat soldiers into the overall FORSCOM battle plan.

Whether it is **Operation Just Cause** in Panama, **Operation Desert Storm** in Southwest Asia, **Operation Restore**

**Hope** in Somalia, or **Operation Uphold Democracy** in Haiti, FORSCOM soldiers are pictured on the front pages of newspapers and referred to in the lead stories on news programs around the world.

Over the past five years, FORSCOM units have provided greatly needed support after Hurricane Andrew smashed Florida; fought forest fires in Montana and Idaho; built dikes to keep back flood waters along the Missouri and Mississippi rivers and in Georgia; provided security and medical help after the California earthquakes; and provided engineering, radar, and surveillance support to U.S. counter-drug agencies.

The history of U.S. Army Forces Command clearly shows that its corporate image is one of heroes: brave, powerful, far reaching. These are America's sons and daughters, some who have died fighting for freedom and democracy. They have fed hungry children with tenderness and care.

The entire FORSCOM family—Active Army, Army Reserve, and Army National Guard, their family members, and civilian employees—is proud to be part of the Atlanta community and is dedicated to serving as "Freedom's Guardian."

Kennesaw State College, the largest senior college in the University System of Georgia, has experienced remarkable growth since it first opened its doors in 1966.

KSC was spotlighted in the 1980s in *Searching for Academic Excellence* as one of 20 colleges and universities in the nation "on the move." In the 1990s, *U.S. News and World Report* named Kennesaw State one of the "best up-and-coming colleges" in the South and a "rising star" among its peer institutions.

With an enrollment of 12,000 students, Kennesaw State offers more than 40 bachelor's degree programs in its five schools: Arts, Humanities and Social Sciences; Education; Nursing; Mathematics and Science; and the Michael J. Coles School of Business. Master's degree programs are available in accounting, business administration, education, nursing, professional writing, and public administration. In addition, hundreds of continuing education courses register more than 18,000 participants annually from

the community, government agencies, business, and industry.

KSC students, who commute to the nonresidential campus for day, night, and

weekend classes, are actively involved in an honors program, as well as in more than 50 campus organizations. The Fighting Owls, winners of national softball and baseball championships, belong to NCAA Division II and compete in the Peach Belt Conference in basketball, cross-country skiing, golf, tennis, softball, and baseball.

Under the leadership of Betty L. Siegel, the president of Kennesaw State since 1981, the college offers a diverse array of cultural enrichment opportunities for the community, including concerts, recitals, art exhibitions, plays, and lectures.

Major construction on the 182-acre campus marks the final decade of the century. But the changing landscape, with yellow-brick buildings rising higher with each new construction project, is memorable for its beautiful grounds, oak-lined streets, manicured lawns, and colorful flower beds.

KSC is located north of Atlanta on Chastain Road, just off Interstate 75, within sight of Kennesaw Mountain.

Pace Academy is located on a cozy 25-acre campus on West Paces Ferry Road in Buckhead. It is fitting that the school's main building, a Tudor castle, is a former residence. What began as a home has become a "home away from home" for children 5 to 18 years old. Founded in 1958, this coeducational, nonsectarian college preparatory day school is recognized today as one of the nation's finest educational institutions.

Pace's "relaxed" family-like atmosphere helps make students feel comfortable and learning enjoyable. With an enrollment of 825 and a student/teacher ratio of 14:1, Pace offers students personal contact with teachers and extensive opportunities for participation in co-curricular and extra-curricular programs.

The school's motto, "to have the courage to strive for excellence," is the cornerstone of the Pace philosophy, and the success of its application may be seen in the numerous accolades received over the years. Through its award-winning service program, state championship sports teams, nationally recognized theater and debate programs, and national merit scholars, Pace continues to demonstrate its commitment to excellence.

This commitment to excellence is also visible in the caliber of the school's faculty and professional staff. The vast majority of the 162 teachers have advanced degrees from the country's leading colleges and universities; their average tenure at Pace is at least 10 years.

The Pace student body comes from a wide cross-section of economic, social, and ethnic backgrounds and falls academically in the above-average to gifted range of the national student population. The average SAT scores of the graduating class have been 1,110, with the top third of the class at 1,320. Pace graduates have been accepted to colleges and universities from Maine to California and have performed with distinction at those institutions.

While Pace has no plans to increase the size of its enrollment in the future, plans are being made to build a new athletic complex to match the state-of-the-art fine arts center that opened in 1990.

*Pace Acadamy—inside or outside—a home away from home*

While Georgia State University, a unit of the University System of Georgia located in downtown Atlanta, has a rich, storied history dating back to 1913, its future expansion plans and new leadership are bringing the school increased attention.

Headed by Carl Patton, who joined Georgia State in July 1992, the university is relocating its School of Music to three buildings in the downtown Fairlie-Poplar district. This expansion includes the old Rialto Theater, which will become the 1,000-seat Rialto Center for the Performing Arts after renovations are completed in early 1996. In addition, the School of Business Administration recently expanded into the former NationsBank building at 25 Broad Street.

The most exciting news, however, is in the area of housing. Thanks to the 1996 Olympics, Georgia State will be transformed from a commuter school to a residential university. In addition to hosting Olympic badminton in its sports arena and offering Olympic officials other assistance, Georgia State is involved in the planning and construction of the Olympic Village on North Avenue, which will house the Olympic athletes and, afterward, Georgia State students.

With the school's campus expansion into new buildings, its role in the Olympics, and the introduction of housing, Georgia State has emerged as an important player in shaping the future of Atlanta and the surrounding area. It is now positioned to meet the growing demands of the students, faculty, and city.

Growth is nothing new to the university. Since it was established in 1913 as the Evening School of Commerce (of the Georgia Institute of Technology) to offer evening business classes in the new field of commercial science, it has relocated several times to handle rapid increases in enrollment. Enrollment in the first class of students totaled 47. Over the next 18 years, the school occupied four rented locations and underwent several name changes.

It was during the tenure of president Noah Langdale, Jr., who led the institution for the 30 years from 1957 to 1987, that the school was renamed Georgia State College (in 1961) and granted university status (in 1969).

A great deal has changed at the school besides its name and locations. One major change is that the university is now composed of six colleges—Arts and Sciences, Business Administration, Education, Health Sciences, Law, and Public and Urban Affairs.

Georgia State has a total of 50 degree programs, and the university's 52 academic departments offer almost 250 majors. In addition to B.A., B.S., and master's degrees, Georgia State offers doctoral programs.

As part of Georgia State's new strategic academic plan, it is striving to reach the twin goals of greater national prominence and enhanced community relevance. By weaving together teaching, research, and service, the university is creating a total learning experience for all students.

Georgia State is already a major player in addressing the critical issues facing cities and states, thanks to its centers in health-care reform, urban education, fiscal policy, and economic forecasting. As for community involvement, faculty, students, and staff support the Atlanta Project, as well as help the working poor appeal IRS audits and teach immigrant mothers English so they can communicate with their children's teachers.

According to fall 1995 figures, GSU's

Courtesy of Georgia State University

enrollment has grown to 24,600 students, making it the second-largest institution of higher learning in the state. The diverse student body has an average age of 26 for undergraduates and 33 for graduate students (who make up 30 percent of the student body). About 80 percent of all the students are employed full or part time, and more than 1,000 international students represent 114 countries. To serve this diverse group, classes are held from 7 A.M. to 10 P.M. While most classes are taught downtown, some are offered at the university's North Metro Center in Dunwoody. In 1996, Georgia State will move that center to Roswell.

So many of Atlanta's movers and shakers are graduates of the school that Georgia State's list of alumni reads like a "Who's Who in Atlanta." In the metro area, more than 100 firms have 30 or more GSU graduates on the payroll. The university itself employs a full-time workforce of about 2,300.

It is Carl Patton's goal to make GSU the premiere urban research university in the nation by developing solutions to problems, serving the community, and preparing students to lead tomorrow.

Courtesy of Georgia State University

Courtesy of Georgia State University

The Presbyterian Church in America (PCA) contributes to the ethos of the Atlanta community by teaching and encouraging its members to integrate life and faith. Unlike many activist organizations that lobby local, state, and federal governments for the enactment of laws, neither the PCA nor its churches attempts to represent its members in public matters. The PCA does encourage its members to be active in political and civic organizations. Consequently, the denomination is well represented in prison ministries, adoption services, pregnancy crisis centers, disaster relief, and many other such organizations in the communities where the churches are located. The PCA does humbly petition the government, when appropriate, regarding the significant moral issues that trouble our communities and nation.

The Presbyterian Church in America also cooperates with other denominations and churches where there are common goals. One example is Quest Atlanta '96, in which 25 denominations and some 1,500 churches are working together. Quest Atlanta '96 is committed to unite the body of Christ to welcome the world during the Olympic Games in an effort to proclaim and demonstrate the love of God.

The Presbyterian Church in America is one of the fastest-growing denominations in the United States. Since its founding in 1973 with 240 congregations and just 40,000 members, it has grown to include 1,277 congregations and 260,885 members. With its successful strategy of planting new churches in population-growth areas, the PCA expects to reach its goal of having 2,000 churches by the year 2000.

"Reformed" defines the doctrinal beliefs of the PCA, which holds that the purist expressions of scriptural doctrine are found in the Calvinistic creeds, particularly the Westminster Confession of Faith.

The PCA's representative form of church government is rooted in its name—presbyterian. Local churches are governed by elders (presbyters) elected by the church members. This form of government extends through the regional presbyteries, which facilitate connectionalism, to the national General Assembly, which expresses PCA's connectionalism and the bond of union between/among all the churches.

Most of the work of the denomination is coordinated in the PCA Office Building in Atlanta. That work is carried out by three program committees—Mission to the World, Mission to North America, and Christian Education and Publication. In addition, there is the Office of the Stated Clerk, which is responsible for the administration of the General Assembly; the PCA Foundation, which teaches more effective stewardship; and the Insurance, Annuities, and Relief Board, which provides health, life, and disability insurance coverage and retirement plans for PCA pastors, lay church workers, and the staffs of PCA committees, agencies, and institutions.

The PCA moved to Atlanta in 1982 and bought its current building at 1852 Century Place in 1987. Two-thirds of the PCA's churches and members are in the Southeast, and 25 churches are located in the Atlanta metro area.

National denominational institutions located outside PCA's headquarters include Ridge Haven, a conference center located close to Rosman, North Carolina; Covenant College, a liberal arts college with over 750 students, located at Lookout Mountain, Georgia; and Covenant Theological Seminary, in St. Louis, Missouri.

The PCA's influence extends far beyond the walls of the local church. Through Mission to the World, about 600 foreign missionaries are working in about 60 nations. Because of the unique relationship between Mission to the World and over 30 mission agencies with which some of PCA's missionaries are working, many people consider PCA's influence to be far greater than its size might indicate. Further, with close to 83 chaplains in the military and in hospitals, the Gospel is proclaimed to a rather large audience around the world not reached through usual ecclesiastical channels. Because of the emphasis on education, many members of the PCA are teachers and professors at all levels of education, including large universities and quite a few theological seminaries.

Mission to North America assists presbyteries and local congregations in their church-planting efforts through vision communication, strategic planning, and the recruitment, assessment, and training of church planters.

Christian Education and Publications' mission is to glorify God by serving the PCA in its commitment to creating disciples. It does this by teaching and training leaders and church members as well as by providing a biblically based Sunday school curriculum for all ages through its publishing house, Great Commission Publications. The Women in the Church is under the oversight and direction of the Christian Education and Publications Committee and provides seminars, retreats, and materials for women.

The Office of the Stated Clerk is under the oversight of the Administrative Committee, whose ministry is service. In addition to planning, coordinating, and arranging facilities and services for the annual meeting of the General Assembly, the ruling body made up of about 1,250 commissioners (ministers and ordained lay leaders), the Clerk's office serves as a liaison between the General Assembly and the presbyteries and sessions, as well as other denominational bodies. Other areas of service include assisting church pulpit committees and pastors in their search for churches and overseeing corporate civil matters, the PCA Historical Center in St. Louis, and the management and operation of the Atlanta headquarters.

Mercer University's influence in the metropolitan Atlanta area has been felt for over 160 years through the thousands of alumni who have made their mark in their respective fields and become actively involved in their communities. A comprehensive educational institution, Mercer prides itself on innovation and its distinction as the only university of its size in the nation to offer such a broad range of academic programs. It's no wonder that for six consecutive years *U.S. News and World Report* has ranked Mercer among the top 15 regional universities in the South.

Mercer's historic Macon campus offers degrees in the liberal arts, business, engineering, education, law, and medicine. The university's Graduate and Professional Center—known as the Cecil B. Day Campus—is strategically located near the intersections of 1-85 and 1-285 in Atlanta. Its offerings in business, pharmacy, education, and engineering provide an important link to Atlanta's business and professional communities.

The second-largest Baptist-affiliated institution in the world, Mercer will broaden its educational programs in Atlanta when it opens a new graduate school of theology on the Cecil B. Day Campus in the fall of 1996. Such expansions are key to the university's regional success and are certainly in keeping with the university's longstanding tradition of providing comprehensive educational opportunities for more than 50,000 graduates and 7,000 current students.

More than 11,000 Mercer alumni make Atlanta their home today, and many hold prominent positions at Atlanta's top businesses and organizations. A number of Mercer's trustees come from the Atlanta area, including board chairman and former U.S. Attorney General Griffin B. Bell.

The university's tradition of educational achievement reaches to virtually every corner of the state, from the historic main campus in Macon to Mercer's off-campus centers in Douglas County, Covington, and Griffin, to its corporate education sites at Atlanta's Georgia Power Company and Grady Hospital.

As Atlanta has solidified its position as a world-class city, Mercer has clearly established itself as one of the South's great private universities.

© Rod Reilly

## ACKNOWLEDGMENTS

Each of the following organizations, educational
and heatlh-care institutions, and government
entities made a valuable contribution to this
project. Longstreet Press gratefully acknowledges
their participation.

Aaron Rents, Inc.
Advanced Control Systems
America's Favorite Chicken Company
ARC Security, Inc.
Atlanta Casualty Company
Atlanta Economic Development Corporation
Atlanta Interfaith Broadcasters, Inc.
Atlanta Journal-Constitution
Atlanta Market Center
Atlanta University Center
AT&T
BellSouth
Best Western American Hotel
Biltmore Suites/Biltmore Peachtree Hotel
Blue Cross and Blue Shield of Georgia
Buckhead Life Restaurant Group
Cadmus Marketing Services
Chick-fil-A, Inc.
CIBA Vision
Coca-Cola Company
Cousins Properties Incorporated
Cox Enterprises
DeKalb Medical Center
City of East Point
Emory University System of Health Care
Ernst & Young
Fleet Capital
Fulton County
Georgia-Pacific Corporation
Georgia Power
Georgia State University
Grand Hotel Atlanta
Holiday Inn Worldwide
Home Depot
Honeywell Network Services
Howell Rusk Dodson—Architects
INVESCO
Jim Ellis Auto Dealerships
Johnson & Higgins
Kennesaw State College
Kimberly-Clark
King & Spalding
Kroger Company
Laing Properties, Inc.
Lanier Worldwide, Inc.
LongHorn Steaks Inc.

Lotus Development Corporation
MARTA
MCI Communications Corporation
Mercer University
Metric Constructors, Inc.
Montag & Caldwell
MSI International
NationsBank
Old Fashion Foods, Inc.
Pace Academy
Peachtree Software
Peterson Dillard Young Asselin & Powell
Piedmont Hospital
Presbyterian Church in America
Pryor, McClendon, Counts & Co., Inc.
Regent Partners
Renaissance Hotels and Resorts
Residence Inn by Marriott
Rich's
Sanderson Industries, Inc.
Scientific Games Inc.
Selig Enterprises, Inc.
Shepherd Center
Simons Engineering, Inc.
Smith Real Estate Services, Inc.
Solvay Pharmaceuticals Inc.
South Fulton Medical Center
Southern Company
Thrasher Trucking, Inc.
United Parcel Service, Inc.
U.S. Army Forces Command

This book was published in cooperation with the
Atlanta Economic Development Corporation
and would not have been possible without the
support of its members. Longstreet Press is
especially grateful to the following individuals
for their commitment and continued assistance:

Walter Huntley, Jr.
Margaret W. McClure
Eleanor Martin
Keith Melton

We would also like to thank the following individuals who contributed in a variety of ways to the quality of *Atlanta: A Vision for the New Millennium.*

Hon. Mayor Bill Campbell
Paula Granger
Carol Grant Muldawer

The following publications and organizations were
excellent sources of information for the text:

**NEWSPAPERS AND MAGAZINES**
*Atlanta* magazine
*Atlanta Business Chronicle*
*Atlanta Journal-Constitution*
*Business Atlanta*
*Creative Loafing*
*Georgia Trend* magazine
*North Side News*

**BOOKS**
*Atlanta: A Chronological and Documentary
    History,* by George J. Lankevich
*Atlanta and Environs: A Chronicle of Its People
    and Events,* by Franklin M. Garrett
*Atlanta Architecture: The Victorian Heritage—
    1837-1918,* by Elizabeth Lyon
*Atlanta: Its Lures, Legends, and Laughter,*
    by Elise Reid Boyleston
*Days in the Life of Atlanta,* by Norman Shavin
*The Legacy of Atlanta,* by Webb Garrison

**ORGANIZATIONS**
Atlanta Chamber of Commerce
Atlanta Committee for the Olympic Games
Atlanta Convention and Visitors Bureau
Atlanta Economic Development Corporation
Atlanta History Center
Atlanta Regional Commission
Buckhead Coalition
Central Atlanta Progress
Chambers of Commerce of DeKalb, Cobb, Fulton,
    and Gwinnett counties
City of Atlanta
Midtown Alliance

ATLANTA — A VISION FOR THE NEW MILLENNIUM

## INDEX TO PROFILES IN EXCELLENCE

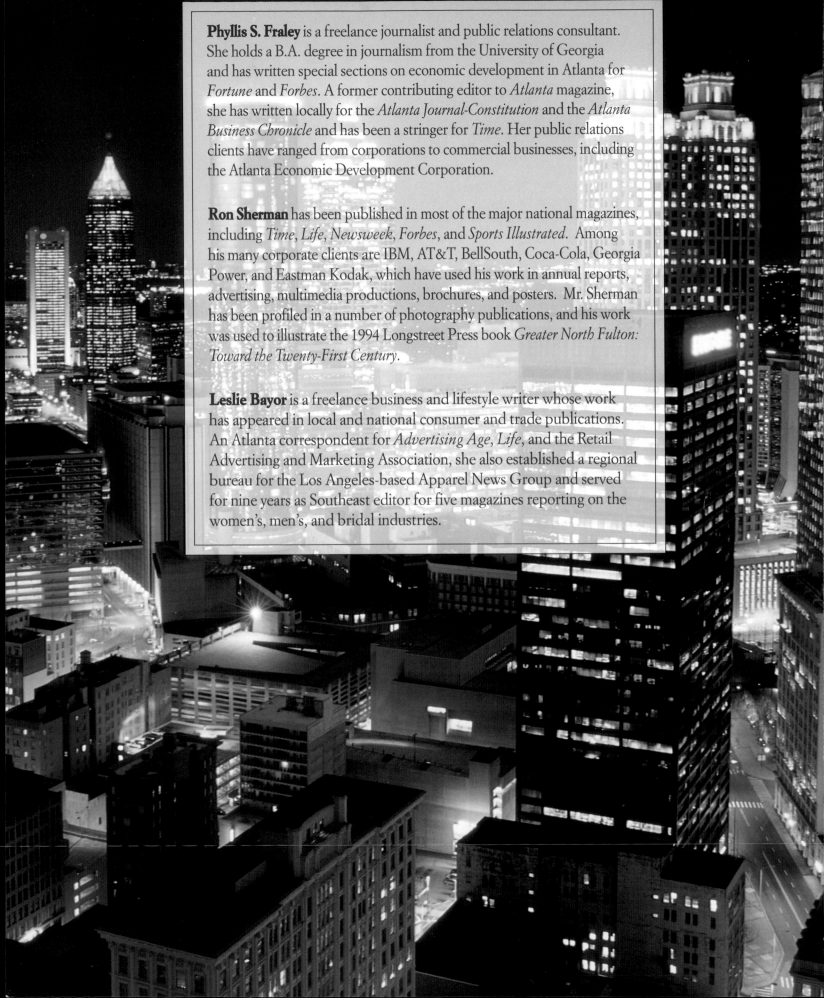

**Phyllis S. Fraley** is a freelance journalist and public relations consultant. She holds a B.A. degree in journalism from the University of Georgia and has written special sections on economic development in Atlanta for *Fortune* and *Forbes*. A former contributing editor to *Atlanta* magazine, she has written locally for the *Atlanta Journal-Constitution* and the *Atlanta Business Chronicle* and has been a stringer for *Time*. Her public relations clients have ranged from corporations to commercial businesses, including the Atlanta Economic Development Corporation.

**Ron Sherman** has been published in most of the major national magazines, including *Time*, *Life*, *Newsweek*, *Forbes*, and *Sports Illustrated*. Among his many corporate clients are IBM, AT&T, BellSouth, Coca-Cola, Georgia Power, and Eastman Kodak, which have used his work in annual reports, advertising, multimedia productions, brochures, and posters. Mr. Sherman has been profiled in a number of photography publications, and his work was used to illustrate the 1994 Longstreet Press book *Greater North Fulton: Toward the Twenty-First Century*.

**Leslie Bayor** is a freelance business and lifestyle writer whose work has appeared in local and national consumer and trade publications. An Atlanta correspondent for *Advertising Age*, *Life*, and the Retail Advertising and Marketing Association, she also established a regional bureau for the Los Angeles-based Apparel News Group and served for nine years as Southeast editor for five magazines reporting on the women's, men's, and bridal industries.